88 AND I

.

88 AND 1

UCLA, Notre Dame, and the Game that Ended the Longest
Winning Streak in Men's College Basketball History

TIMOTHY BOURRET

Essex, Connecticut

An imprint of Globe Pequot, the trade division of
The Rowman & Littlefield Publishing Group, Inc.
4501 Forbes Blvd., Ste. 200
Lanham, MD 20706
www.rowman.com

Distributed by NATIONAL BOOK NETWORK

British Library Cataloguing in Publication Information available

Library of Congress Cataloging-in-Publication Data
ISBN 978-1-4930-8121-9 (paperback)
ISBN 978-1-4930-8122-6 (e-book)

∞™ The paper used in this publication meets the minimum requirements of American National
Standard for Information Sciences—Permanence of Paper for Printed Library Materials, ANSI/
NISO Z39.48-1992.

88 and 1 is dedicated to Niels Aaboe, senior acquisitions editor at Global Pequot/Lyons Press, who developed the concept of this book and first contacted me about being the author. Niels had a 40-year career in the publishing business that ended when he passed away in April 2023. No one was more invested in his profession and easier to work with. My thoughts are with his family and friends.

CONTENTS

CONTENTS

FOREWORD

Digger Phelps coached Notre Dame for 20 years, from 1971 through 1991, winning 393 games and taking the Fighting Irish to its only Final Four appearance to date in 1978. He won 20 or more games 14 times and, at the time of his retirement, shared the NCAA record for most upsets over a No. 1 team with seven, beating UCLA in 1974, San Francisco in 1977, Marquette in 1978, DePaul in 1980, Kentucky in 1980, Virginia in 1981, and North Carolina in 1987.

But the game that will always define him will be that 71–70 victory over top-ranked UCLA on January 19, 1974, before a frenzied, sellout crowd of 11,343 at the Joyce Center in South Bend that broke the Bruins' 88-game winning streak and showed the first cracks in a Bruins dynasty that had lasted seven consecutive seasons.

It also turned out to be the most memorable road trip I ever made as a young sportswriter with the *Philadelphia Daily News*.

I fell under the spell of UCLA basketball during the Lew Alcindor/Kareem Abdul-Jabbar era. I got a chance to watch him play three times in college—twice at the old Madison Square Garden against Holy Cross and Boston College, and again during his senior year at the 1969 Holiday Festival Classic in the new Garden over Pennsylvania.

If Kareem was the most dominant college player I ever watched in person, Bill Walton was the most fundamentally sound superstar.

After watching him shoot a near perfect 21-for-22 and score 44 points against Memphis State as a junior when UCLA completed another unbeaten season in the 1973 tournament at St. Louis, I figured the Bruins were a mythological beast who might never lose again as long as John Wooden was coaching.

Notre Dame was a program that had just entered the national spotlight under Phelps, the 32-year-old rising star in his profession. I got to know Digger when he was the coach of Penn's 26–0 freshman team in 1969. He recruited the nucleus of the Quakers' third-ranked 1971 team that won 28 straight games before losing to Philadelphia Big 5 rival Villanova in the NCAA East Regional finals before taking the Fordham job in 1971.

Phelps coached Fordham to a 26–3 Sweet 16 season in his only year in the Bronx before accepting the challenge of replacing Johnny Dee at Notre Dame. In just three years, he built the Irish from a 6–20 team into an unbeaten national power ranked No. 2 in the AP poll.

Phelps wanted to build Notre Dame's profile as soon as he arrived, so he scheduled UCLA twice a year, at Westwood and South Bend, convincing Wooden, whose first coaching job was at South Bend Central High School, it was a chance to come home to Indiana.

The first meeting in 1972 in Los Angeles was a disaster. UCLA won, 114–56, that day. The Bruins won the first four games of the series easily, including an 82–63 win over Notre Dame in 1973, the day they broke San Francisco's previous college record of 60 straight victories.

But the Irish had gotten more competitive as Phelps used his Eastern connections to fill his roster with five-star players like Adrian Dantley from DeMatha Catholic (Hyattsville, Maryland); center John Shumate from Elizabeth, New Jersey; and Gary Brokaw from New Brunswick, New Jersey.

There was no film exchange at the time, so Phelps scouted UCLA in person against Iowa in Chicago the Thursday prior to meeting the Bruins, and felt the Irish had a legitimate chance to upset the Bruins and emulate football's ultimate success that occurred a month earlier when the Irish defeated Bear Bryant's Alabama Crimson Tide, 24–23, to win the national championship at the Sugar Bowl.

It was also a chance to relive the Irish's 89–82 upset victory over the Bruins at home in 1971. It was the last time UCLA lost—in a game where All-America guard Austin Carr scored 46 points, including 15 of Notre Dame's last 17.

UCLA had gone 1,092 days since then without a defeat.

The 1 vs. 2 matchup was must-see TV on the TVS network of stations, but I wanted to experience it in person.

I got a rare chance to make the pilgrimage when Jimmy Murphy, a former Penn basketball player, called out of the blue and asked if I wanted to take a private plane with him and Bob Levy, a generous Penn trustee who was into horse racing, built the squash pavilion on campus, and was a huge supporter of Penn basketball. He was close friends with Digger and had done business with Ara Parseghian, another friend of his who had coached the Irish to a national college football championship that previous fall.

I jumped at the chance.

Four of us—including Don McBride, the assistant principal and soccer coach at the Haverford School—made the trip.

The flight that Saturday took two hours and landed at 11 a.m. There was snow on the ground, but we drove right to the arena. By the time I got to my seat on press row the place was filled with students, who had been waiting all week for this. I sat next to Ken Denlinger, a columnist for the *Washington Post* who had spent close to a week on campus because Dantley had been a high school legend in Washington, DC. This was the biggest game of his career.

Kenny was there at the end of practice Wednesday when Phelps called the team together and instructed them on cutting down the nets after they won the game. He wanted forward Gary Novak to go to the far basket and Shumate to the near basket. He even had specific assignments for who would lift Novak and Shumate up to cut down the nets. That day he got his players to believe in mission impossible.

In my mind Digger never gets enough credit for being a great big game coach. He was at the top of his game in the '70s, when coaches like Wooden, Bob Knight, Al McGuire, Dean Smith, Ray Meyer, Joe B. Hall, Dave Gavitt, and Lou Carnesecca were bigger-than-life personalities. Phelps at the very least deserves a spot in the College Basketball Hall of Fame.

I was just glad both teams had a complete roster for the game. For a brief moment, it looked like Walton, who had a back injury and didn't even take it to Chicago Stadium for the Iowa game that Thursday, might not play. But Walton, a student of history, had watched Carr and Notre Dame defeat UCLA when he was a senior in high school, and there was no way he was going to miss the game. He was one of eight future NBA players to participate.

In fact, after Dantley elbowed Walton in the face on UCLA's first possession, it only served to antagonize the big 6-foot-11 redhead, who was wearing a corset to protect his back, and who proceeded to take the game over. Walton made six of his first seven shots and UCLA shot 70 percent in the first half when the Bruins took a 43–34 lead.

UCLA looked like they had the game under control after guard Tommy Curtis hit a jumper from the right corner to give UCLA a 70–59 lead with 3:32 to play and Phelps signaled a timeout 10 seconds later.

Then, the world turned upside down. There was no shot clock. All the Bruins had to do was run out the clock. But the Irish scored the last 12 points of the game.

There are two things that stood out to me during that frenzied stretch. One, Phelps went to a small three-guard lineup with freshman Dice Martin replacing small forward Billy Paterno, and he switched up the press, playing the 6-foot-8 Shumate at the top in place of the smaller 6-foot-3 Brokaw so UCLA couldn't just inbound the ball high to Walton. Second, UCLA's iconic coach John Wooden never called time out when the game was on the line.

The Bruins looked uncharacteristically tentative and unfocused during the comeback.

After a Shumate jumper and two layups off steals cut the lead to five, I remember leaning over to Kenny and saying, "Damn, this is happening."

After Brokaw, playing with four personals, shook free from Keith Wilkes for two straight jumpers, it was 70–69 with 1:25 to play. Walton flashed a timeout signal to Wooden, who waved it off because he thought it was a sign of weakness.

After Dwight Clay, whose nickname was "The Iceman" because he made a game-winning shot against Marquette the previous year to end their 81-game home winning streak, nailed a huge shot from the deep right corner to give the Irish a 71–70 lead with 29 seconds left.

Walton had enough. He, not Wooden, called timeout so UCLA could compose itself and to set up the final shot.

But Walton missed his only shot of the second half. Pete Trgovich missed a follow and David Meyers missed a tip just before the buzzer. When Shumate secured the ball and time ran out, pandemonium broke out.

Luck of the Irish? Maybe. But definitely part of Notre Dame folklore.

I was so into the game I didn't see the avalanche of fans coming out of the stands and using press row as a steeple chase on the way to mid-court for a classic court storming. I could see them flying over my head.

The scene on the floor was wild. Novak did his part to cut down the nets at one end. But Shumate was out of the picture, having been knocked down in the crush.

So, students lifted Clay Dantler and Martin up so they could take over the other net.

When the dust had settled and I finished up in the locker room, Bob Levy took me over to the football offices to meet Ara Parseghian, who was pretty happy since quarterback Joe Montana and tight end Ken MacAfee, two future Irish immortals on Notre Dame's 1977 national championship team, picked that day to make their official visits.

After that we went to Digger's house for a party in his basement. It was a cast of thousands, including Indiana governor Otis Brown. The party went on until two in the morning and there were reports every bar in South Bend had run out of beer before midnight.

We were long gone by then, flying to Columbia, South Carolina, to see the Penn vs. South Carolina game. We got there just before tipoff.

We arrived back in Philly just as the Palestra doubleheader was letting up. We then met up with friends at Cavanaugh's, across from the old Bulletin building near the 30th St. train station.

It all seems like a blur to me today.

Neither UCLA nor Notre Dame won the national title that season. The Bruins lost to David Thompson and eventual national champion North Carolina State in double overtime during the national semifinals at Greensboro. Notre Dame lost to Michigan in the Sweet 16 behind an incredible performance by Campy Russell.

I eventually moved on to work for the *New York Daily News* and have covered 50 Final Fours. If I've learned anything from the sport, it's that some games will always stick with you.

Dick Weiss

An award-winning columnist, Dick "Hoops" Weiss is a member of the National Sportswriters Hall of Fame and a recipient of the Naismith Basketball Hall of Fame's Curt Gowdy Award.

Acknowledgments

The title of this book is *88 and 1*, the same name as the documentary produced by ESPN in 2014 in conjunction with the 40-year anniversary of UCLA's 88-game winning streak. This book is not connected with that video or with anyone at ESPN. The video was a useful tool in the documentation of facts cited in this book.

I would like to thank Digger Phelps for his contributions through his recall of events and countless interview hours. The same holds true for former Notre Dame player Ray Martin.

I would like to thank the sports information offices from the University of Notre Dame and UCLA for their production of outstanding media guides and resources over the years. The media guides produced in the early 1970s by Vic Kelly at UCLA and Roger Valdiserri at Notre Dame were especially helpful.

Gene Sullivan's book, *A Frame of Mind Game*, on the Austin Carr era was also helpful in the first chapter.

I would also like to thank Curry Kirkpatrick of *Sports Illustrated*, whose articles in the magazine throughout this era of college basketball were useful tools throughout the book.

Special thanks to Clemson head football Coach Dabo Swinney and his discussion on John Wooden quotes he still uses today. Also special thanks to John Fineran for his article on John Wooden's incredible day of golf as a high school coach in South Bend, Indiana.

Thanks also to the *Los Angeles Times*, *South Bend Tribune*, the *Notre Dame Observer*, and *NCAA Basketball Record Book*.

.

Introduction

I was there on January 19, 1974.

I was a freshman sitting in the last row of the upper deck behind the Notre Dame bench of the Athletic and Convocation Center on the Notre Dame campus.

I was in college athletics as a sports information director for over 43 years, including three years as a student assistant in the SID office under the great Roger Valdiserri. It is still the greatest atmosphere I have experienced at an athletic event and the most historically significant game I have witnessed in person.

That was the day that Notre Dame ended one of the great streaks in sports history, the 88-game winning streak recorded between 1971 and 1974 of John Wooden's UCLA basketball teams. The previous record was 60 consecutive wins by the San Francisco Dons of Bill Russell and K. C. Jones of the 1954–56 era, and in the 50 years since UCLA's accomplishment the top win streak is just 45 games by UNLV in the 1989–91 era.

There aren't many streaks or records in sports where a new record exceeded the old mark by 47 percent, and in a 50-year period since establishing the new mark, no one has come within 49 percent of the existing record.

The title of this book, *88 and 1*, is appropriate because this publication is about the streak and its incredible accomplishment in almost a game-by-game accounting. It centers on the accomplishments of John Wooden's senior laden team of 1970–71, then focuses on the "Walton Gang Era" that ran UCLA's streak of national championships to seven and the streak to 88 consecutive wins before it ended.

As a 43-year veteran of the sports information field, I was always fascinated by interesting facts and unusual circumstances that brought attention to an event or person. This book is filled with them. This streak was bookended with losses in the same building to the same team in the same city where John Wooden coached at the beginning of his career at the high school level. UCLA broke San Francisco's record in the same building as well.

This book goes into pregame preparation and game detail of those two Notre Dame victories.

While I am a second-generation Notre Dame graduate, I always had great respect for UCLA's basketball program. Like many of my classmates, we rooted for the Bruins because it made the games against Notre Dame more meaningful. That was never more the case than the game of January 19, 1974.

Digger Phelps always felt the way to build a program was to beat the best. He took his lumps against Wooden's teams twice a year in his first two years in South Bend, including a 58-point loss in Pauley Pavilion in his first year as Notre Dame head coach (1971–72). But just two years later, he had recorded the greatest basketball victory in Notre Dame history.

While many Notre Dame fans rooted for the Bruins in this era, it was hard to root for All-American center Bill Walton at times. He was a rebel with a cause, and that rubbed many people across the country the wrong way.

Times have changed over the years and many hold him in high regard, including me, or at least find him entertaining. I urge you to watch *The Luckiest Guy in the World*, the four-part 30 for 30 documentary on Walton that premiered on ESPN in the summer of 2023.

One of those who holds him in high regard is Digger Phelps.

When Phelps was inducted into the Notre Dame Ring of Honor in 2014, a video was produced and Walton played a major role in the final version presented. He gave a humorous account of their relationship, and in recalling Notre Dame's 71–70 victory that ended the 88-game streak.

"January 19, 1974, Digger Phelps ruined my life."

On December 8, 2018, Walton was broadcasting the Notre Dame at UCLA game in Pauley Pavilion and Phelps called in to be a guest on the broadcast for a segment. After Phelps had hung up, Walton asked broadcast partner Dave Pasch, "Was that Digger Phelps?" Pasch responded in the affirmative. Walton then said after a pause, "I thought he was dead!"

Classic Bill Walton.

My overall goal in writing this book was to create something Notre Dame and UCLA fans would enjoy. The review of Notre Dame's 71–70 victory on January 19, 1974, is in chapter 8. The book continues with a review of the rest of the 1973–74 season, which had a disappointing ending for both programs.

Later chapters document John Wooden's final season that concluded with a surprising national championship, and a review of Notre Dame's 1977–78 season, when Phelps finally got the program to the Final Four, still the only Final Four in school history.

Whether you watched college basketball in this era and watched this game on television or in person, or are a youth interested in basketball history, I hope you enjoy reading about one of the greatest accomplishments in team sports history, and how the streak ended in a most dramatic fashion.

CHAPTER 1

The Austin Carr Game

THERE HAVE BEEN MANY SIGNIFICANT VICTORIES IN NOTRE DAME BAS-ketball history. Even the most ardent college basketball fans reading this book might be surprised to learn that Notre Dame ranked eighth in total college men's basketball victories in the history of the game entering the 2023–24 season, not far from the school's number-four ranking for total football victories in the history of the game, nor UCLA's number-five ranking in total college basketball wins.

You could certainly make the claim that the victory documented later in this book when Notre Dame ended UCLA's 88-game winning streak is the most important, and certainly the most famous. But, as far as looking at a victory that put Notre Dame on the map nationally, one could say the 89–82 victory over a number one ranked UCLA team, at the front end of the longest winning streak in men's college basketball history, is just as important.

Until the Notre Dame vs. UCLA game of January 23, 1971, the Irish had been considered a respectable and often feared team in the Midwest. As of January 1971, Notre Dame had been to the NCAA Tournament nine times, among the top 10 nationally in tournament appearances.

Notre Dame had upset a fifth-ranked Houston team and All-American Elvin Hayes at the Notre Dame Fieldhouse four years earlier, but the game was not televised and played before just 4,000 people. And on top of that, Notre Dame didn't make the 1967 NCAA Tournament, an appearance that would have brought attention to that Houston win.

Just a year later the Cougars defeated UCLA in the Astrodome in a game that brought many eyes to the college game in an era when the Final Four was not televised live. The Cougars went on to the Final Four that year.

Notre Dame's 1970–71 team needed a victory that would capture the nation's attention. Beating the four-time defending national champion UCLA who had not lost yet in 1970–71, had won 46 straight non-conference games, and lost only four times in the last four years would do the trick. And being led by senior generational player Austin Carr with the performance of his life would certainly add to the attention.

UCLA was a veteran outfit led by All-American Sidney Wicks, Carr's chief rival for 1970–71 National Player of the Year honors. John Wooden's team also featured future NBA players Curtis Rowe and Steve Patterson in the front court, and Henry Bibby in the back court. The only starter who did not go on to the NBA was fleet-footed guard Kenny Booker.

UCLA entered this game with a 14–0 record, and had a 19-game winning streak overall with the last loss coming at home the previous season against Southern California, 87–86 on March 6, 1970, the Friday night of a Friday–Saturday back-to-back set.

Coaches would never play on consecutive nights today in the conference season, never mind with both games on the road. But that was the scheduling philosophy of the Pac-8 in those days, which makes UCLA's 88-game winning streak even more amazing.

UCLA had started the season with wins by 31 over Baylor and 46 over Rice. Their first road game was 350 miles away at Pacific in game three, and it was a close high scoring game with the Bruins coming out on top, 100–88.

Having won four consecutive national championships and six of seven at the time, it would have been easy for Wooden to schedule all home non-conference games in December and January leading up to the league slate. But, to his credit, Wooden took his team on road trips back east and he did so in December 1970. They played on consecutive nights in Pittsburgh against William and Mary and Pittsburgh and won both by double digits.

After a non-conference 24-point win over a Dayton program who had played UCLA in the national championship game in 1967 in Louisville, the Bruins began the conference schedule with home wins over Washington (78–69) and Washington State (95–71).

The closest game of the season to that point was a 58–53 win at Stanford on January 15. A victory the next night at California by 18 points, was the final Pac-8 game before heading to the Midwest for a weekend trip that would see the Bruins face Loyola of Chicago on Friday night in the Catholic school's tiny Alumni Gym, before the bus ride to South Bend late that January 22 night.

That Cal game on January 16, 1971, would be the last conference game for the Bruins until February 6. Conference teams had large gaps in their schedules in those days as there were only eight schools in the Pac-8 and teams played 14 conference games on a 26-game regular-season schedule.

UCLA handled a Loyola team that would finish 4–20 by an 87–62 count, then boarded the bus to South Bend for the next day's afternoon game against the Irish. The Bruins were 14–0 with an average winning margin of 17.8 points per game. They had played just one game that was decided by five points or less and just two by less than a dozen.

As much as Wooden was not afraid to face top non-conference opponents (see the 1973–74 schedule when they played four games against non conference teams ranked in the top four in the nation), they had not faced a ranked team to this point in the 1970–71 season.

The Irish were ranked ninth in the latest AP poll with an 8–4 record, but three of the four losses had come against top 15 teams. Notre Dame had finished the 1969–70 season with a number-nine national ranking and Johnny Dee's last Irish team was number five in the AP preseason poll.

With the return of Austin Carr and five other experienced seniors, Dee stacked the Irish schedule with strong clubs from around the nation. Notre Dame would play eight games against top 20 teams in the regular season compared to just three for the Bruins. As an independent in those day, that was the formula needed to get an NCAA bid.

Four of those games against ranked teams took place prior to the January 23 UCLA game, so Notre Dame had experience against national brands.

The Fighting Irish season began in Crisler Arena against a Michigan team that was unranked, but would finish 19–7 overall and 12–2 in the Big Ten. The Irish won that game 94–81 behind 38 points and 13 rebounds by Carr.

South Carolina, ranked second in the nation behind All-American John Roche, came to South Bend for a matchup of top five teams. The previous year, South Carolina had won, 83–82, in the Sugar Bowl Classic in New Orleans. But Carr had burst on the national scene by scoring 43 against the third-ranked Gamecocks by shooting 19-for-24 from the field, including one stretch when he made 14 straight field goals.

But this year was Roche's year to shine, as he made 16 of 16 free throws, to this day the highest perfect free throw performance against the Irish in the Athletic and Convocation Center, and he "held" Carr to 27 points. South Carolina handed the Irish their first loss of the year, 85–82.

Notre Dame continued its strong schedule in games five and six. First, Indiana came to South Bend led by future ABA legend George McGinnis and won in what resembled an ABA game, 106–103. Carr scored 54, his high total of his senior year, and added 12 rebounds from his guard position, but it was not enough.

In game six, Notre Dame won at eighth-ranked Kentucky, 99–92, behind 50 points from Carr. Adolph Rupp always believed in playing teams straight up. If a team had a great player, he felt he was going to get his points, but shut down the other four. It had worked against Pete Maravich, who never beat Kentucky in six tries at LSU. Maravich scored 64 points against the Wildcats during his senior year, but UK won by 15 points.

The strategy did not work against Carr and the Irish, however, and Notre Dame had a rare win over the Wildcats in the state of Kentucky at Louisville's Freedom Hall.

Notre Dame's fourth game against a ranked team of the 1970–71 season was against Al McGuire's Marquette Warriors. McGuire's team was always tough in Milwaukee and once won 81 consecutive home games, a streak that was stopped by Dwight Clay and the Irish in 1972–73, the first of Digger Phelps's noted streak breakers.

But on this January Saturday, Marquette avenged a thrilling Notre Dame double overtime victory from the year before, 71–66. The previous year Marquette had the ball up two with just five seconds left when Jim Hinga stole the ball and fed Carr for a layup at the buzzer to send the game into a second overtime. Notre Dame went on to win, 96–95.

Notre Dame was not coming off a high point entering this UCLA game. After the loss at Marquette, Notre Dame trailed at the half against a 4–5 University of Detroit team. Carr was off in the first half, scoring just nine points. But he responded with a Notre Dame record 38 points in the second half and the Irish won, 93–79.

The Monday before the UCLA game the Irish traveled Pittsburgh to face Duquesne, and they dropped an 81–78 game to a then 4–2 team. At season's end it was not a terrible loss, as the Dukes went on to a 21–4 season, an NCAA Tournament appearance, and a top 15 finish in the AP poll. Duquesne has been to the NCAA Tournament just once since.

But at the time, Notre Dame was not a team one would think could rise up and defeat the number-one team in the nation, a team that had not lost a non-conference game since losing in the Astrodome to Houston in 1968.

Notre Dame's preparation for this game emphasized breaking UCLA's vaunted full-court press, a defense that was the prime reason for Notre Dame's 31-point loss (108–77) at Pauley Pavilion the previous season.

On defense, Dee spent much time developing a plan to limit Wicks's touches. He had the perfect practice player to simulate what he wanted to do. John Shumate was a freshman that season and freshmen were not eligible until two years later (1972–73). Shumate played Wicks in practice and gave Notre Dame frontcourt players Collis Jones, Sid Catlett, and John Pleick an excellent preview of what they would be facing on Saturday afternoon.

Shumate could not play in this 1971 game, but he had quite an effect on the outcome against the Bruins three years later.

The good week of practice was nearly ruined near the end of Friday's session. Before one of the drills, Dee put lines on the court that ran from the free throw lines at either end to about six feet outside the free throw lane on the baseline. Dee instructed that he did not want anyone other than Carr and Jones to shoot from outside the taped lines.

The suggestion did not go over well. The players were sick of hearing from the media that they were a two-man team, and when Coach Dee basically confirmed that with the taped court lines, it hit close to home. Practice did not go smoothly after Dee made the statement and it was obvious feelings needed to be aired.

A mid-practice meeting was called. The late Gene Sullivan, who went on to become a successful coach at Loyola of Chicago, recalled the scene in a book he authored after his career as the top assistant to Dee:

> Jackie Meehan revealed he didn't particularly like it when Dee was quoted as saying he could get three kids out of the student body to play with Jones and Carr.
>
> Collis Jones said he did not see why Tom Sinnott (his classmate) should not be allowed to shoot, while Doug Gemmell voiced that he had gone into a slump because he was gun-shy about shooting because he was not given any confidence by the coaches.
>
> Finally Carr took over. By now the entire team, even the freshmen, were involved in the meeting.
>
> Carr said, "I think everyone is too worried about getting me the ball. I think we would be better off if you [the coaches] just let everyone worry about themselves and their own game. I have played with these guys for four years now and I know they can play."

That was all that was needed. Dee rescinded the shooting restriction, pulled up the tape and the team returned to practice with a new, refreshed attitude. That meeting had done more for the team than all the X and O work on the court over the last four days.

Notre Dame was known for its legendary student support in this era, especially during academic years when the football team was also on a roll. Ara Parseghian's gridders had just upset No. 1 Texas in the Cotton Bowl 24–11 behind Joe Theismann to end the Longhorns 30-game winning streak, leading to a number-two final ranking for the Irish just 21 days earlier.

It was a great time to be a Notre Dame student with Joe Theismann, who finished runner-up for the Heisman Trophy race to Stanford's Jim Plunkett, and Carr, who would win National Player of the Year honors in basketball. The student enthusiasm was at an all-time high and they arrived at the Athletic and Convocation Center an hour before tipoff.

More often than not the winner in this series had gotten off to a good start. UCLA had taken a 13–2 lead in the first four minutes the previous year in Los Angeles and Dee knew it was important for his team to jump out quickly to get the home fans lathered.

Twenty-four seconds after the opening tip Collis Jones banged home a jumper off the backboard from the left side to give Notre Dame a 2–0 lead. Four minutes later Carr scored after a long pass to give the Irish a 10–3 advantage and UCLA called timeout, something Wooden rarely did, as you will see 88 games later.

The student crowd was already at fever pitch. They stood the entire game and shouted "REBOUND, REBOUND, REBOUND" with every UCLA field goal attempt. Dee had cited the importance of rebounding in an article in the Notre Dame *Observer* the day before.

Unlike the Convocation Center dedication game two years earlier when Lew Alcindor (Kareem Abdul-Jabbar) had led UCLA to an 88–75 victory, Notre Dame's frontcourt players were holding their own with Wicks and Rowe. Point guard Jackie Meehan was playing the defensive game of his life on future NBA guard Henry Bibby.

Center John Pleick, a native of El Segundo, California, was also playing with abandon underneath. He once out-hustled Wicks and Rowe to score an impossible lunging tip-in that started the Irish on a new scoring run.

While UCLA had four future NBA players on its roster, the Bruins struggled when Wicks was not in the game. With eight minutes left in the first half, Wooden took Wicks out for a breather. Notre Dame led 26–23. When he returned just 1:52 later, the Irish were up 12 and eventually got the lead to 39–26.

With Wicks back on the floor, UCLA cut the lead to 43–38 at intermission. What gave Irish supporters optimism at intermission was the fact that Notre Dame had shot just 39 percent, yet had a five-point lead.

That optimism was wiped out just a couple of minutes into the second half when Catlett and Pleick both picked up their fourth foul with 18 minutes still showing on the clock. Catlett had been playing solid defense in the front court and didn't seem the least bit nervous.

Catlett had played in big games during his high school career at DeMatha High in Washington, DC, including joining forces with former Notre Dame pivot Bob Whitmore to defeat Alcindor and Power Memorial during his high school career. That 46–43 DeMatha victory ended Power Memorial's 71-game winning streak.

At one point in the second half, Catlett flipped a perfectly executed behind-the-back pass to Jones. Even though Jones missed the shot, it was a confidence builder for the team and the crowd went crazy.

Fearing UCLA might blow the game open with Catlett and Pleick out of the lineup, Dee kept both in the game. Pleick lasted just two more minutes and fouled out with the score tied at 47. The crowd gave him a standing ovation, as he had battled for nine points and seven rebounds in 24 minutes.

Dee replaced the 6-foot-8 Pleick with 6-foot-3 Gemmell, who now had to guard Curtis Rowe. Catlett moved to the middle to guard center Steve Patterson and Jones guarded Wicks.

The teams traded baskets for the next eight minutes. It was a time to shine for the Notre Dame players who had been told at one point the day before they couldn't take a shot more than six feet from the basket.

First, senior Tom Sinnott, who Jones had supported in the team meeting the day before, knocked down a 20-footer from the right side to give Notre Dame a 54–49 lead. Then Gemmell, who had his confidence back, swished a 20-footer from the left corner to give the Irish a 60–50 lead with 12 minutes left.

The Bruins made a comeback to cut the lead to 64–62 before Catlett hit a 17-footer from the right elbow to put the Irish back up by four. Gemmell then battled Curtis Rowe for a rebound. The ball was batted by both players, but went into the hoop to give Notre Dame a 70–62 lead. When that shot went in Irish fans thought it just might be their day.

Then Meehan took matters into his own hands and drove through the Bruins defense down the lane for a floater to put the Irish up 72–64.

They were all key scores to keep Notre Dame ahead.

Wooden had unsuccessfully tried three different players on Carr. So with 6:35 left he brought in then unknown sophomore forward Larry Hollyfield, a player who was not on the Notre Dame scouting report. It was not an oversight by the Irish staff. Hollyfield had rarely played to this point in the season.

Thirty-two seconds after his entrance into the contest, Hollyfield hit a soft jumper from the left to bring UCLA to within a bucket. Defensively, he guarded Carr for a couple of possessions, but he couldn't stay with him. It was one drive to the basket after another.

But offensively Hollyfield made two more baskets, keeping UCLA in the game. He finished with six points in seven minutes. He would score just 19 points the entire season and appear in just 11 of the 30 games.

The final 5:40 of the game became an Austin Carr highlight film. He made drives to the hoop, created his own shot for short jumpers, rebounded, and made steals. He would score 15 of Notre Dame's final 17 points.

Late in the game, Carr sped past Wicks in a matchup of All-Americans and all the Bruin forward could do was foul him, his fifth foul of the game and third in the last three minutes when he was attempting to guard Carr. An article on the game in *The Sporting News* quoted Wicks as saying to Coach Wooden, "I told you not to put me on him."

With seven seconds left Carr was fouled again. As he went to the line, the students chanted "We're number one." Uncharacteristically, Carr raised his right index finger to the crowd after he sank both free throws, the 45th and 46th points in his scoring column.

While Carr was at the foul line, Wooden left the UCLA bench and walked to the Notre Dame bench to congratulate Dee. Wooden knew meeting Dee after the final buzzer would be impossible as the Notre Dame student body was about to rush the floor like it never had before.

The postgame scene was a classic moment in Notre Dame history as the fans hoisted Carr to their shoulders in a scene broadcast to the national television audience (on the TVS network produced by Eddie Einhorn) after a commercial. They brought Carr to the basket closest to the Notre Dame locker room where he cut down the nets, establishing a tradition that is still carried on today whenever the Irish pull off an upset of the nation's top team.

Carr had become the first Notre Dame athlete to "shake down the thunder" without the use of a football. He had scored 46 points against UCLA and the legendary coach John Wooden, the most points by an individual opponent in Wooden's 27-year UCLA career.

The media besieged Carr and Dee in the locker room as soon as they entered (no postgame interview rooms in those days).

"I know UCLA did not play as well as it can," said Carr. "They played last night in Chicago and didn't get here until 3:00 a.m. and that had to affect them.

"But we had them well scouted. They did all the things we thought they would. We overloaded one side and that left the whole right side open for me. I just drove to that side time and again.

"Yes, I do think the students had an effect on the game. You can be sure that they gave us 15 of 18 points out there today,"

John Wooden was gracious in defeat . . . but did have one statement that would have made him trend on Twitter today. "We were simply outplayed. That is what usually happens when you lose and it happened today. We are not unbeatable and today we met a team that played better than we did.

"Austin Carr is tremendous. Actually, Kenny Booker did a good job on Carr defensively at the start of the game. We told him to overplay Carr and to expect help if he drove to the basket. Unfortunately, we didn't get the inside help from our big men. Carr got too many easy baskets on drives."

Wooden continued and gave some props to Pleick. "The Notre Dame player that surprised me the most was John Pleick. Being from California I am sure he was giving a little extra."

When asked about playing Notre Dame again in the NCAA Tournament, Wooden gave a frank answer that would wrinkle an eyebrow or two in the Notre Dame locker room, but would prove to be correct.

"I would like to play them again in the NCAA Tournament on a neutral site, but I don't think that will happen. *Notre Dame will not go far in the tournament because they depend on one guy to score all the points, and teams like that never have won it.*

"Even when we had Lew Alcindor we had balanced scoring."

While Wooden would prove to be correct at season's end, this day belonged to Notre Dame and Carr. While Notre Dame didn't win a championship this day, it did bring unprecedented attention to the program and certainly help future Fighting Irish coaches in the recruiting process when it came to program credibility.

And it was probably the most important game in Carr winning National Player of the Year honors at season's end by the *Associated Press*, *United Press*, the Naismith Award, and the Helms Foundation.

He had scored a still record 61 points in the NCAA Tournament against Ohio University the previous year and would end his career with nine games of at least 50 points, 23 with at least 40, out of the 74 games he played. He scored at least 20 points in each of his last 58 games.

But this was the signature game of his career and a contributing factor to his selection as the top draft choice of the NBA the next summer.

Carr finished the afternoon with 46 points on 17 of 30 from the field and 12 of 16 from the foul line. Jones added 19 points and 14 rebounds, as both Notre Dame stars played the full 40 minutes. They scored 65 of Notre Dame's 89 points. But that was about their average for the season. Carr finished 1970–71 averaging 38 points a game, while Jones averaged 24 per contest, by far the highest scoring duo in Notre Dame history over the course of a season.

UCLA was the more balanced team on this day with four players in double figures led by Wicks's 23 points and 11 rebounds. Patterson had a double-double, also with 15 points and 10 rebounds. Rowe and Bibby both finished with 16.

Austin Carr drove through the UCLA defense for 46 points, still the most ever against a UCLA team. *Notre Dame Archives*

On the plane ride back to Los Angeles, Wooden had to plan his practice schedule and what he would say to his team coming off a loss. It would be the last time he had to do that for a long time.

Most Points Scored by an Opponent vs. John Wooden Coached UCLA Team

Player	Opponent	Date	Pts
Austin Carr	Notre Dame	1-23-71	46
Billy Knight	Pittsburgh	1-22-72	37
Freddie Boyd	Oregon State	1-7-72	37
Mike Sylvester	Dayton	3-14-74	36

NOTE: CARR'S 46 IS MOST EVER AGAINST ANY UCLA TEAM

THE AUSTIN CARR GAME
Notre Dame 89, UCLA 82
January 23, 1971
at Notre Dame, IN
Athletic and Convocation Center

UCLA (82)

Name	FG-A	FT-A	Reb	Ast-TO	F	Pts
Sidney Wicks	8-19	7-10	11	5-6	5	23
Curtis Rowe	6-13	4-6	9	4-4	4	16
Steve Patterson	7-11	1-2	10	4-5	3	15
Henry Bibby	6-12	4-5	4	2-0	4	16
Kenny Booker	3-4	0-1	3	1-4	3	6
Terry Schofield	0-1	0-0	1	0-0	0	0
John Ecker	0-0	0-0	0	0-1	1	0
Andy Hill	0-0	0-0	0	0-0	1	0
Larry Hollyfield	3-5	0-0	1	0-0	1	6
Rick Betchley	0-0	0-0	0	0-0	0	0
Team			5			
Totals	33-65 (.502)	16-24 (.667)	44	16-20	22	82

Notre Dame (89)

Name	FG-A	FT-A	Reb	Ast-TO	F	Pts
Collis Jones	6-19	7-9	14	1-4	4	19
John Pleick	3-8	3-3	7	2-1	5	9
Sid Catlett	2-9	0-0	5	2-1	4	4
Austin Carr	17-30	12-16	5	0-3	1	46
Jackie Meehan	1-3	1-2	1	6-5	4	3
Doug Gemmell	3-3	0-1	5	1-1	2	6
Tom Sinnott	1-1	0-1	0	2-0	0	2
Jim Regelean	0-0	0-0	1	0-0	0	0
Team			6			
Totals	33-73 (.452)	23-32 (.719)	44	14-15	20	89

Score by Half

UCLA	38	44	82
Notre Dame	43	46	89

OFFICIALS: DON WEDGE, RICHARD WEILER

ATTENDANCE: 11,343 (CAPACITY)

CHAPTER 2

UCLA Runs the Table

UCLA DROPPED TO NUMBER TWO IN THE *ASSOCIATED PRESS* POLL THE Monday after its seven-point loss to ninth-ranked Notre Dame. Johnny Dee's team improved to seventh and Al McGuire's 14–0 Marquette team jumped into the number-one spot. UCLA was still ranked second ahead of crosstown rival Southern California, who was 14–0.

After the trip to the Midwest to play Loyola and Notre Dame, the Bruins had a week off. Most expected Coach John Wooden to practice the team hard and get the squad refocused with a blowout against UC Santa Barbara, a solid team that would finish the season 20–6, but was just 9–4 entering a January 30, 1971, contest at Pavilion.

But the Gauchos had a two-point lead at the half, because the Bruins committed turnovers against the Santa Barbara pressure defense. UCLA came back to take the lead in the second half, but it was still just an eight-point margin with eight minutes left. In the end, UCLA won 74–61 thanks to veterans Curtis Rowe and Sidney Wicks who played well with 28 and 19 points, respectively.

Wooden was not satisfied with a 13-point win in a non-conference home game. He began his postgame meeting with the media by stating, "I am going to initiate this conversation by saying that I am not at all pleased. We didn't play well today and we didn't play well last weekend.

"We're not seeing the open man on offense. We're not sliding well on defense. And today, we looked as if we'd never seen a press before.

"If we play the way we're playing right now against Southern California, we don't have a chance."

So, the Bruins were not in a great mindset heading into the February 6 rivalry game with Southern California, now ranked second in the latest AP Poll. Perhaps the worst thing that happened to the Trojans was that February 1 poll because Southern California moved ahead of UCLA, who dropped to third after the lackluster home win over UC Santa Barbara.

Marquette was still number one, but Southern California's No. 2 ranking was its highest ever—and still is as I write this book in May 2023.

USC was 16–0 coming into the game and had three wins over top 20 teams to zero for the Bruins. Bob Boyd's team was led by future Naismith Hall of Fame player Paul Westphal and Mo Layton, a 6-foot-1 guard who would play five years in the NBA and ABA. *Sports Illustrated* had called the USC backcourt the best in the nation earlier in the season.

The Trojans had beaten top 20 teams from Florida State, LSU, and Illinois and also had wins over eventual NCAA tournament teams BYU and Houston. A 122–75 win over Alabama and Coach C. M. Newton brought the program national attention as well.

Despite these résumé advantages and the USC home court advantage, UCLA was installed as a two-and-a-half-point favorite by the folks in Las Vegas.

Southern California had a 38–37 lead at the half and held a 59–50 lead with about 10 minutes left. The LA Sports Arena home crowd was in a frenzy that resembled the enthusiasm of a USC home football crowd.

"Frankly, I was scared," said Wooden when discussing that situation in his postgame media meeting.

But shockingly, the Trojans went cold and scored just one point in the last 9:30 of the game. With five minutes left Kenny Booker stole the ball from Westphal and put the Bruins up, 61–59.

UCLA got the ball back and went into a stall for three minutes, certainly a rarity for a John Wooden–coached team, but he would use it a couple of times in key situations during this season. It would be a big reason UCLA was 7–0 in games decided by five points or less in 1970–71. The Bruins won 64–60.

Wicks finished with 24 points and 14 rebounds, and Booker had 14, including the most important bucket of the game.

With the win, UCLA jumped back to number one in the AP poll. Most felt the Bruins were on their way with such an emotional win. But on the trip to Oregon the following weekend (February 12–13), it looked like there was a hangover instead of an infusion of energy.

On Friday night in Eugene, UCLA trailed by five points with two minutes left. Just as Booker had done in the previous game against Westphal, Henry Bibby made a key steal from Bill Drozdiak with just 43 seconds left and scored a layup. Oregon star Stan Love sent Bibby into the stands with a hard foul after he made a basket, and a technical foul was called on the Ducks forward who had played high school basketball just a few miles from the UCLA campus in Inglewood, California.

It proved to be the deciding play as Oregon, trailing 69–68, held for one shot over the last 43 seconds. Len Jackson's shot missed and the Bruins had the victory.

The next night at Oregon State proved to be another cliffhanger in a battle of Hall of Fame coaches. Coming into the game, first-year Beavers head coach Ralph Miller had been 3–0 against Wooden in coaching stints at Wichita State and Iowa. Oregon State had a 14-point lead in the first half and had a three-point lead at intermission.

The game was close throughout, but once again a veteran Bruin made the winning play. This time it was Wicks who hit a jumper from the top of the key with just three seconds left for a 67–65 victory.

So, as you can see, the 88-game winning streak could have lasted just one, two, or three games, because the Bruins had three wins decided by four points or less within the first four games after the Notre Dame loss, with all three decided in the last minute.

The following weekend the Oregon schools returned the trip to Los Angeles and the Bruins won by 30 over Oregon State on Friday thanks to Wicks who had a 20–20 performance (25 points and 21 rebounds), and by seven on Saturday over the Ducks thanks to 28 more points by Wicks, who was reaffirming his candidacy for National Player of the Year.

UCLA's struggles on the road continued the next weekend in Washington, but again UCLA came away with a pair of victories.

On Friday night, February 27, UCLA had another road win that was a struggle. This time Rowe had an off game with a line score that said just six points on 2-for-9 shooting. Wicks had another strong game with 16 points and 11 rebounds, and Patterson was a big factor with 13 and nine.

It was a two-point game with seven seconds left when Terry Schofield was fouled. The force of the foul caused him to leave the game. Wooden looked to his bench and saw seldom used but 87 percent free throw shooter John Ecker staring at him. He gave him the nod and he made both free throws to give the Bruins a 57–53 lead and victory. Once again, the Wizard of Westwood made the right call.

On Saturday night, March 1, UCLA again survived an opponent's last second game- winning attempt. Rowe made a jumper over Washington State's Louis Nelson to give UCLA a one-point lead with 29 seconds left. Nelson then drove the lane on Washington State's next possession, but missed with two seconds left.

Patterson again had a great game with 17 points and 12 rebounds and he held Washington's star center Steve Hawes to a career-low seven points.

UCLA returned to its dominant ways in wins over California and Stanford on March 5 and 6, respectively. On Friday, the Bruins gave Wooden the 500th victory of his career with a 103–69 triumph, as Wicks had another 20–20 (21 points and 22 rebounds). He could have had a 30–30, as he sat out the last nine minutes. On Saturday night, the Bruins defeated Stanford 107–72.

This set up the regular season finale and senior night game for Wicks, Rowe, Patterson, and Booker against Southern California. UCLA was back at number one in both polls and Southern Cal was third. Both teams had not lost since the first meeting on February 6.

Even though UCLA had won the previous meeting at the LA Sports Arena, the Trojans were confident because they had beaten UCLA teams that had gone on to win the national championship each of the last two years. They had won at Pauley Pavilion the previous year in an up-tempo game against a top-ranked Bruins team, 87–86, which gave Westphal and company confidence they could run with the talented Bruins.

There were some quotes in the local media that told you the Trojans were a little too confident. A couple of players had said UCLA was lucky when they won earlier in the year by four points.

There was a lot on the line for these teams who had lost a combined two games coming into the contest. Prior to 1974–75, only the conference champion (any conference, not just the Pac-8) could go to the NCAA tournament. If Southern California could win this final game, both schools would be 13–1 in the Pac-8 and both teams would have won a game head-to-head. To break the tie there would be a one-game playoff the next day at Pauley Pavilion.

There would be no playoff needed as the Bruins raced to a 19-point lead at halftime. They went 12 minutes without a field goal in the second half that allowed Southern California to make a comeback thanks to a 20-rebound performance by Ron Riley, who is still the only UCLA opponent to have two 20-rebound games against UCLA. But the Bruins pulled away at the end to win, 73–63.

When we look back at it today, we wonder what the NCAA was thinking. Southern California had gone 24–2 with the only two losses coming to the nation's top team and couldn't go to the NCAA Tournament.

It took a similar situation in the Atlantic Coast Conference three years later to wake up the NCAA and allow more than one team from a conference to go to the tournament. In the 1974 ACC Tournament, North Carolina State defeated Maryland, 103–100, in what is still regarded as the greatest ACC Tournament game in history. Maryland finished the season 23–5 and ranked fourth in the nation. Lefty Driesell's team had lost three times to number-one ranked N.C. State, once to UCLA by a point in Pauley Pavilion, and once to North Carolina.

Maybe the ACC media made a louder cry than the Pac-8 media at the impropriety of the rules. The following offseason, the rule was changed.

A FIFTH STRAIGHT NATIONAL CHAMPIONSHIP

Until 1975, the NCAA Tournament had a regional aspect to its pairings. That meant UCLA stayed in the West (actually called the Far West Regional) and played against teams from the West until the Final Four. The Bruins had a first-round bye in the 25-team tournament and met BYU in its first tournament game on March 18, 1971.

In recent years, UCLA had benefitted from a home court advantage in the NCAA Tournament, something that doesn't happen at all today. In 1968, the Final Four was held at the Los Angeles Sports Arena, Southern California's home court, but just a few miles from the UCLA campus. The Bruins' first two games of the 1969 tournament were held on their Pauley Pavilion home court. UCLA won all four games easily.

But, in 1971, UCLA's path to the NCAA title started in the state of Utah at the home of the Running Utes. Their first opponent was BYU, whose campus was just 51 miles away. If the Bruins won two games at Utah, they would then have to win two games at the Final Four in the Astrodome in Houston, where the Bruins had suffered a nationally televised loss to Houston three years earlier. Entering the tournament Houston was one of the favorites to get to Houston.

BYU had won 18 games, including the WAC championship, and was ranked 20th in the AP poll entering the NCAA Tournament. Their résumé had included a 102–93 win over Villanova in a December tournament in Hawaii. That Villanova team would go on to the NCAA Championship game.

BYU featured the unique Kresimir Cosic, a 6'11" player who was capable of playing all five positions. He was the first European to be named to the United Press International All-America team, and would be inducted into the Naismith Hall of Fame in 1996, just the third international player so honored. He was a sophomore in 1970–71 and averaged 15.1 points and 12.6 rebounds per game.

The Cougars also featured Bernie Fryer, the team's leading scorer at 19.2 points a game, who later played in the NBA.

BYU had beaten 16th-ranked Utah State in a first-round game, 91–82. In those days with many teams receiving byes in the first round, it set up the question, are you better off playing a first-round game and getting a rhythm, or better off with a couple extra days of rest?

For UCLA the rest was a bigger factor as the Bruins won rather easily, 91–73. UCLA led 41–32 at the half and won the second half, 50–41. It was a balanced performance for Wooden's club. Bibby led the way with 15 points and nine rebounds, quite a total for a 6-foot-1 guard. Wicks had 14 points and added 20 rebounds, while Patterson had a double-double with 13 points, 11 rebounds, and four assists. Rowe had one of his best all-around games with 13 points, nine rebounds, and six assists.

Cosic was outstanding with 18 points, 23 rebounds, and five assists. It is still the most rebounds against a UCLA team. His all-around abilities contributed to his promotion for the next two years as one of the top college players in the nation, and as a player who would change the college game by enticing college coaches to look across the pond for talent more often.

That Bruins victory set up a regional final against Long Beach State and young dynamic head coach Jerry Tarkanian. He was in just his second year as head coach at the Division I level with the 49ers after posting a 67–4 record in two years at Pasadena City College.

Tarkanian had recruited Ed Ratleff from the state of Ohio to Long Beach and he became an instant star. He was at the top of Wooden's scouting report. Ratleff was just a sophomore in 1970–71, but was the team's leading scorer with a 19.9 average.

After a preseason No. 20 AP ranking, Long Beach State stubbed its toe early in the season against ranked teams Kansas and Marquette, and unranked clubs from Tulsa and UNLV. After the loss at Las Vegas, where Tark would become head coach just two years later, the 49ers went on an 18-game winning streak, including an 11–0 record in winning the Pacific Coast Athletic Conference.

Tarkanian had the reputation of running a high-octane offense at UNLV, but when he began at Long Beach State he relied on defense. In 1970–71, his team was 95th in the country in scoring offense, but sixth in scoring defense. He was noted for coming up with special defenses for the opposition, and he had a special zone defense for the Bruins.

We are not sure if it was a 1-2-2, a 2–3, or an amoeba defense, but it sure worked in the first half when Bibby, Booker, and Patterson were a combined 0-for-17 from the field. Long Beach held a 31–27 lead at intermission and it grew to 44–33 in the second half. On top of that, Wicks had four fouls.

During a possession with just 5:46 left and Long Beach State up by seven points, Ratleff was called for his fifth foul, a debatable call according to many media covering the game. The 49ers ace had fouled out with 18 points.

UCLA kept working its way back and cut the margin to two at 52–50. It was a struggle for the Bruins who would end the game 18-for-62 (.290) from the field as a team with Bibby making just 4 of 18, Patterson 2 of 8, and Wicks 5 of 13.

But Wicks was clutch from the foul line, hitting 4 of 4 in the final 25 seconds. UCLA never had the lead until 25 seconds remaining after he made two free throws. Wicks made two more with 12 seconds left to give the Bruins a 57–55 lead.

With Ratleff out of the game there were other options for Long Beach State in its attempt to tie the game. George Trapp had scored 15 points and collected 16 rebounds.

But the ball ended up in the hands of 6'2" reserve guard Dwight Taylor, who had averaged just 5.5 points per game and shot just .346 from the field for the season. He had taken only one shot in the game and missed it. His last-second jumper missed and UCLA was on to the Final Four.

It was a tough ending for Taylor in that game and he had a difficult ending to his life. In 1992, he was killed at the age of 42 during the beginning of the Rodney King riots in Los Angeles. He was the unfortunate victim of a stray gunshot when he was exiting a supermarket. He had run into the store to simply buy a few groceries for his family.

It was a difficult loss for Tarkanian, who would lead UNLV to the national championship 19 years later. "We did everything we had to do," said Tarkanian after the game. "We stopped UCLA's inside game. We shut them off outside, we kept our hands in their faces, we stayed close. . . . We did everything we wanted to do to win."

While UCLA shot just 29 percent from the field, it did hit 21 free throws and won the rebounding margin by eight.

THE FINAL FOUR

The Final Four was still played on a Thursday night and a Saturday night in 1971. The event was played at the Astrodome in Houston, regarded as the Eighth Wonder of the World when it had opened in April 1965.

The Astrodome got the Final Four because of an epic game between UCLA and Houston on January 20, 1968. It was the most publicized regular season college basketball game to that point, and it had an epic result as Houston and Elvin Hayes upset UCLA and Lew Alcindor, 71–69 to end the Bruins' 47-game winning streak.

More than 52,000 fans attended that game and the NCAA thought it could draw a similar crowd for a Final Four, so it didn't take long for the national governing body to put a Final Four in the relatively new facility that at the time was the home of the Houston Astros and the Houston Oilers.

As had been the case for that Houston vs. UCLA regular season game three years earlier, the court was placed in the middle of the field, something that would never happen today. There wasn't a good seat in the house according to many, including the fans who paid top dollar to sit close to the court.

The court was four feet above the floor of the stadium, making it difficult for those fans to see over photographers and courtside personnel. There was also some concern about players running off the end or sides of the court going after a loose ball and getting injured as a result of the four-foot drop that was just 10 feet off the court.

At the half, teams had to walk a long distance through the baseball dugouts used by the Astros, then make their way to the locker rooms. There wasn't much time for halftime adjustments. As soon as they arrived it was about time to turn around and go back to the court for shooting prior to the second half.

Each school at the Final Four that year received $60,000, at the time a much larger purse than had been received previously, so teams were benefitting from the unusual setup.

The Bruins faced Kansas in the second semifinal game on Thursday night. Like UCLA, Ted Owens's Jayhawks had lost just one game all year, at Louisville on December 20. The Jayhawks entered on a 21-game winning streak and had a 27–1 overall record.

Kansas was not well received in Houston because the Jayhawks had beaten Houston in the regional, 78–77, and that kept the Cougars from having a true home court advantage for the Final Four.

Against Houston, Kansas star Dave Robisch had 29 points, 16 rebounds, six blocks, and four steals in one of the best all-around performances anyone had seen that year.

That performance had UCLA coaches a bit concerned because they didn't have Lew Alcindor in the post to guard him. Robisch would end the semifinal game with 17 points, but Wicks, Rowe, and Patterson combined to limit him to 7 of 19 shooting.

UCLA led 32–25 at the half, but Kansas made a run early in the second half. With the score 39–37 in UCLA's favor, Robisch hit a jump shot to tie the score, but one of the officials whistled him for traveling and wiped out the goal. It was an extremely controversial call and Robisch said in an interview later in life that he probably remembers that play above all others in his career that included 930 professional games.

UCLA eventually got its lead to 15 points after that "turnover" and went on to the 68–60 victory. Wicks and Rowe were superb, as the former had 21 points, and the latter had 16 points on 7-for-10 shooting while adding 15 rebounds. Bibby was the top player in the backcourt with 18 points on 6-for-9 shooting from the field and 6-for-6 from the line.

Bibby's contribution was more than just points and assists. At one point in the game assistant coach Denny Crum wanted to send guard Terry Schofield into the game. Crum was the assistant coach in charge of substitutions on that staff that included future UCLA head coach Gary Cunningham.

Coach Wooden said no to Schofield's entry into the game, but Crum sent him in anyway and Wooden threatened to send Crum to the end of the bench. Both coaches were hot and Bibby intervened to try to calm both of them.

According to *Sports Illustrated*, Wooden said to Crum at a later point in the game, "I'm the coach of this team, and don't tell me how to coach my team."

All seemed fine after the game and the next day when both coaches attended a luncheon. But at the end of the season, Crum left UCLA to become the head coach at Louisville, where he won two national titles and had a Hall of Fame career.

A look to the final stats shows that UCLA won the game by dominating the boards 42–29 and the Jayhawks made just 12 of 23 free throws. Kansas stayed in the game by forcing the Bruins into an uncharacteristic 24 turnovers, while committing just 11.

UCLA met Villanova in the national championship game on Saturday, March 27. The Wildcats of Philadelphia, Pennsylvania, had lost six games during the regular season and were attempting to be just the second NCAA champion since Kentucky's Rupp's Runts of 1958, and just the second overall, with that many losses.

Villanova was an up-tempo team under Jack Kraft and they would average 86 points per game at season's end. They dressed only nine players at the Final Four, but that had been the situation most of the year. Five players averaged at least 13 points a game for the season, led by Howard Porter who had a 23.5 scoring average and 14.8 rebounds per game. Not bad for a 6'8" pivot.

Unlike UCLA, Villanova had a key win over Notre Dame at mid-season. They had "held" Austin Carr to 37 points. After beating the Irish, Villanova lost just one more game the rest of the regular season. The late season run against eastern teams gave Villanova a 23–6 record and No. 19 AP ranking entering the NCAA Tournament.

Villanova dispensed with St. Joseph's (Pennsylvania) in the first round, then downed Digger Phelps's upstart Fordham team, 85–75. In the East Regional final, the college basketball world took notice of its 90–47 domination of Pennsylvania, at the time the largest victory margin in the history of the tournament.

That brought Villanova to a national semifinal game against Western Kentucky and 7'1" All-American Jim McDaniels. The battle between McDaniels and Porter was epic. McDaniels had 22 points and

17 rebounds, while Porter had 22 and 16 rebounds. Villanova won the game in double overtime after McDaniels fouled out, 92–89.

That semifinal proved to be a matchup of players who had taken money from agents before the end of the tournament and both Villanova and Western Kentucky were later forced to vacate their participation in the 1971 NCAA Tournament.

Porter had scored at least 22 points in each NCAA Tournament game so he was obviously a focal point of UCLA's scouting report. While the Bruins were certainly favored, there was concern on the UCLA side because Steve Patterson was not playing well and would be going against the eventual tournament Most Outstanding Player in Porter.

Patterson had started off the tournament well with a double-double against BYU and Cosic (13 points, 11 rebounds), but in wins over Long Beach State and Kansas he was just 5-for-19 from the field and had just 11 total points.

What resulted was one of the most unpredictable great individual performances in a championship game in tournament history.

Villanova had decided to take a page out of Long Beach State's game plan and played a zone against UCLA. That opened some areas for Patterson, who made 9-for-13 shots from the field in the first half and scored 20 points, leading to an 11-point Bruins lead.

In the second half Wooden decided to hold the ball and bring Villanova out of its zone. After a period of time, Kraft went man-to-man, but they did well in those matchups. Porter and Hank Siemiontkowski hit shots and cut the UCLA lead to four with 4:53 left. UCLA made just three field goals during an eight-minute span and Villanova later cut the lead to three twice inside the final minutes.

But Patterson hit his 13th and final field goal with 38 seconds left, giving the Bruins an eight-point lead and UCLA had its fifth straight national title, its 28th straight NCAA Tournament win, and 15th straight win to end the 1970–71 season.

Patterson finished with 29 points on 13-for-18 shooting from the field, added eight rebounds and four assists in his final game and most important performance as a Bruin.

He needed to record those numbers because Wicks and Rowe were non-factors in their final college games. Rowe had eight points, but took just three shots (making two) in playing all 40 minutes. Wicks had just seven points on 3-for-7 shooting in 40 minutes. Bibby was also a key with 17 points.

Porter finished with 25 points, giving him 133 points for the five games in the tournament. In defeat he was named the tournament's Most Outstanding Player. Although the award was later listed as vacated because of his NCAA violations with an agent, Porter and Houston's Akeem Olajuwon (1983) are the only players on the losing team to win the award since 1971.

Coach Wooden on the 1970–71 Season

Amazing poise, incredible courage and extraordinary discipline were qualities consistently exemplified by the 1971 Champion UCLA Bruins throughout the entire season. These qualities along with an exceptional defense and outstanding rebounding enabled us to gain the pinnacle to which we aspire.

Although the headlines usually, and deservedly, went to Sidney Wicks and/or Curtis Rowe, both of whom performed superbly, Steve Patterson (what a championship game he had against Villanova), Henry Bibby (his clutch steal at Oregon saved us as did his outstanding shooting in other games), Kenny Booker (his play in the first game against USC averted defeat), Terry Schofield (his outstanding shooting against zones and some key steals were instrumental in many victories), John Eckler (pressure free throws at Oregon), Larry Farmer (his essential rebound in the closing minutes against Long Beach State) and the daily practice performances of Rick Betchley, Jon Chapman, Andy Hill and Larry Hollyfield were all very important to the ultimate accomplishment of the team.

I salute and thank them all and wish them continued success in every pursuit.

Irish Eliminated in Sweet 16

While Wooden and the Bruins were running the table in January, February, and March 1971, Notre Dame was playing well, hanging around the top 20 every week.

Carr was as consistent as ever. He averaged 37.9 points per game through the UCLA game (the team's 14th game) on January 23, then averaged 38.0 over the final 15 games to finish with an overall average of 37.9, second in the nation to Johnny Neumann of Mississippi.

The Irish did not have a letdown in the game following the upset of No. 1 UCLA as they defeated Michigan State 104–80 behind 36 from Carr, who shot 15-for-21 from the field.

But an 18th-ranked Illinois team downed Notre Dame 69–66 on January 30. The Irish went 3–1 over the next four games before heading to New York City to take on Digger Phelps's Fordham team, who had captivated the city with a remarkable season. They were ranked 18th nationally and defeated the Irish in front of a sellout crowd at Madison Square Garden, 94–88 (more on that game in chapter 3).

But that would be the last regular season loss for Carr and the Irish, who won their final five regular-season games, including a 92–79 victory over St. John's in a return trip the Garden.

On senior night at the Joyce Athletic Center, Carr scored "just" 31 points, but Notre Dame downed Western Michigan, 110–79. It was Carr's last home game and afterward he was carried from the court by the students and brought to the scorer's table. He was given the microphone into which he proclaimed, "On to Houston!"

Carr had 52 points in the NCAA opening round win over TCU, but Drake upset Notre Dame in the round of 16 with a 79–72 overtime victory, ending the dream of a trip to the Final Four.

Carr scored 47 in his final college game against Houston in the regional consolation game to end the season. He scored 1,106 points as a junior and 1,101 as a senior, becoming the second player in college history to score over 1,100 points in consecutive seasons. He scored at least 20 points in every game his junior and senior seasons, 58 consecutive games. His 34.6 career average is topped only by Pete Maravich in college basketball history.

Carr was named the winner of the Naismith Award as college basketball's top player, beating out Wicks. He was then the top pick of the 1971 NBA Draft by the Cleveland Cavaliers. He played 10 years for the

Cavs and has become a legend in their organization as the color commentator on local television broadcasts.

1971 NCAA Championship Game
12UCLA 68, Villanova 62
March 27, 1971
at Houston, Texas
Astrodome

UCLA (68)

Name	Min	FG-A	FT-A	Reb	Ast	F	Pts
Curtis Rowe	40	2-3	4-5	8	2	0	8
Sidney Wicks	40	3-7	1-1	9	7	2	7
Steve Patterson	40	13-18	3-5	8	4	1	29
Henry Bibby	40	6-12	5-5	2	3	1	17
Kenny Booker	5	0-0	0-0	0	0	0	0
Terry Schofield	26	3-9	0-0	1	4	4	6
Rick Betchley	9	0-0	1-2	1	0	1	1
Team				5			
Totals	200	27-49 (.551)	14-18 (.778)	34	20	9	68

Villanova (62)

Name	Min	FG-A	FT-A	Reb	Ast	F	Pts
Tom Inglesby	40	3-9	1-1	4	7	2	7
Hank Siemiontkowski	37	9-16	1-2	6	0	3	19
Chris Ford	40	0-4	2-3	5	10	4	2
Clarence Smith	40	4-11	1-1	2	0	4	9
Howard Porter	40	10-21	5-6	8	0	1	25
Joe McDowell	3	0-1	0-0	2	1	0	0
Team				4			
Totals	200	26-62 (.419)	10-13 (.769)	31	18	14	62

Score by Half

UCLA	45	23	68
Villanova	37	25	62

TURNOVERS: UCLA 13, VILLANOVA 10

OFFICIALS: JIM BAIN, IRV BROWN

ATTENDANCE: 31,765

CHAPTER 3

Wooden and Phelps,
the Faces of Their Programs

IF YOU SEARCH ON YOUTUBE TODAY FOR THE FINAL FOUR MINUTES OF the January 19, 1974, Notre Dame vs. UCLA game, Hall of Fame announcer Dick Enberg puts the contrast between John Wooden and Digger Phelps in perspective.

With 45 seconds left in the game, Notre Dame took over the ball after an offensive foul on senior forward Keith (Jamaal) Wilkes when he hooked freshman guard Ray Martin on a drive to the basket.

Just as the Irish inbounded the ball on the ensuing possession, Enberg said, "John Robert Wooden, 63 years old, when he went into the US Navy in the Second World War, Digger Phelps was being born. Sixty-three and thirty-two (years of age), the contrast between the veteran Wooden and the electric young coach of the Irish."

There were more drastic differences between the two coaches in this historically important game than just age.

The most glaring difference might have been their respective playing careers.

Wooden was a star basketball player from an early age, earning All-State honors in Indiana his last three years of high school. He led Martinsville High to the 1927 state championship and runner-up honors in 1926 and 1928. That was quite an accomplishment because there was just one state basketball champion in Indiana until the 1997–98 academic year.

Wooden's high school success led to a scholarship at Purdue, where he was a three-time consensus All-American, the first on record. (Notre Dame's Moose Krause, who would become the school's athletic director between 1948–80, was the second from 1932–34.)

Wooden played for Piggy Lambert, who would be a great influence on his coaching career. The coach and star player led the Boilermakers to Big Ten titles in 1930 and 1932 and a mythical national championship that final year when Wooden averaged a Big Ten–best 12.8 points a game and led a Purdue defense that allowed just 23 points per game.

Nicknamed the "Indiana Rubber Man," when *Street & Smith* magazine did a special publication on the 100 greatest college basketball players in 2003, Wooden was ranked No. 81. He and Hank Luisetti (1934–38 at Stanford) were the only representatives in the Top 100 who played in the 1930s. Wooden and Rick Mount were the only Purdue alums on the top 100, and Wooden was one of just seven players who grew up in Indiana.

Wooden was elected to the Naismith Hall of Fame as a player in 1960. Note that selection was made before he won any national championship as a coach, so his fame as a mentor at UCLA had no impact on his selection. When he was inducted again in 1973 as a coach, he became the first person inducted into the Naismith Hall of Fame as both a player and a coach. (There are now five with dual membership, with Lenny Wilkins, Bill Sharman, Tom Heinsohn, and Bill Russell on that select list.)

Wooden went on to play two years in the NBL, the professional league at the time that lasted 12 years and was a forerunner to the NBA. Somehow, he found time to both play in the NBL and coach high school basketball during the 1937–38 season, the first year of the league. He earned first-team All-NBL honors for the Whiting Ciesar All-Americans. At one point he made 134 consecutive free throws, which is still ahead of the current NBA record of 97 in a row by Michael Williams who set that mark in 1993. (We are not aware of a consecutive-made free throw record in any competition that is longer than Wooden's 134.)

Digger Phelps grew up playing all sports in Beacon, New York. He was an all-county basketball player at Beacon High School where he also ran track for one year and played baseball for two. After graduating from Beacon High in 1959, he made the two-hour drive to Rider College in Lawrenceville, New Jersey.

Phelps was a two-sport athlete at Rider. You probably haven't heard much about his college basketball career as a player, but an even smaller number probably know he also played college golf at Rider. He once competed in a golf match for Rider at the famed Aronimink Golf Club in Philadelphia.

Phelps played on the varsity team at Rider in 1960–61, 1961–62, and 1962–63. The Broncs posted a 20–8 record his senior year in 1962–63 when they made the NAIA national tournament in Kansas City.

Phelps was known for his aggressive play, especially when it came to chasing down rebounds. Over his last two years he played 45 games and had more rebounds (184) than points (179). He averaged 4.9 points and 5.0 rebounds as a junior, and 3.1 points and 3.2 rebounds as a senior.

He was known to some for his defensive play, and on January 9, 1963, when Rider met Seton Hall and national scoring leader Nick Werkman, Phelps was assigned to him. "I think I held him to 42," says Phelps today with a laugh.

Phelps then jumped into his coaching career the next season as a graduate assistant at his alma mater.

During that year Rider played NYU, then a nationally known team thanks to the play of future NBA star Happy Hairston. This game was to be played on NYU's campus, a rarity as NYU played most of its home games at Madison Square Garden.

This game was played on March 3, 1964, and NYU had not lost at home at their Alumni Gym since 1941, a streak that stretched 57 games. Phelps was charged with scouting NYU and he saw them play two games, one against Iona and one against Hofstra.

Ever the realist, but also an optimist, Phelps told head coach Bob Greenwood he thought Rider could win the game and he had a game plan to do it.

The Rider team worked on Phelps's scouting report for two days. After the score was tied at 29 at halftime, Rider won 66–63 thanks to some great defense by Nick Valvano, brother of Jim Valvano, late free throws and rebounds by Dick Kuchen, Phelps's future longtime assistant coach at Notre Dame, and a career-high 32 points from Dick Endres.

"That was where the tradition of the upsets started," says Phelps. "That game early in my career gave me confidence that I could do this."

As stated earlier, Digger Phelps was on the varsity golf team at Rider. John Wooden was not on the golf team at Purdue, but he had an incredible accomplishment on the golf course, one that has been duplicated by only 12 other people anywhere.

That golfing accomplishment took place at Erskine Golf Club in South Bend, Indiana, of all places, just 5.1 miles from where Notre Dame plays its home basketball games . . . just 5.1 miles from where Wooden and his UCLA Bruins set the all-time college record for consecutive wins with a victory over Notre Dame on January 27, 1973.

And, of course, just 5.1 miles from where the longest men's college basketball winning streak would end in 1974.

On Monday, June 26, 1939, Wooden played a friendly round of golf with some teachers from South Bend Central High School where he was the head basketball coach and an English teacher.

At the time 28 years old, Wooden was an avid golfer who took lessons from John Watson, the golf professional at Erskine Golf Club in South Bend. Watson was a renowned teacher from Scotland who went on to be head pro at South Bend County Club.

While his final score of 75 was not his career best (he was a six handicap at the time), what he accomplished on two of the holes that day was remarkable.

First, on the par-3 sixth hole that measured 175 yards, he made a hole-in-one with a five iron. "I didn't see the ball go in the hole, but I knew it had gone in based on the reaction by the next group that was standing near the green," said Wooden in an interview with *Golf Digest*, four months before his death in 2010.

Later in the round he made a double eagle 2, on the par-5 15th hole that measured 504 yards. He made the second shot on the hole with a three wood.

A hole-in-one and an albatross in the same round is something that has been accomplished just 12 times in history, anywhere, according to the latest reports by *Golf Digest*.

As a high school teacher at the time, he was not the most famous coach in Indiana, never mind the country. Few knew about the accomplishment until he did that interview 71 years later with *Golf Digest*.

It was not until his daughter, Nan Muehlhausen, found the scorecard after he passed away while going through his belongings in his modest Encino, California, condominium that the story received national publicity. Nan found the scorecard from the round in a box that Wooden had kept all these years. It was signed by six people, the three he was playing with and the three-some playing in front who had seen both shots go into the cup.

Golf media outlets from all over the world made mention of the accomplishment that is now listed with other documented occasions of someone making a hole in one and an albatross in the same round.

Wooden Still Influencing Coaches Today

John Wooden has an incredible legacy when it comes to winning championships. He has a terrific legacy in helping to develop outstanding players for professional basketball. He also has a significant legacy when it comes to guiding the careers of outstanding professionals when it comes to broadcasting, doctors, lawyers, just about any profession you can think of over his 40 years as a coach.

But one of the most nationally well-known aspects of his legacy is his ability to motivate coaches, and thus teams, through his widely quoted philosophies of leadership, team building, and motivation.

While there is no data to back it up, one has to believe John Wooden is the most widely quoted coach by other coaches in all sports.

Dabo Swinney, a two-time national champion of college football at Clemson, is one of the more prominent coaches in college sports who routinely quotes Wooden to his players, his coaches, his administration, and the general public when making a speech.

In February 2023, Swinney gave a talk at an Anderson University football fundraiser in nearby Anderson, South Carolina. Anderson is a four-year institution that will be starting a football program in 2024. During his keynote address at the school's opening fundraiser, he related some of the tenets of his program that has won two national championships, six College Football Playoffs (football's Final Four), eight conference championships, and 11 consecutive top 15 seasons.

Swinney said to the Anderson group, "One of my favorite quotes by John Wooden stated, 'It takes talent to win, but it takes character to repeat.'"

Swinney takes pride in his program's success on the field, but he takes just as much pride in his program's success in the classroom. Clemson has ranked in the top 10 percent in the nation among Division I programs in APR scores and graduation rates 11 of the last 12 years, something only Duke and Vanderbilt have also achieved.

Those statistics are an indicator of his student-athlete's character.

Each July, Swinney resets his entire coaching and administrative staff with a weeklong retreat. He reviews every aspect of the program from a coaching and administrative standpoint. The manual he distributes to the staff includes four quotes from John Wooden at various points of the book. He has used those quotes every year he has been a head coach (15 years).

"Whether it be a speech to any group, or my team or staff, I often talk about character building as a major part of our program's culture," said Swinney. "It is important to build a culture with high character student-athletes and it is important that it last. That was also a key to Coach Wooden's team's culture and success.

"You can get to the top, but to stay there you need to have high character. That was one of his main messages."

Here are some other Wooden quotes Swinney uses in his All-In Manual:

"If you don't have time to do it right, when will you have the time to do it over."

"Be more concerned with your character than your reputation, because your character is what you really are, while your reputation is merely what others think you are."

"Talent is God-given. *Be humble.* Fame is man-given. *Be grateful.* Conceit is self-given. *Be careful.*"

"You can't have a perfect day without doing something for someone who will never be able to repay you."

"Do not let what you cannot do interfere with what you can do."

One of the most famous images of Wooden's philosophy was his Pyramid of Success. A similar pyramid is posted at the entrance to the Clemson football practice field outside the team locker room at the Reeves Football Facility on the Clemson campus. Every player comes by that pyramid every day on the way to practice.

"I got the idea to display that pyramid from another coach, but I am sure the idea for it originated with Coach Wooden. I put some of my own tenets in the blocks, but the one at the top is the same as the one at the top of coach Wooden's Pyramid . . . Competitive Greatness."

Swinney also pointed out that he has often used the Seven-Point Creed that Wooden received from his father when he was a youth when he meets with his Clemson team:

Dad's Seven-Point Creed
1. Be true to yourself

2. Help others

3. Make each day your masterpiece

4. Drink deeply from good books, including the Good Book

5. Make friendship a fine art

6. Build a shelter against a rainy day

7. Pray for guidance, count and give thanks for your blessings each day.

Swinney has also referred to Wooden's two sets of threes as axioms of life to live by:

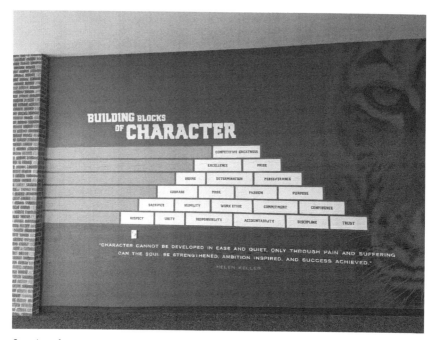

Coaches from around the nation in all sports still use John Wooden quotes and teaching methods. Pictured is Dabo Swinney's version of the Pyramid of Success Clemson football players see every day at their practice facility. *Author photo*

Wooden's Two Sets of Threes

1. Never lie

2. Never cheat

3. Never steal

4. Don't whine

5. Don't complain

6. Don't make excuses

It is interesting to point out that entering the 2023 season, Swinney was the winningest active coach in Division I college football with a .805 winning percentage (161–39). John Wooden finished his career with

664–162 record, an .804 winning percentage. Wooden is fifth in NCAA basketball history in winning percentage and Swinney is sixth (minimum of 150 wins) in Division I football. Swinney had a streak of 11 consecutive final top 15 Associated Press finishes and Wooden had a run of nine in a row and 16 overall.

"John Wooden's philosophies are timeless," said Swinney. "Coaches will be talking to their teams in all sports about his Pyramid for Success and other quotes as long as we have sports."

Wooden was presented with the Presidential Medal of Freedom in 2003, the third coach in any sport to receive the honor (Bear Bryant and Earl Blaik preceded Wooden. Pat Summitt, Dean Smith, and Lou Holtz have received it since). Perhaps someday Swinney will join the list.

JOHN WOODEN COMES TO UCLA

In the April 17, 2017, issue of *Sports Illustrated*, the magazine did a "what if" feature. It examined what would have happened over sports history if some different decisions had been made that would have significantly changed the course of sports history.

One of the pictures used in the issue was a mock cover depicting John Wooden in a 1940s era University of Minnesota basketball sweater.

In reality it almost happened, for the legendary career of John Wooden almost didn't happen in Westwood. Would the University of Minnesota have celebrated 10 national championships in the rafters of Williams Arena had he become the Gophers head coach in 1948? We will never know.

As crazy as it sounds, a 1948 snowstorm in the state of South Dakota altered the course of college basketball history.

After the 1947–48 season Wooden was a hot item when it came to coaching openings. He had been the coach at Indiana State in Terre Haute, Indiana, for the 1946–47 and 1947–48 seasons and taken the NAIA school to great heights.

In his first year he led Indiana State to a 17–8 record and a bid to the NAIB postseason tournament in Kansas City. But Wooden declined the invitation because one of his players was an African American named Clarence Walker. While not a rule in writing, there was a "gentleman's agreement" at the time that African American players were not allowed to play in the national tournament in Kansas City.

The next year, the "gentleman's agreement" was eliminated and Walker was allowed to play. Wooden's second Sycamores team raced to a 22–6 regular season record. It is interesting to note that one of the losses was by 16 points to Notre Dame, coached by Moose Krause.

Indiana State then won its first five games of the national tournament in Kansas City to reach the championship game against Louisville. But Louisville won 82–70, the only time John Wooden lost a national championship game.

With a 44–15 record in two years, Wooden was pursued by UCLA and Minnesota after the season. Having grown up in the Midwest with a résumé that included coaching high school in Ohio and Indiana, it was common knowledge that Wooden and his wife Nell preferred to stay in the Midwest.

But he was also in the stage of his career where it was time to move from the NAIB level to a bigger program.

The negotiations with Minnesota went well and Gophers athletic director Frank McCormick offered Wooden the job. Wooden told McCormick he would come to Minneapolis, but only under the condition that he could bring his assistant coaches with him.

These were certainly different times and money was much tighter. McCormick was hopeful Wooden would keep Dave MacMillan, the Gophers' recently fired head coach, on his staff for at least a year because the school owed him another season under his contract. To make this happen McCormick had to get permission from university president James Morrill.

During the process, McCormick traveled to South Dakota to visit a friend. He never dreamed that trip would change the course of college basketball.

A snowstorm in South Dakota knocked out the phone lines and he could not get through to Wooden to tell him he had gotten approval from Morrill to pay off MacMillan's last year without him being on Wooden's staff.

Had he not gone to visit that friend in South Dakota his call would have gone through because the weather in Minneapolis that April day was 64 degrees.

When Wooden did not hear from McCormick on April 17, 1948, he assumed McCormick could not get the situation approved. So, when UCLA called later that night, Wooden accepted their offer.

How text messaging would have changed the course of Minnesota and Big Ten athletics.

One other note for the "what if" list concerns the 1948–49 Minnesota roster. The Gophers hired Ozzie Cowles after Wooden took the UCLA position. Cowles was a native of the state of Minnesota who had been the Michigan head coach the previous two years.

Cowles was successful from the first year, and even seven years into his tenure at Minnesota he had a 69 percent winning mark, just below Wooden's 71 percent mark at UCLA for his first seven years.

Cowles led the Gophers to an 18–3 record and a number-six final ranking in the AP poll that first season. In fact, they were ranked in the top six by the Associated Press (first year of the poll) the entire year. The third leading scorer on that team was future NFL Hall of Fame coach Bud Grant. So, had Wooden gotten that phone call and accepted the Minnesota job, one of his starters and top players would have been the future Pro Football Hall of Fame coach.

Wooden went on to win 10 national championships in 12 years between 1964 and 1975, still the greatest run in NCAA basketball history. But it did take him 15 years to win a title. He was tempted to leave Westwood one more time, after the 1949–50 season.

His alma mater, Purdue, came calling and he was certainly tempted. As he was quoted as saying years later, "Nellie didn't like Los Angeles and there was a lot more money being offered by Purdue.

"But UCLA reminded me that I was the one who insisted on a three-year contract [when he accepted the job]. That was true. So I talked it over with Nell and I said, 'You know I gave my word.' And I haven't broken it yet."

So, he called Purdue and said he would stay at UCLA.

Wooden and Phelps both had quick rises in the coaching profession. Wooden went from being a high school coach early in 1946 to becoming the head coach at UCLA in the spring of 1948.

This short brief from the Elkhart (Indiana) *Truth* newspaper in the winter of 1946 puts his swift rise in perspective.

A short blurb was written about a local sports banquet that had just taken place.

"John Wooden, the head coach at South Bend Central High School, a recent service returnee, came to speak at the Elkhart Winter Sports Banquet. They had hoped to line up some prominent college coach."

WOODEN NOT ONE TO SCOUT THE OPPONENT

One difference between John Wooden and Digger Phelps was the use of scouting. Digger studied film of the opposing team and personally went to games to see the other team in person. He did that when he was the coach at Fordham and scouted Notre Dame at a Marquette game in 1971. He was to play the two teams on consecutive Thursday nights in Madison Square Garden.

Wooden was the opposite. Bill Walton told a story in a first person 1994 *Sports Illustrated* article that summarized his approach. "His philosophy didn't include scouting. He taught us to play against an idea, not an actual opponent.

"He would come in the locker room before a game with his rolled up program and say, 'Men, I've done my job. We've practiced all week. We're ready. The rest is up to you.

"That was it, it wasn't uncommon for us to ask the ballboys to go fetch a game program so we could see the names and faces of the opposing players."

DIGGER PHELPS COMES TO NOTRE DAME

The week after Notre Dame's 29–3 football victory over Navy on October 30, 1965, head coach Ara Parseghian received a letter from a first-year high school coach at a small Catholic school in Hazelton, Pennsylvania. The letter from the twenty-four-year-old basically told Parseghian that he wanted to be the head basketball coach at Notre Dame someday. Even though he had never seen the campus, it was his dream job.

Parseghian, who was in the middle of his second year at Notre Dame, received a lot of letters like this from football coaches interested in getting into his chosen profession, but never had he received a letter from a basketball coach about being the Notre Dame basketball coach. Well, at least this guy wasn't after his job. He had a file for such correspondence called "Crazy Letter File." And that is where he placed it.

Less than six years later, in May 1971, a now twenty-nine-year old Richard "Digger" Phelps, the author of that letter, joined Parseghian as basketball coach on the head coaching staff of legendary Notre Dame athletic director Moose Krause.

Phelps was the first Notre Dame head coach who was not a Notre Dame graduate since 1943, but he probably had twice as much passion for the school as any of his predecessors.

"I loved the essence of Notre Dame and what the University stood for," recalled Phelps about his letter to Parseghian. "It does seem crazy today that I wrote a letter to the football coach about becoming the basketball coach. But Ara had such charisma. He was the most visible face of the school and I identified with him.

"When I thought about Notre Dame then, I thought of Ara Parseghian. To some extent I still do that today even though he is no longer with us."

That letter was just one of the examples of Phelps's personal mission to be the head basketball coach at Notre Dame at an early age. A native of Beacon, New York, he was surrounded by New York "subway alums" and he remembers as a youth the city's excitement when the Notre Dame football team came to Yankee Stadium to play Army.

"When I was a kid and we played pickup football games in the neighborhood, I was always Johnny Lujack," he said of the 1947 Heisman winner who passed away in 2023. Phelps was just six years old when Lujack won the Heisman.

When Phelps became the head coach at St. Gabriel's High School in 1965, he designed the uniforms and wanted to incorporate something about Notre Dame into the game attire. "Even though our primary color was purple, I put a green shamrock on our game pants."

Phelps coached at St. Gabriel's for one year and won the state Class C championship. He then became the freshman coach at the University of Pennsylvania, a position he held for four years, and helped recruit many of the players who eventually took the Quakers to a 28–1 record, a number-three final ranking in the AP poll, and a trip to the Elite Eight of the NCAA Tournament in 1970–71.

One of those Penn recruits was Corky Calhoun, who lived in Waukegan, Illinois. In the fall of 1968, on one of his recruiting visits to Illinois for the Quaker program, Phelps made a side trip to Notre Dame. He had a strong relationship with Johnny Druze, who had been one of the Seven Blocks of Granite at Fordham with Vince Lombardi, and later an assistant coach at Notre Dame under Frank Leahy and Terry Brennan.

"Johnny called Moose Krause and arranged for me to meet him. But, before I met Moose, I went to Notre Dame Stadium and walked to the middle of the field. I mentally flashed back to my youth. I could hear Bill Stern calling games on WOR radio in New York. I had goose bumps standing in the middle of that field. The visit only confirmed to me that this is where I wanted to be."

Two years later Phelps, with the help of Druze, was named the head basketball coach at Fordham. He took over a team that had been 10–15 the previous year and shocked the college basketball world by taking the Rams to a 26–3 record and number-nine final ranking in the AP poll.

Two key games on Fordham's 1970–71 schedule were consecutive late February Thursday night games against Notre Dame and Marquette, respectively, in famed Madison Square Garden.

In those days, there was no film exchange and coaches, usually assistants, scouted games involving future opponents in person. Notre Dame played at Marquette on January 12, 1971, so Phelps decided he could scout both teams with one trip to Milwaukee.

Instead of calling Marquette to get a scouting pass, he called Eleanor Van Der Hagen, Krause's secretary. He had made a point of striking up a friendship with Eleanor when he visited three years earlier.

Digger was the master at paying attention to detail and cultivating relationships. "Eleanor was a wonderful person," recalled Phelps. "I called her and asked if she would call Marquette and see if they could give me a seat next to [Notre Dame sports information director] Roger Valdiserri on press row. In addition to scouting the game, I knew it would give me a chance to spend some time with Roger, who was one of the most respected athletic administrators in the country."

There were rumors that Johnny Dee, who had been Notre Dame's head coach since 1964, would retire at the end of the year. Sure enough, Eleanor pulled it off and Phelps spent the entire game in Valdiserri's ear.

On February 18, 1971, Phelps had his chance to impress more than just Valiserri as Notre Dame came to MSG to face his 14th-ranked Fordham Rams. Thanks to several interviews with New York's most popular sportscaster, Howard Cosell, Phelps and the Rams were the talk of New York and a sellout crowd of 19,500 was in attendance for the 9 p.m. tipoff.

The Irish had beaten No. 1-ranked UCLA behind Austin Carr's 46 points just three weeks earlier (see chapter 1) and were a virtual lock for an NCAA bid. Both Fordham and Notre Dame were ranked in the top 20 of the AP and UPI polls entering the game.

Prior to the game, Phelps enhanced his relationship with Valiserri and his chances of getting the Notre Dame job:

> It was just 30 minutes before the game and I was in the runway with Roger and Johnny Druze. Johnny asked me how I was going to stop Austin Carr.
>
> Roger said he wouldn't run to the locker room and tell Johnny Dee my plan because it was too close to the game. So, I told them Notre Dame had struggled against a zone in five of their six losses. We hadn't played a zone defense all year, but we were going to use it for this game because Notre Dame wouldn't expect it. I told him we were going to double team Carr and let Sid Catlett shoot from the outside. We wanted someone other than Carr to beat us.

That is a strategy directly opposite of John Wooden's theory, as noted in the first chapter of this book. Wooden felt the approach would be to let

Digger Phelps coached Fordham to a 26–3 record and NCAA bid in his only year at the New York City–based school, including a win over Notre Dame in a sold-out Madison Square Garden. *Fordham University Athletics*

Carr get his normal point total, but shut down the other four players on the court.

The strategy worked and Fordham defeated Notre Dame that night, 94–88. It was its only loss over the last eight games of the regular season. The victory also gave Phelps a common accomplishment with Parseghian. Ara had impressed Notre Dame administrators by beating Notre Dame as Northwestern football coach four straight years from 1959 to 1962 before he was hired by Fr. Ted Hesburgh. Now Phelps had beaten the Irish on the most national stage of college basketball.

"That night I sold New York City on Fordham's basketball program. And I sold Roger Valdiserri that I could be the next coach at Notre Dame."

Phelps was the hottest coach in the country at the end of that 1970–71 season and was approached by Virginia Tech and Pennsylvania. Both were willing to pay $35,000 a year for four years. But Phelps was going to wait on Notre Dame. He talked with Valdiserri often and he told him Dee's retirement was on the way.

On April 30, 1971, as Valdiserri was putting out a press release on Dee's retirement, Phelps was interviewing with Fr. Edmund Joyce at the

Detroit Airport. "He told me he expected us to graduate our players, never get in trouble with the NCAA and to be competitive. I asked him, 'What do you mean by competitive? He said, about 18 wins a year. I had just won 26 at Fordham. Surely, I could win 18 at Notre Dame."

At the conclusion of the interview, Fr. Joyce told Phelps the job paid $18,000 a year, plus an additional $3,000 for radio and TV, plus a car. That was just a little over half of what Penn and Virginia Tech were offering.

"That didn't matter," recalled Phelps. "I would have taken that job for food coupons for my wife and kids at the North Dining Hall."

In fact, that initial four-year contract would be the only multi-year contract he had at Notre Dame. He worked on a year-to-year basis after the 1975 season until he retired in 1991.

Phelps was announced as Notre Dame head coach on May 4, 1971, and a press conference was held in South Bend the next day. He still resides in South Bend, less than a mile from campus.

CHAPTER 4

1971–72: Wooden's Best Team?

WITH SIDNEY WICKS, CURTIS ROWE, KENNY BOOKER, AND STEVE PAT-terson graduating from UCLA's 1970–71 national championship team, the national media was looking for a new story in college basketball. UCLA had won five consecutive national championships and seven of the last eight and quite frankly many people had grown tired of seeing John Wooden's team cut down the nets.

The national preview of the NCAA's official collegiate basketball guide had the title, "Will UCLA Fall Right on its Crown? Many Teams Think the Time Has Come."

The article written by Jeff Prugh of the *Los Angeles Times*, the president of the US Basketball Writers Association at the time, started with the following sentence. "At last, there is hope—real live 'We're gonna be No. 1!' hope—pervading the entire college basketball world."

He continued.

Maybe, just maybe this is going to be the season when somebody finally knocks the UCLA Bruins right on their NCAA crown. East Coast, West Coast, all across the land, there is a horde of challengers restlessly plotting to overthrow the defending five-time champion Bruins, the mightiest dynasty the collegiate game has ever seen. . . .

Whoever finishes on top, it will have to do it by surviving what promises to be the game's most hotly competitive winter in several years.

Also, particularly comforting for many coaches is the fact that there won't be any Sidney Wicks, Curtis Rowes and Steve Pattersons punishing them on the backboards anymore, either.

Who then will be wearing those UCLA wrist watches at the finish?

In Prugh's defense, UCLA had lost four starters off its 29–1 team, key players for the last three championship runs. Freshmen were not eligible to play with the varsity until 1972–73, so college squads had freshman teams.

Freshman teams received some attention, but it wasn't like the games were on TV. Statistics were kept and sports information offices reported the scores and did game stories, but no one really paid attention until these young players were eligible to play with the varsity.

UCLA's 1970–71 freshman team featured 6'11" redhead Bill Walton and 6'7" forward Keith Wilkes. There were other terrific players as well. But if you look back at the old recruiting magazines of the era you didn't read a lot about them as being generational talent. Don't get me wrong, they were highly regarded, but Walton was not considered to be another Lew Alcindor and Wilkes was not the second coming of Curtis Rowe when they were in high school.

Walton and Wilkes certainly proved to be that, however, as both are today in the Naismith Hall of Fame. How many recruiting classes at the same school have had two Naismith Hall of Famers?

If you read a couple of quotes from Wooden in Prugh's preview, you can certainly see why he wrote his lead. "*There is no way in the world* we should be favored to win everything this season," said Wooden. The above phrase was in boldface when it originally appeared in the 1971–72 NCAA Media Guide.

"Everybody knows for example that USC in our own conference will have better material—and more experience—than we will."

Coach Wooden was correct in that Southern California was a good program. It had beaten the Bruins in 1968–69 and 1969–70 and finished 24–2 in 1970–71 with a final No. 5 ranking in the AP poll. The only two losses had come to UCLA. In those years only the conference champion could go to the NCAA Tournament, so USC's season ended with the regular season final loss to UCLA in Pauley Pavilion.

You might have thought the early ending of Southern California's season would have stimulated the NCAA to change the rules and allow more than one team from a conference to reach the NCAA Tournament. They lost to UCLA that year 73–62 and 64–60, and won the other 24 games against a good Pac-8 conference that included future Hall of Fame coaches Marv Harshman at Washington and Ralph Miller at Oregon State.

In closing the section about the Pac-8, Prugh said, "What is significant to remember about UCLA is that Walton is no Lew Alcindor and Wooden realizes that there are more question marks on his team than exclamation points."

It wouldn't take long for that opinion of the Bruins to change.

Despite these quotes from Wooden and other national media preview articles trumpeting other programs, UCLA was the preseason No. 1 team in the AP and UPI polls.

The "Walton Gang" era opened on December 3, 1971, with a 105–49 win over The Citadel at Pauley Pavilion. Walton had 19 points and 14 rebounds in his first game, while senior Henry Bibby led the way from his guard position with 26. Wooden actually got 35 points from the center position as Swen Nater, who was a junior college transfer from Cypress JC in California, had 16 in a reserve role behind Walton in his first game with the Bruins.

After the game, sophomore guard Greg Lee met with the media and was asked if playing The Citadel was like playing a high school team. Lee responded, "No, more like playing a junior college team." Coach Wooden was not happy with that comment, and it would not be the only time he was not happy with Lee.

The Citadel actually had a decent season, finishing 12–13 and averaging 78 points per game with four double-figure scorers. Three weeks later they played 11th-ranked Virginia and lost by only five points, 77–72.

That was the first of seven victories in which the Bruins scored at least 100 points to open the season. It is still the UCLA record for consecutive games scoring at least 100 points at any point in a season.

The second game of the year was against Iowa the next night. Iowa was supposed to be more of a challenge because the Hawkeyes had a seven-foot center named Kevin Kunnert, who would average 18.2 points and 14.7 rebounds that year, would become the 12th pick of the 1973 NBA draft by the Chicago Bulls, and played 10 years in the NBA.

But Kunnert was smothered by Walton and Nater and had just 11 points and four rebounds, as the Bruins won 106–72 thanks to 32 points by Bibby.

The next weekend, December 10–11, had two more blowouts against major conference teams. UCLA beat Iowa State, 110–81, and Texas A&M, 117–53. The 64-point win against the Aggies was the largest victory margin in the 88-game streak. Walton had his most dominant game to date with 23 points, 18 rebounds, and eight blocks, while Wilkes had 22 points and 17 rebounds.

With the Christmas holiday approaching, UCLA actually played a game on a Wednesday night, December 22, against Digger Phelps and his first Notre Dame team. We are sure there was a point spread on this game at some hotel in Las Vegas, but there is no record of it. If we could find one it would have been at least 40 points.

Notre Dame had lost its top six players, including All-American Austin Carr off the previous year's team that was the last to beat the Bruins. Notre Dame had already lost to Indiana and first year head coach Bob Knight by 65 points (more on that game later in this chapter).

When the Notre Dame team landed at LAX, Phelps bought a copy of the *Los Angeles Times* and a story about the game included a cartoon that had a Notre Dame player about to face a guillotine. "Watch a live execution in person," was the headline.

It didn't take long for UCLA to dominate, as the Bruins started the game with a 17–0 run and there were many possessions the Irish couldn't get the ball over half court against the UCLA zone press. It was 53–16 at the half and it got worse from there. Bibby finished with 28 points and Walton had an efficient 20 points and 19 rebounds.

Phelps was complimentary in his postgame press conference, saying, "This is the greatest team John Wooden has ever had. Walton is the best big guy in the country. They don't have any weaknesses."

Digger did a good job of hiding his anger in front of the media. With eight minutes left and UCLA up 41, Wooden was still pressing and had his best players in the game. The Bruins won 114–56.

At some point during the final moments, Phelps was in a crouch in front of his bench and looked down at the UCLA bench. He caught assistant coach Gary Cunningham's eye and he mouthed two words to him. It wasn't thank you, but the second word was you. Cunningham did a double take, then Phelps mouthed, "and the guy next to you, too!"

After the game and after both coaches had met with the media, Wooden sought out Phelps. Cunningham had obviously told him Digger was upset with the Bruins' pressing defense with a 40-point lead.

"Now Digger, this past week we were in final exams and we didn't have time to practice much. We have our conference season starting soon so I needed to work on my press."

Phelps thought that was baloney and that Wooden was running up the score as revenge for last year's Notre Dame win in South Bend. In classic Phelps fashion he responded to Wooden, "John, you do anything you have to to beat me, because some day I am going to kick your ass." Phelps then turned and walked off.

It might be the only time on record a rivalry was born from a game decided by 58 points. (Although we must note the Notre Dame vs. Miami [FL] football rivalry in the 1980s was born from a 58–7 Hurricane victory in Gerry Faust's last game as Notre Dame coach in 1985.)

The Bruins then beat TCU by 38 (119–81) the next night before taking the Christmas break. After watching UCLA beat Notre Dame by 58, many of the TCU coaches felt it was a moral victory to lose by just 38.

The Bruin Classic was held at Pauley Pavilion December 29 and 30. UCLA played Texas in the first round and won 115–65 as Walton had 28 points and 24 rebounds. UCLA had a school record 84 rebounds in the game. When looking back this was one of the more impressive performances by UCLA that year because Texas finished 19–9, won the Southwest Conference, and made the NCAA Tournament.

The game the national media was looking forward to was the December 30, 1971, contest with Ohio State. The Buckeyes were ranked sixth in the AP poll after finishing 10th with a berth in the Elite Eight of the NCAA Tournament the previous year.

Ohio State featured the guard and center combination of Alan Hornyak and Luke Witte, respectively, that many thought could stay with the young Bruins. Hornyak had gained national attention in high school by scoring 86 points in one game, and he averaged 22.5 a game as a sophomore in 1970–71, his first year with coach Fred Taylor's varsity.

Witte was a seven-footer who many felt would give Walton his biggest test. He had been first-team All-Big Ten the previous year when he averaged 19 points and 12.7 rebounds a game. William F. Reed of *Sports Illustrated* was among the media throng at Pauley to see the game.

Ohio State was 6–1 and defeated Arizona 90–47 in the opening round of the Bruin Classic, which added more intrigue to the game.

Reed said of Walton and UCLA, "It is led by redheaded Bill Walton, a 6'11" sophomore center who does everything, but help the Bruin pom-pon girls with their dance routines."

The Bruins once again got off to a great start leading 11–1 and 30–10. When asked about the start Taylor said, "I felt like getting up and going to Disneyland."

Ohio State thought they had a chance when Walton picked up his fourth foul with 18:07 left in the game. He had been dominant to that point and finished the game with 17 points and 13 rebounds in just 18 minutes. He was also dominant on defense in the first half when he blocked six shots, some of them by Witte.

Witte would end the game with a respectable 19 points and 13 rebounds, but many of those stats were recorded when Walton was out of the game. Hornyak, who would end the season averaging 21.6 points a game, did not have a field goal against the Bruins, who won by 26 points even though starting point guard Greg Lee was out with an injury.

After the game Walton was asked if Witte was the best defensive center he had played against. "No," said Walton. "Swen Nater is the best."

UCLA began its run through the Pac-8 conference on January 7, 1972, at Oregon State. The Beavers gave the Bruins their most difficult game until the NCAA Championship game. It was a surprise at the time as Oregon State was unranked, but they were just two games removed from losing a heartbreaker to Florida State, who would go on to play UCLA in the NCAA Championship game.

Freddie Boyd, a 6–2 guard, scored 37 points to keep Oregon State in the game the entire contest. It would be tied for the second most points scored against a Wooden coached UCLA team. He helped force 30 UCLA turnovers, but UCLA still won, 78–72.

Did this result lead to doubts about the Bruins? If there were any, they lasted just a few hours as the next night UCLA won at Oregon by 25 points. Walton had 30 points and 17 rebounds and Nater added 14 points off the bench.

The next four games between January 14 and 22 were routs contested in Pauley Pavilion. There was a 118–79 win over Stanford when the Bruins scored exactly 59 points in each half. Walton had 32 points and 15 rebounds, leading Howie Dallmar, the head coach at Stanford, to compare Walton to Bill Russell in his postgame press conference.

It had taken just 11 games for an opposing coach to jump right over Alcindor to compare Walton to the greatest winner in NBA history.

The following night UCLA held California to 24.6 percent field goal shooting in an 82–43 victory. In 1971–72 the official NCAA boxscore didn't keep blocked shots, but postgame articles claimed Walton blocked 14. The boxscore did reveal he had 20 points and 21 rebounds.

The term *triple double* was not used until the early 1980s when Los Angeles Lakers public relations staffers were looking for a way to document Magic Johnson's unique all-around abilities. Since there was no official listing of blocked shots on Walton's stat line against California it is not considered a triple double, but it sounds like he accomplished the feat for the first time in this game.

After a 35-point win over Santa Clara and a 47-point win over Denver, the Bruins made their annual trip to the Midwest to face Loyola of Chicago and Notre Dame.

There was actually more attention on the Loyola game because UCLA had already beaten Notre Dame by 58, and the Ramblers featured senior 6'11" center LaRue Martin. Martin was a skinny 210 pounds, but he was athletic and NBA scouts were interested to see how he would do against Walton.

Well, he did pretty well, scoring 19 points and pulling in 18 rebounds. The performance probably led to Martin being selected first overall in the 1972 NBA Draft by Portland. He did not go on to a great NBA career, lasting just four years and he averaged just 5.3 points and 4.6 rebounds. But on this January 28, 1972, night at Chicago Stadium he held his own against the National Player of the Year.

Playing back-to-back games was the norm for UCLA as a member of the Pac-8 in the 1970s. They must have gotten to South Bend, Indiana, at 3 a.m., but it didn't make any difference against an undersized Notre Dame team.

Phelps's goal was to keep the point spread under 50 and he accomplished that by holding the ball in the 57–32 Bruins win. It was the fewest points scored by an opponent (and probably the fewest possessions) during the 88-game winning streak.

"In those days there was no shot clock," said Phelps. "I knew Wooden would play man-to-man, but wouldn't chase Walton away from the basket. So, we just held the ball for long periods of time with Gary Novak [6'7" center] dribbling the ball by the 28-foot mark on the court.

"I know we missed two TV timeouts because of it and a couple of times Novak caught Walton napping and drove by him for a basket. It was boring, but we didn't lose by 50."

The USC vs. UCLA games brought national media in the late 1960s and early 1970s, but a season-ending knee injury to Trojans star guard Paul Westphal stole some of the luster from this February 5, 1972, game. Southern California jumped out to a 10–2 record, but Westphal's season-ending knee injury made the Trojans a mediocre team. The future member of the Naismith Hall of Fame had averaged 20.3 points a game for the 14 games he played.

The Trojans lost three in a row against non-conference teams from Providence, Seattle, and Santa Clara leading up to this game.

UCLA had another fast start, a 5–0 lead just 27 seconds into the game and that quick start led to win number 32 in a row. Walton held USC star center Ron Riley without a field goal for the first 27 minutes and he finished with just 12 points.

The UCLA schedule called for the next four games to be played against Washington and Washington State, two against each team, home and away. First, Walton had another 20–20 (25 points and 21 rebounds) in a 31-point win against Washington State.

The next night, February 12, Walton dominated Steve Hawes and the Huskies. Walton blocked Hawes's first three shots and held him to four points for the night. Walton's column finished with 27 points and 24 rebounds, the first time in his career he posted back to back 20–20 games.

But the very next game, Hawes had one of his top games of the season with 30 points and 18 rebounds. Walton had 31 points and 15 rebounds, so it was a virtual draw between the big men. It was a more important game for Hawes, who was a senior and would be taken as the 24th pick of the draft by Cleveland in the spring of 1972. He would go on to play 12 years in the NBA.

UCLA won the game at home by 109–70 and won the game at Washington 100–83. Hawes's improvement cut UCLA's victory margin in half, but still not enough to make the game close.

The Bruins won the game at Washington State to complete the sweep of the state of Washington portion of the schedule, 85–55, their 11th victory by at least 30 points in 1971–72.

For some reason teams didn't try gadget defenses against the Bruins. We can only imagine it was because opposing coaches thought Wooden just had too many weapons.

Washington State did try a 1-2-2 zone in this game that double teamed Walton. The defense held Walton to just seven shots and 15 points, but four other Bruins scored in double figures, led by Wilkes and Hollyfield with 16 points apiece.

Oregon and Oregon State came to Pauley February 25 and 26 for the final two home games of the year. While it was Senior Weekend for Bibby, Walton had a season-high 37 points against Oregon, the most by a UCLA player since Alcindor had the same total against Purdue in his final game as a Bruin, the 1969 NCAA Championship game. It was becoming more and more noteworthy to compare Walton to Alcindor.

Bibby played his final game as a Bruin at home against Oregon State. The Beavers had come within six points of UCLA in the first meeting back in early January thanks to 37 points by Fred Boyd. Bibby scored just 13 points in this game, but held Boyd to just one field goal in the first half while the Bruins took a 19-point lead at the break. The two teams played even in the second half and Wooden's team finished the home season with a 91–72 victory.

UCLA had to go on the road for the last three games of the regular season. As dominant as they had been, UCLA did not clinch the Pac-8 title until the victory over California on March 3. The sophomore duo of Walton and Wilkes combined for 42 points and 30 rebounds in the 14-point win.

For the second time this year UCLA dominated Stanford, this time at The Farm with a 102–73 victory. It was the Bruins' 12th game with at least 100 points in 1971–72.

UCLA completed the perfect regular season (26–0) with a 79–66 win at Southern California in a game that had some controversy. It was a classic 1970s game where low post play was the name of the game. Walton and Southern California center Ron Riley both had at least 20 points and 20 rebounds. In fact, Riley's 22 rebounds are still the second most in history against UCLA.

At one point, Walton accused Riley of intentionally hitting him in the mouth. After the game Wooden was quoted as saying that Riley should have been kicked out of the game.

NCAA TOURNAMENT

UCLA entered the NCAA tournament on a 41-game winning streak over two years. The Bruins were the number-one ranked team in the nation according to AP and UPI, a position it had held since the preseason poll. There was no seeding of teams in those days, but had there been, UCLA would have been the No. 1 overall seed.

For the second straight year, the Bruins had to travel to the state of Utah to open defense of their NCAA championship, this time at the Marriott Center in Provo, Utah. And they would have to play a team from the state of Utah in the first game, Weber State.

As was the case in this era, UCLA got a bye to the Final 16 of the 25-team NCAA Tournament by virtue of its Pac-8 championship.

Weber State was coming off the top upset of the first-round games, defeating a 12th ranked Hawaii team that was 23–3 entering the game. Not only did they beat the Rainbow Warriors, but they also trounced them 91–64 thanks to a defense that allowed Hawaii to shoot just 31 percent from the field. Hawaii had averaged 88 points per game during the season, but Weber State held them 24 points under their average.

That performance got Wooden's attention and apparently the entire team.

Walton got into early foul trouble and would only play 20 minutes and finished with a season-low four points. He took just one shot from the field, but did have 12 rebounds in those 20 minutes.

Five other Bruins scored in double figures, including Nater, who had 12 points in 20 minutes. Bibby led the way with 17 points and Larry Farmer had 15. Shoutout to reserve Andy Hill, who had 10 points in just six minutes.

That 90–58 victory set up a rematch with Jerry Tarkanian's fifth-ranked Long Beach State team. The previous year the 49ers had given Coach Wooden's team all it could handle in an Elite Eight game before the Bruins won, 57–55. Many felt UCLA was lucky to win because Long Beach State star Ed Ratleff fouled out after scoring 18 points. The Long Beach State defense had held UCLA to 29 percent shooting from the field.

Ratleff was back, but the Bruins were ready for him. He did score 17 points, but he made just 7 of 19 shots from the field and was the only 49er to score in double figures. Bibby took the matchup with Ratleff as a personal challenge and led UCLA with 23 points. Walton added 19 points and 11 rebounds on the inside. UCLA led by just five at the half, but won going away, 73–57.

It was on to a sixth straight Final Four for UCLA.

The Final Four was in Los Angeles at the Los Angeles Sports Arena, a facility just 13 miles from UCLA's home facility, Pauley Pavilion.

Wooden and the UCLA players were very familiar with the coach of their national semifinal opponent, fourth-ranked Louisville. The Cardinals were in their first season under head coach Denny Crum, who had been an assistant coach under Wooden the previous four years (1967–71), all national championship seasons. He had personally recruited many of the current UCLA players.

Crum had done a remarkable job in his first year, leading Louisville to a 26–3 record and number-four national ranking entering the Final Four.

Many in the media felt Crum didn't have the best of relationships with Wooden and there was a famous substitution disagreement during the Final Four in Houston the previous year that added to the speculation.

But the pregame press conferences were cordial. Wooden was quoted as saying, "I'm tickled Denny is here. It is just too bad one of us has to lose."

Crum said, "I like to play friends for fun, not for real."

In Curry Kirkpatrick's story on the Final Four in *Sports Illustrated* the following week, he witnessed an encounter between UCLA players and Crum just before the teams came on the court for the opening tip. "Walton playfully grabbed Crum and said, 'Coach where's the money you promised me last year under the table?'" Greg Lee kidded Crum about his "pitiful sideburns."

It must have felt strange for Crum to watch all these players he recruited to Westwood playing against him. In many ways it was one of the top five UCLA performances of the season as the Bruins finished shooting 57.6 percent from the field, 77 percent from the line, and won the rebounding battle, 48–28. It could have been worse as UCLA did lose the turnover margin by 10 (21–11).

Walton was motivated for sure playing against the coach who recruited him and in comfortable surroundings just a few miles from where he lived. In the first 10 minutes of the game, he personally outscored Louisville, 16–14.

But UCLA led by just eight at the half, the closest the score had been at intermission all year. It could have been much closer because Louisville was successful in breaking UCLA's vaunted zone press. According to Kirkpatrick's article, nine times Louisville broke UCLA's press and nine times they missed jump shots when they had the man advantage.

The Bruins scored 57 points in the second half and won easily, 96–77. Walton finished with 33 points thanks to 11-for-13 field goal shooting and he added 21 rebounds. Jim Price, a future Los Angeles Laker, was Louisville's top scorer with 30, but many came late in the game when the outcome was decided.

UCLA's opponent in the championship game on Saturday, March 25 would be Florida State. The Seminoles were a surprise team in that they had finished the previous season under Hugh Durham with a 17–9 record, including a 5–5 mark in the last 10 games.

They were ranked 10th in the nation in 1971–72 after a 24–5 regular season. But what a run they had in the NCAA Tournament. They defeated 11th ranked Minnesota, 18th ranked Kentucky, and second-ranked North Carolina to reach the championship game.

They had defeated Adolph Rupp (today the seventh winningest coach in college basketball history with 876 wins), in the regional final and Dean Smith, the fifth winningest coach in college basketball history with 879 wins in the national semifinal. The 19-point win over Kentucky would be the final game of Rupp's Hall of Fame career.

As if Florida State didn't have enough problems preparing for the mighty Bruins, the afternoon of the game, National Association of Basketball Coaches President Bill Wall held a press conference and called Florida State's appearance in the finals "a disgrace" because of recent NCAA rules violations.

Despite all of that, and with UCLA a 16-point favorite, Florida State went up 21–14 in the first half, making seven consecutive field goals. It was the first time UCLA trailed by as many as four points at any point in a game in 1971–72.

But, as expected, it was an up-tempo game with a lot of possessions. Florida State averaged 84 points a game and UCLA 96 entering the contest. When Florida State got in some foul trouble, the Bruins made a run behind Tallahassee, Florida, native Tommy Curtis. The Bruins went from down seven to up 11 (50–39) at halftime.

UCLA was in good shape most of the second half, but Walton got into foul trouble. Florida State kept fighting and cut the margin to 79–72 late in the game. But the Seminoles had three costly turnovers in the last two minutes and UCLA won, 81–76.

The five-point margin was the smallest for UCLA all year.

Walton finished with 24 points and 20 rebounds, and cut down the nets. But in the postgame press conference he had a "disturbing, almost disdainful attitude," according to Curry Kirkpatrick. "He told the press he 'was not elated.'"

"He felt as though he had lost the game," said Kirkpatrick in his April 3, 1972, *Sports Illustrated* story. "We don't like to back into things," Walton continued. "We didn't dominate the way I know we can."

Walton had set high standards, so perhaps you can see his reaction. But he did lead the Bruins to a perfect 30–0 record with the 30 wins coming by an average of 30.3 points per game. It remains the NCAA record for scoring margin in a season. North Carolina was second that year at +17.7 points per game.

Walton finished fourth in the nation in field goal percentage at 64 percent and averaged 15.7 rebounds per game, another top 10 national average. He had won the Naismith Award, the AP and UPI Players of the Year, and the Rupp Award. Bibby had also been named a consensus first-team All-American.

There was much concern about comparing Walton with Lew Alcindor (Kareem Abdul-Jabbar) when the season began. But it is interesting to note that on the final season stat sheet Walton had 466 rebounds, the exact same total Alcindor had when leading the Bruins to the national championship and a 30–0 record as a sophomore in 1966–67.

When asked to give his synopsis of the 1971–72 season, Wooden said the following in the 1972–73 UCLA media guide:

Considering their extreme youth, their inexperience and certainly, the unfair pressure to be placed on them due to the remarkable success of recent UCLA teams, no realistic or knowledgeable basketball person could possibly have foreseen the success of the 1971–72 Bruins.

The undefeated championship was a result of their development of excellent teamwork and their youthful enthusiasm for hard work. This probably was the most versatile of all my teams. They became quite proficient in the set offense, the fast break, the set defense and the pressing defense.

Bill Walton insured a strong inside game while Henry Bibby, Greg Lee and, at times Larry Farmer gave us outside strength. Walton and

Keith Wilkes not only provided the nucleus for an excellent rebounding team, but their smooth all-around play was amazing considering their age and inexperience.

The inspirational efforts of Bibby and Tommy Curtis, the relief Sven Nater gave to Walton, the occasional brilliant work of Larry Hollyfield, and the daily effort of Vince Carson, Jon Chapman, Gary Franklin and Andy Hill were all of vital importance and very instrumental in the overall accomplishments of the team.

NOTRE DAME'S 1971–72 SEASON

While UCLA could not have had a more perfect season, Notre Dame's 1971–72 campaign could not have been worse.

The bad luck of the Irish started on August 8, 1971, when Doug Gemmell, the captain of Digger Phelps's first Notre Dame team, suffered a broken leg in a motorcycle accident near his home in New Jersey. The injury was so bad he later had to have the leg amputated.

Then, in early November, just a month before the start of the season, it was learned that sophomore center John Shumate, the leading scorer

The Walton Gang outscored opponents by 30 points a game in 1971–72, still an NCAA record. *Public domain, via Wikimedia Commons*

on the preceding year's freshman team, would be lost for the season due to a blood clot near his heart.

That left Phelps with five sophomores for his starting lineup with the biggest player 6–7 Gary Novak, who by today's standards would be a small forward.

Freshmen were ineligible until the 1972–73 season, so future stars Gary Brokaw and Dwight Clay watched from the sidelines as members of the Irish freshman team.

On December 1, 1971, the Digger Phelps era began against a Michigan team that would finish third in the Big Ten. The Irish started an all sophomore lineup, one that had not played a single minute of varsity basketball previously. One of the starters was Tom Hansen, a Notre Dame baseball player.

The team played a gutty first half and led Michigan at intermission, 49–47. Legendary Michigan coach Johnny Orr had to be shocked at the success of this undersized Notre Dame team, especially when he saw Notre Dame had a 20–19 rebounding edge at the break.

But Michigan's physical advantage took over in the second half and the Wolverines won 101–83, the first of 20 losses for the Irish in 1971–72.

Phelps believed from the start that to be the best you have to compete against the best. His first Notre Dame team faced eight teams ranked in the top 20, five against top 10 teams, and of course two games against number-one ranked UCLA.

One of those top 10 teams was Indiana, ranked 10th in the nation under first-year head coach Bob Knight. Not only was it a rivalry game, the December 18, 1971, game was the dedication game of Assembly Hall, Indiana's new basketball arena.

It was a perfect storm for an Indiana celebration. The Irish made two of their first four shots and led, 5–4. They then shot 1-for-30 for the rest of the half. That is not a typo, one-for-thirty. It was 44–13 at intermission.

Some of the statistics of that game remain standards for Notre Dame basketball futility. Notre Dame finished 8-for-61 from the field, 13 percent, the worst field goal percentage on record in school history. Starting guards John Egart and Bob Valibus were a combined 0–16 from the field.

The Irish finished with 29 points and 29 turnovers, the only game in Irish history those two numbers were the same in the final box score. Indiana forward John Ritter outscored the entire Notre Dame team, 31–29.

Indiana closed the game with a 19–2 run over the last 6:23 to win, 94–29. The 65-point margin was, and still is, the worst margin of defeat in Notre Dame history.

"The next day I got calls from my buddies in New York," said Phelps. "'Digger, the wires service switched the digits on your score against Indiana.'

"I told them we had lost at the buzzer [94–92]."

The very next game was at No. 1 ranked UCLA and as we documented earlier, the Bruins won by 58, still the second largest margin of defeat in Notre Dame history.

On December 28, the Irish traveled to Freedom Hall in Louisville, Kentucky, to face Adolph Rupp's Wildcats. They were ranked 12th in the nation and would go on to the Elite Eight of the NCAA Tournament.

But the Irish hung with the Wildcats for most of the game before losing, 83–67.

With it being a night game and the team on semester break, Notre Dame spent the night in Louisville. When Phelps got back to the hotel he got a call from Rupp.

"When I first heard the voice on the other end, I figured Coach Rupp was calling to congratulate me on playing his team tough, and that he was going to encourage me to hang in the rest of the season."

But that was not what Rupp said.

"Digger, what is wrong with my team?"

Digger responded, "What do you mean, coach?"

"Well Indiana beat you by 65 and UCLA beat you by 58, we should have beaten you by 50. What is wrong with my team?"

"I was surprised by the call and basically told him I didn't know. I had problems of my own to figure out."

The Irish finished the season with a 6–20 record, including six losses in a row to close the season. Phelps told a writer from the *Chicago Tribune* near the end of the season, "We have to scrimmage every day so I know what it feels like to win."

The only Power Five conference schools with a worse record than Notre Dame that year were Oklahoma State (4–22) and Northwestern (5–18). Oregon, Arizona, and Georgia Tech were also 6–20.

Despite the difficulties of the season, 29-year-old Digger Phelps was his ever-optimistic self. He knew John Shumate would be back for the 1972–73 season and the freshman team had gone 12–5. Lightning quick guard Gary Brokaw had averaged 28 points a game and Dwight Clay 16.

They still had a Notre Dame basketball banquet at the end of the season. Over 500 people showed up and Digger greeted every person at the front door upon their arrival.

Top Season Scoring Margins in NCAA History

Rk	School	Year	Off	Def	Mar
1.	**UCLA**	1971–72	94.6	64.3	+30.3
2.	NC State	1947–48	75.3	47.2	+28.1
3.	Kentucky	1953–54	87.5	60.3	+27.2
4.	Kentucky	1951–52	82.3	55.4	+26.9
5.	UNLV	1990–91	97.7	71.0	+26.7
6.	UCLA	1967–68	93.4	67.2	+26.2
7.	UCLA	1966–67	89.6	63.7	+25.9
8.	Houston	1967–68	97.8	72.5	+25.3
9.	Duke	1998–99	91.8	67.2	+24.6
10.	Kentucky	1947–48	69.0	43.9	+24.1

1972 NCAA CHAMPIONSHIP GAME
UCLA 81, Florida State 76
March 25, 1972
at Los Angeles, California
Los Angeles Sports Arena

UCLA (81)

Name	Min	FG-A	FT-A	Reb	Ast	F	Pts
Larry Farmer, F	33	2-6	0-0	6	0	2	4
Keith Wilkes, F	38	11-16	1-2	10	3	4	23
Bill Walton, C	34	9-17	6-11	20	2	4	24
Greg Lee, G	16	0-0	0-0	2	4	0	0
Henry Bibby, G	40	8-17	2-3	3	1	2	18
Tommy Curtis	24	4-14	0-1	4	6	1	8
Larry Hollyfield	9	1-6	0-0	2	3	2	2
Sven Nater	6	1-2	0-1	1	0	0	2
Team				2			
Totals	200	36-78 (.462)	9-18 (.500)	50	19	15	81

Florida State (76)

Name	Min	FG-A	FT-A	Reb	Ast	F	Pts
Reggie Royals, F	33	5-7	5-6	10	2	5	15
Rowland Garrett, F	37	1-9	1-1	5	0	1	3
Lawrence McCray, C	23	3-6	2-5	6	3	4	8
Ron King, G	31	12-20	3-3	6	1	1	27
Greg Samuel, G	31	3-10	0-0	1	7	1	6
Ron Harris	26	7-13	2-3	6	1	1	16
Otto Petty	9	0-0	1-1	0	2	1	1
Ottis Cole	10	0-2	0-0	?	1	1	0
Team				6			
Totals	200	31-67 (.463)	14-19 (.737)	42	17	15	76

Score by Half

UCLA	50	31	81
Florida State	39	37	76

TURNOVERS: UCLA 13, VILLANOVA 10

OFFICIALS: JIM BAIN, IRV BROWN

ATTENDANCE: 15,063

CHAPTER 5

1972–73: UCLA Wins
Seventh Straight Title

UCLA ENTERED THE 1972–73 SEASON WITH A 45-GAME WINNING streak, and held the preseason number-one ranking in every preseason magazine and wire service poll. How could you not be No. 1 with four starters returning from a national championship team that won every game by an average of 30 points per game, still the largest average victory margin in NCAA history.

While the streak had been discussed the previous year, it received much more attention in the preseason for 1972–73 now that Wooden's team was just 16 games away from breaking San Francisco's mark of 60 that had been set by Bill Russell and K. C. Jones–led teams between 1954 and 1956.

When the Bruins schedule came out, quick math revealed that the 16th game of the season would be in South Bend, Indiana, against Notre Dame. It just worked out that way, but what a story.

It didn't take long for the national television broadcaster of college basketball in those days, TVS, to announce it would show the game on its national network of local stations.

It was just too good a story. John Wooden, a native of Indiana, who used to coach high school basketball in South Bend, would attempt to break the all-time record for longest college winning streak in the same building where he last lost a game. Not to mention the facility was just a few miles from where he lived in the 1940s as a high school coach at

South Bend Central High School. Not to mention it was just a few miles from where he once made a hole-in-one and an eagle in the same round. (Well, no one really knew about the last accomplishment in 1972, but we can marvel at it now.)

While the UCLA streak was on the national conscience, media pundits were preoccupied with finding a reason UCLA might not win the national championship for the first time in six years. Many of those scribes were quite frankly tired of UCLA winning the title every year, and many of the non-UCLA fans were too.

The preseason narrative for a possible end of the streak involved the adoption of a new rule by the NCAA. And it was a major one. For the first time since the early 1950s, freshmen would be eligible to play with the varsity in 1972–73. It was the rule for all sports, not just basketball.

Many of the preseason basketball articles were being written as college freshmen football players were playing in meaningful games on national television. One of the noteworthy freshman footballers was Notre Dame defensive tackle Steve Niehaus.

But, by and large, freshmen football players were not having a big impact.

Most thought basketball would be a different story, just because of the nature of the sport. Only five players are on the court in basketball, but in football there are 11 at a time, and really 22 starters when you consider it is a two-platoon sport.

Because freshmen were not eligible the previous season, that meant two classes of new players would be on varsity teams for the 1972–73 season.

In *Sports Illustrated*'s preseason issue, Curry Kirkpatrick theorized this could make it more difficult for UCLA to continue its reign. At least that was what he was hearing.

"Basketball coaches prefer to think freshmen were allowed to play primarily for basketball, and more specifically to help them get UCLA," wrote Kirkpatrick.

While the theory might have had some merit, the freshman class of 1972–73 was not stocked with talent. In Kirkpatrick's preview of the season he listed Wally Walker of Virginia, John Lucas of Maryland, Alvin

Adams of Oklahoma, Ticky Burden of Utah, and Major Jones of Albany State as possible freshmen of influence.

There was no mention of freshman Robert Parish of Centenary, who went on to become a Hall of Famer, but of course Centenary was a very small school. Nor was there any mention of Phil Sellers, who had committed to Notre Dame. He was to be Phelps's first major recruit. But he ended up at Rutgers and had a strong freshman year. He later took Rutgers to its only Final Four appearance in his senior year, 1975–76.

The magazine opted to put a freshman on the cover instead of Walton, Wooden, or some other nationally known player or coach. The cover featured Walter Luckett of Kolbe High school in Bridgeport, Connecticut, who had averaged 39 points a game as a high school senior. Luckett had enrolled at Ohio University, a school best known for giving up 61 points to Notre Dame's Austin Carr in the first round of the 1970 NCAA tournament, a total that is still the all-time NCAA Tournament single-game record.

A 6'4" guard, Luckett was a very good player, but he would average just 13.6 a game his freshman year for the Bobcats. He did average 20.6 points a game over his three years at Ohio and was a second-round pick in the 1975 NBA draft, but he never played in an NBA game.

The leading freshman scorer that year nationally was James "Fly" Williams of Austin Peay, who averaged 29.4 points per game, sixth best in the nation. But he took 800 shots over the course of the season to reach that number.

The top freshman athlete in the nation that year was Quinn Buckner, who started as a defensive back for the Indiana football team in the fall, and for Bobby Knight's basketball team in the winter. He led the Hoosiers in interceptions on the gridiron with five, then quarterbacked the basketball team to the Final Four in March, where they played UCLA.

In the 1973–74 academic year he played for Lee Corso on the gridiron and Bobby Knight on the hardcourt. Talk about a topic for book!

There were actually far more threats to UCLA's streak from the crop of players who had played freshman basketball in 1971–72 and were eligible for the first time to play with the varsity in 1972–73.

One player in that sophomore class was NC State guard David Thompson. The native of Shelby, North Carolina, averaged 35 points a game for the Wolfpack freshman team in 1970–71. His legend grew by the game as his leaping ability for a 6'4" player was jaw-dropping.

There was one problem, however: the Pack would not challenge UCLA for the title. NC State was on probation for the 1972–73 season, the result of violations committed during their recruiting process for Thompson, who was from a family of 11 children in rural North Carolina.

NC State would go 27–0 in 1972–73 and win the ACC Championship with a 76–74 victory over Maryland, but their season ended that March 10 Saturday night in Greensboro.

Wooden and the Bruins would worry about Thompson and the Wolfpack the following year.

It had been an interesting summer for Bill Walton. He twice received national headlines that did not help his popularity with some fans, including UCLA supporters, particularly the older generation. In May, he was arrested for his participation during a Vietnam antiwar rally in Los Angeles.

He was released after paying a $50 fine. There was fear he would be suspended from school, thus jeopardizing his participation on the basketball team because he reportedly said some things to Chancellor Charles Young during the incident that were not complimentary. The university gave him a conditional probation for two years, but it still allowed him to play basketball.

"That was one of the two times Coach Wooden was the most mad at me," Walton said during an interview on ESPN in 2020. "The other was when I gave his home phone number out at an event attended by 25,000 people."

In the spring of 1972, Walton declined an invitation to try out for the 1972 US Olympic team. His decision was partly due to his feelings on the Vietnam War. But he also had a bad experience when he tried out for the 1970 United States World University Games team when he was in high school. "For the first time in my life, I was exposed to negative coaching and the berating of players and the foul language and the threatening of people who didn't perform."

Walton and David Thompson both declined to try out for the team and the United States lost an Olympic basketball game for the first time at the 1972 Games in Munich, Germany, when Russia won a controversial gold medal game by one point.

The 1972–73 season was John Wooden's 25th in Westwood. UCLA was the preseason No. 1 team, the 23rd consecutive AP poll they had been ranked number one since losing at Notre Dame on January 23, 1971.

Wooden's Bruins looked like a number one team in the season opener against Wisconsin, and Walton looked like the number one player in the nation.

Walton had many incredible games in his UCLA career, but the season opener his junior year against Wisconsin might be the most impressive statistically. In just 25 minutes he had 26 points, 20 rebounds, eight blocked shots and seven assists.

Statistics for assists were spotty in the early 1970s and it was even more rare to see blocked shots in a box score. But some games included assists, and this might have been the closest a Bruin player has come to a quadruple double. And he played just 25 minutes in the 94–53 victory. We must only wonder what he would have done had he played 35.

How rare is a quadruple double in college basketball? There has been only one recorded in games when all statistics were recorded. It was accomplished by Lester Hudson of UT Martin against Central Baptist on November 11, 2007. Hudson had 35 points, 12 rebounds, 10 assists, and 10 steals.

Bradley head coach Joe Stowell, who had been a member of the Bradley team of 1949–50 that finished as the national runner-up to CCNY in both the NIT and NCAA tournaments, thought he would try a stall against UCLA in the second game of the year. Surprisingly this had not been tried often by UCLA opponents during the streak. Only Digger Phelps had really done it for a long period of time in the game at South Bend the previous year.

Bradley held UCLA to 28 points in the first half, but the Braves only scored 10, hitting just 4 of 20 shots from the field. Bradley called off the stall in the second half and Walton got the ball enough to score 16 points and pull in 17 rebounds as UCLA won, 73–38.

The next night, December 2, 1972, Stan Morrison brought his Pacific team to Pauley Pavilion. He would later bring Southern California to Pauley Pavilion for seven consecutive years starting in 1979 when he was coach of the Trojans.

It was the 1,000th game of Wooden's career including high school games and games at Indiana State. It was over in a hurry as UCLA took a 24–4 lead, something that happened often to UCLA opponents because they just couldn't simulate UCLA's zone press defense in practice. They didn't have the athletes and they didn't have the experience in dealing with the Bruins' sixth sense about jumping in the passing lanes.

For the first time in his career as a head coach, John Wooden missed a game when the Bruins played UC Santa Barbara on December 16, 1972. The then 62-year-old Wooden was suffering from a mild heart condition, but it did require him to stay in the hospital.

Wooden had put in a busy summer working on multiple books that talked about his basketball theories on the court and keys to success in life. They were very successful, but added to his busy schedule and thus stress level, which was already great due to the winning streak. Gary Cunningham ran the team in his absence.

Here is what Wooden said about the issue in a season review in a later UCLA media guide:

> A mild heart problem, which caused me to miss my first game in 38 years of coaching, the problems involved with the maintenance of a long consecutive game winning streak, which has now reached an unbelievable total of 75, the normal pressures that are to be expected from being "at the top" for such an unprecedented period of years, and the additional burden brought on by the publication of several books pertaining to UCLA basketball and my personal life, all contributed to making the 1972–73 season one of the most "trying" in my experience.
>
> However, the end result was extremely gratifying and made this one of the most cherished of all of our championships.

Walton made sure his head coach didn't suffer any stress while following the game from a hospital, as he scored 30 points and pulled in 22 rebounds. Hollyfield had 18, Farmer 17, and Wilkes 16 as the Bruins won, 98–67.

The following weekend, December 22–23, was a Friday–Saturday night weekend set against Pittsburgh and Notre Dame. On Friday night, Wooden was back in good spirits and he was presented the *Sport Illustrated* Sportsman of the Year Award for 1972. He told the crowd, "I am perfectly all-right."

Walton had another noteworthy all-around performance with 18 points, 16 rebounds, and nine assists in the 89–73 win over Pittsburgh, the 50th consecutive win for the Bruins.

It is unfortunate that the NCAA did not keep assists for every game in that era. There are lists of seven different games this season that Walton had at least seven assists. One must wonder if he also holds every assist record for a Bruins big man.

Digger Phelps did not receive an early Christmas present this December 23 evening at Pauley Pavilion. UCLA won easily over the Irish, 82–56. John Shumate did a good job on Walton, holding him to just 12 points, including four in the first half, but Wilkes scored 18 and Hollyfield added 15 in a 26-point Bruins win. Shumate outscored Walton 18–12 to further gain some national attention individually, and give him some confidence going forward. But the loss moved the Irish to 1–5 for the season, 7–25 in the Phelps era.

Those who were at this game never would have dreamed what would take place just 13 months later.

Instead of playing host to the Bruins Classic, Wooden decided to broaden his team's horizons by traveling to New Orleans for the Sugar Bowl Classic. Whether it be a Christmas hangover or just playing the first two games of the year away from home, the Bruins did have their most challenging games of the young season against Drake and Illinois on consecutive nights in the Crescent City.

UCLA led by just four points at the half against Drake before Walton took over. He finished with 29 points and 14 rebounds. The next night Illinois had a 19–18 lead in the first half. UCLA won 71–64, its closest game of the season to that point and just the third game decided by seven points or less over the last two years and 39 games.

The Pac-8 season began on January 5 and 6, 1973, when the teams from Oregon came to Pauley Pavilion on consecutive nights.

For the second time this season, a team tried to hold the ball against the Bruins and for the second time the strategy failed. Bradley had tried that strategy on December 1 in the second game but the Braves scored just 38 points and lost by 35 points. Oregon attempted the strategy in the first league game of the year and also scored just 38 points in a 26-point Bruins win.

Oregon, coached by Dick Harter, actually stayed with UCLA, who led by just 18–14 at intermission. But Coach Wooden went to a three-guard offense, playing Greg Lee, Larry Hollyfield, and Pete Trgovich together for much of the stanza and the result was a 46-point second half and a 64–38 UCLA win.

The next three games—wins over Oregon State at home and road wins at Stanford and California—were all typical, relatively easy wins. UCLA led by 12 at the half against the Beavers on January 6, then Hollyfield scored four of the team's first five baskets of the second half. Sophomore Dave Meyers had his best game of the year with 10 points off the bench.

Stanford had an outstanding center in Rich Kelley, who went on to an 11-year NBA career and would face Walton many times as a pro. But the Walton Gang stymied the seven-footer, holding him to just nine points and 0-for-6 shooting in the second half. UCLA won by 15.

For the first time all year, UCLA trailed at the half in the game in California. But Hollyfield came alive in the second half with his left-handed jumpers from the left side and the Bruins went on to a 60–50 win.

After the 4–0 start in the Pac-8, the Bruins had a run of four straight non-conference games between January 19 and 27, the final four non-conference contests of the regular season. Three of the four games were against teams that were playing their best basketball at the end of the season. Two of them would reach the Elite Eight of the NCAA Tournament and another would reach the finals of the NIT.

On January 19, a date that a year later would become synonymous with the Notre Dame vs. UCLA series, the Bruins faced San Francisco at Pauley Pavilion. This game had obvious historical significance because San Francisco still owned the all-time longest Division I winning streak and certainly wanted to keep the Bill Russell and K. C. Jones teams of the mid-1950s at the top of the record book.

But, as was the case with most Bruins opponents, they could not contend with Walton, who had 22 points, 22 rebounds, and seven assists. Wooden was quoted as saying after the game, "Overall, I rather think this was our best game of the season." His point was proven as the season went on, because the Dons would not only make the NCAA Tournament, but they would also reach the West Regional Final before losing to UCLA again.

It was win number 58 in the streak.

Wooden was never afraid to play a strong non-conference schedule, but most of the time the opponent came to Pauley Pavilion. And he was known to bring in teams with celebrated players. Pete Maravich and LSU, and Austin Carr and the Irish had come to Los Angeles in 1969–70.

Providence College and entertaining guard Ernie DiGregorio came to Pauley on January 20, 1973. Ernie D was the talk of the East Coast because of his flamboyant style that included multiple behind-the-back passes in every game. He was a 5'11" version of Maravich in many ways.

The Friars also featured athletic center Marvin Barnes, who would be a first-round pick two years later. DiGregorio scored 22 points and had 13 assists, and Barnes held Walton without a point the first 12 minutes of the game. But Walton caught fire in the second half and had another incredible all-around game. He finished with 18 points, 24 rebounds, and eight assists, leading the Bruins to a 101–77 victory.

This victory became more and more impressive as the season went on because the Friars would join the Bruins at the Final Four in St. Louis.

If UCLA was to break San Francisco's record they would do so on the road in the Midwest. It was fitting because that was where Wooden's roots, as a player and a coach, were formed.

On January 25, 1973, UCLA met Loyola of Chicago, and Notre Dame met Illinois, in a doubleheader at Chicago Stadium. It was a "game note fest" for the sports information directors of the schools, including Notre Dame's Roger Valdiserri.

On this night UCLA was trying to tie San Francisco's record of 60 consecutive wins by beating Loyola. San Francisco got its 60th consecutive win over Loyola in a game in Chicago in December 1956. Loyola was coached by George Ireland, a former Notre Dame player who was on the Irish teams when Wooden was living in South Bend as the head coach of South Bend Central High School.

Illinois was also in the building and they were the school that ended San Francisco's 60-game winning streak, three nights after the Dons had beaten Loyola. And of course, Notre Dame was the last school to defeat UCLA.

Is your head spinning?

Walton continued his incredible run of legendary games in the 87–73 win over Loyola with 32 points on 14-for-19 shooting and a career best 27 rebounds. A check of the 2024 NCAA Record Book shows that there have been just three games in NCAA history where a player has had at least 30 points and 30 rebounds in the same game. Walton was just three rebounds short of accomplishing the feat.

Win number 60 was in the books.

UCLA made the short drive from Chicago to South Bend after the game. Wooden was used to playing games on consecutive nights, even when the opposition didn't have a game. In this case, the Irish played Illinois at Chicago Stadium the same night the Bruins played Loyola, so that evened up the rest factor.

Wooden had learned a lesson two years previously when he suffered his last loss. The Bruins played a game on Friday night in Chicago against Loyola and didn't get to South Bend until 3 a.m. on Saturday for an afternoon game against Austin Carr and the Irish. The result was an 89–82 Notre Dame win. This time they had a day off to prepare and rest.

Walton enjoyed playing in front of hostile crowds and he would get one at Notre Dame. Digger Phelps, in his second year, already had the ability to get the Irish fired up and there was a pep rally on campus the night before the game.

The Irish stayed with the Bruins for a half, which was better than what they had done the previous three meetings of the Phelps era, but UCLA pulled away at the end to win by 19, 82–63. Walton had 16 points, 15 rebounds, and according to some media members who kept the stat (but it was not listed in the final box score), had 10 blocked shots. Wilkes was actually the top scorer with 20 points and he shut out Notre Dame forward Gary Novak from the field.

The game got a bit physical in the second half and Wooden came over to Phelps's side of the court for a discussion. Wooden thought Peter Crotty (whom UCLA players referred to as Peter Karate) and Shumate were being rough with Walton.

Digger made light of the meeting in the postgame press conference. "John asked me if I had read his book," laughed Digger. "I told him I had." Wooden's book, *They Call Me Coach*, had just been published.

In his book, *Digger Phelps's Tales from the Notre Dame Hardwood*, he told the story:

"Near the end, and with the game going on, he motioned for me to meet him at the scorer's table. He said, 'Tell John Shumate to lay off the rough play on Walton, or I'll put Swen Nater into the game.' He was implying he was going to put Nater in to play rough.

"I didn't back down. I said, 'Go ahead, and bring in Nater. I've got three football players at the end of my bench (Willie and Mike Townsend, and Frank Allocco), and I'll put them in and take on your entire team.'

"I just turned and walked away. He was either shocked that I stood up to him, or he thought I was crazy enough to do it."

The game continued without incident.

During the offseason Wooden sent a letter of apology to Phelps over the issue.

At the end of the game Phelps retrieved the ball and presented it to a smiling Wooden at virtually the same spot they had just had an argument. "I congratulated him and said send this ball to the Hall of Fame."

Wooden said in a TV interview after the game that he was pleased with his team's performance, but it was just another game. "My thoughts

Digger Phelps presented John Wooden with the game ball after UCLA won its 61st consecutive game, a victory at Notre Dame in January 1973. *Associated Students of UCLA, Public domain, via Wikimedia Commons*

today are more on the ceasefire announced in Vietnam." (President Nixon had announced earlier in the day that there had been a ceasefire in regard to the Vietnam War. Unfortunately, the United States was the only side to honor it and the war continued until April 1975.)

After the game, Curry Kirkpatrick of *Sports Illustrated* caught up to Walton as he was headed to the bus. He asked Walton if he would remember this game for a long time. After a pause he told Kirkpatrick no. "I will remember the game we lose."

The following week, UCLA was on the cover of *Sports Illustrated* in the form of an action shot of Walton pulling in a rebound. The headline said, "61 The Record Busting Walton Gang."

At the bottom left corner of the picture is a Notre Dame student who actually lived in the Athletic and Convocation Center. By living there, he had the run of the place, and worked his way to a place under the basket to watch this historical game.

The student was Rudy Ruettiger, who had not yet joined the Notre Dame football team, but would someday be the subject of the movie *Rudy*.

One of the incredible aspects of the streak was Wooden's ability to keep his team focused after a big game. The Bruin players didn't talk about the streak that much when it was going on. There was no ESPN to publicize it every day of the season as they would do now.

But there were obviously stories leading up to the last two games and the subsequent accomplishment.

You would think there might have been a letdown after the streak was broken. But that was not the case even for a big game against rival Southern California at their home court the next weekend.

UCLA was as focused as ever and Walton again led the team with 20 points and 17 rebounds. He didn't even play the last five minutes after a collision with Southern Cal's John Lambert.

The 79–56 victory was the 600th of Wooden's career as a college coach.

The following weekend the Bruins made the trip to the state of Washington for a Thursday (February 10) and Saturday (February 12) set.

On Thursday night, first year Washington State head coach George Raveling tried to stall, but UCLA still scored 34 points in the first half. The Bruins would win by 38 (88–50) as Walton had 17 and 13, and Lee had 10 assists.

So, to this point in the season, three teams had tried a stall tactic against UCLA, at least in the first half, and those three finished the game with an average of 42 points scored and lost by an average of 33 points per game.

Washington played well and lost by just 76–67, just the second team to keep the final score under double digits this season. The Huskies' center was 6-foot-10 freshman Lars Hansen from Denmark, the first prominent freshman big man the Bruins had faced.

As one could have predicted, it was a learning experience for Hansen, who did make it to the NBA for one year. Walton finished with another 20–20 (29 points and 21 rebounds).

The following weekend the Washington schools came to Pauley Pavilion and it was two more 30-point victories. Hansen again was no match for Walton on Friday night, as he scored just four points, while Walton had 26. On Saturday, Raveling did not try to stall and Washington State trailed by 20 at the half. Walton and Nater combined for 43 points and 29 rebounds in the 96–64 win.

UCLA had won consecutive 26-point games over the Oregon schools to open the Pac-8 season, but seven weeks later it was a different story on the road.

Oregon had won four in a row under Dick Harter, who had been the head coach at Penn four years earlier and had a freshman coach named Digger Phelps. It seemed Harter took a similar approach to what Phelps had done earlier in the season against the Bruins. Or Wooden was just anticipating it having known the connection between the two coaches.

UCLA won, but by just 11, 72–61. Wooden said in his press conference it was the roughest game he had seen. "It was wrestling. . . . We showed tremendous self-control."

While media had talked about facing freshman Lars Hansen two weeks previous, Oregon freshman Ron Lee got a lot of publicity after he scored 31 against the Bruins.

Two nights later at Oregon State, UCLA won by just six, 73–67, its closest game of the season to date. At a pivotal point with 7:12 left, Walton scored on a put-back that the home crowd thought was offensive goaltending. The game was delayed as Beavers fans threw paper on the court. Order was restored and Walton would finish with 21 points and 19 rebounds, while Hollyfield added 18.

The Pac-8 title (no postseason tournament in those days) was clinched at home versus California on March 2 with a 90–65 victory. Walton got into foul trouble, but it only allowed Nater, who would go on to average a double-double over 11 years in the NBA, to show his capabilities as the backup pivot with 10 points, 12 rebounds, and four assists.

The next night versus Stanford, Rich Kelley played much better than the first meeting between the two teams. He played as well against Walton as any player had all year and the Indians (now Cardinal) had a seven-point lead at the half. Kelley finished with 15 points and 15 rebounds, but Walton came on strong in the second half with 23 points and the Bruins won, 51–45.

UCLA finished off the regular season with a 76–56 win over Southern California. The Trojans were an NCAA Tournament team by today's standards, but not in 1973. They were headed to the NIT where they would be the first Pac-8 school to compete in the tournament. They were not given any favors in the tournament draw, however, as they would face Notre Dame in New York City on St. Patrick's Day.

Walton finished off the regular season with his seventh double-double with at least seven assists and Wilkes added 17.

THE NCAA TOURNAMENT

The NCAA Tournament still didn't have pre-tournament seeding, but all believed the Bruins were not only the top team in the West, but also the favorite for the entire tournament.

Not only that, but Pauley Pavilion had also been selected as the West Regional site.

Arizona State, who was not yet in the Pac-8, liked the up-tempo style under head coach Ned Wulk. They had beaten Arizona 110–105 late in the season, then scored 103 in the first round NCAA Tournament win over Oklahoma City. They were ranked 16th in the nation with an 18–8 record and were champions of the Western Athletic Conference.

But running with the Bruins did not work as UCLA had 29 assists on 43 made field goals. Walton made 13 of 18 shots and scored 28 points, pulled in 14 rebounds and had six assists. Hollyfield continued his hot outside shooting and scored 20, while Wilkes added a double-double with 12 and 10.

Wooden and his coaching staff were probably putting more time in on preparation for Jerry Tarkanian's 26–2 Long Beach State team that was ranked third in the nation. But Long Beach State star Ed Ratleff was injured against San Francisco and shot just 4-for-18 from the field and San Francisco pulled off the upset, 77–67.

San Francisco was no slouch. They were 23–4 coming into the game with UCLA and ranked 20th in the final AP poll prior to the NCAA

Tournament. They had lost earlier in the season to UCLA by 28 points as Walton had a double 22 (22 points and 22 rebounds).

This time they put in more emphasis making someone other than Walton beat them. The Bruins' center did have 14 rebounds, but shot just seven times and scored just nine points. Larry Farmer led the team with 13, while Tommy Curtis and Wilkes had 12 apiece.

UCLA got off just 56 shots after getting 80 against Arizona State. The result was a 54–39 Bruins win, as the two teams combined for just 93 points after combining for 156 in the first meeting. Every San Francisco starter played all 40 minutes and future pro Phil Smith led the way with 17 points.

UCLA celebrated winning the regional in its own building and looked to face Indiana and second-year head coach Bobby Knight in St. Louis, Missouri, on March 24.

Knight had taken the Hoosiers to a No. 6 AP ranking and a 21–5 record entering the contest. The Hoosiers featured five future NBA players, just one less than the Bruins.

Indiana was led by Steve Downing, a 6'8" center who averaged 20.1 points and 10.6 rebounds for the season. It didn't look that way early in the game, but Downing proved to be a worthy opponent.

UCLA led 40–22 at the half. Just another easy 20 minutes left before moving on to the championship game.

But we all know the fire and brimstone of motivation techniques of Coach Knight. He must have given quite a charge at halftime. In the first 10 minutes of the second half, Indiana was on fire behind Downing and the press-breaking abilities of freshman guard Quinn Buckner.

From a 40–22 deficit at the half, the Hoosiers scored 32 points in the first 10 minutes of the second half. At the end of the segment was a 17–0 run, which must have been the longest run against the Bruins during their 88-game winning streak. Incredibly, Indiana took a 54–51 lead.

Then, with 7:57 left, and the margin still close, Walton drove across the lane and collided with Downing. Referee Joe Shosid blew his whistle. Both players had four fouls. Shosid looked at Downing and he was gone from the game.

Indiana still hung in, trailing by just two with 5:51 left. But UCLA went on a 10–0 spurt inside the last five minutes and won going away, 70–59. Downing finished with 26 points on 12-for-20 shooting in a head-to-head battle with Walton, who had 14 points, 17 rebounds, and nine assists.

Tommy Curtis was the real hero for UCLA, scoring 22 points off the bench on 9-for-15 shooting.

It was a meeting of Hall of Fame coaches that was closer than the score indicated and it was an indication Bobby Knight was going to have quite a coaching career. It would be their only meeting as head coaches.

The win over Indiana moved UCLA into the national championship game for the seventh year in a row, this time against a Memphis State (now Memphis) program that reached the Final Four for the first time in its history. In fact, the three wins so far in the tournament were its first wins in history in the event.

For the second time in the tournament UCLA's opponent was a surprise. The Tigers had defeated Providence in the other semifinal. While UCLA had beaten the Friars and star players Ernie DiGregorio and Marvin Barnes by 24 points in Pauley back in December, Dave Gavitt's team had not lost since, winners of 16 in a row, and had risen to No. 4 in the polls.

The East Coast media had flocked to St. Louis to see if the Friars could end UCLA's winning streak in the championship game. Many felt Marvin Barnes at least had a chance to compete with Walton.

But 12th-ranked Memphis State, the Missouri Valley champion, ruined that dream by defeating Providence, 98–85. The Friars played a great first half and led 49–40 at intermission. But late in the half, Barnes, who averaged 18 points and 19 rebounds that year, went down with a knee injury that would keep him out the rest of the game.

With Barnes sidelined, Memphis State won the second half, 58–36, and the Friars were on to the consolation game where they played without Barnes and lost to Indiana. Larry Kenon (28 points and 22 rebounds), Ronnie Robinson (24 and 16), and Larry Finch (21) all went over 20 to lead the balanced Memphis State team that beat South Carolina, No. 9 Kansas State, and No. 4 Providence to reach the finals.

The NCAA had moved the Final Four from Thursday night and Saturday afternoon to Saturday afternoon and Monday night.

Even with UCLA being a 15-point favorite and without the wizardry of Ernie D, the game was very attractive. According to the *2023 NCAA Final Four Record Book*, the game had a 20.5 rating on NBC-TV with a 32 share. The share is still the eighth largest for an NCAA Tournament game. It was seen by an estimated 39 million people.

The NCAA and television partners were pleased with those numbers and the championship game has been played on a Monday night ever since.

Memphis State coach Gene Bartow made the decision before the game to have Larry Kenon guard Walton straight up with no help, no gimmick defenses. Bartow was quoted in the pregame press conference as saying, "Half of his [Walton's] game is passing. He is a great passer. We'd like to make a shooter out of him tonight."

Bartow backed up his strategy by saying that a lot of NBA teams had used this same strategy against Wilt Chamberlain. "Who knows, maybe he won't score 70 points," said Bartow. "Actually, I think the highest number of points he has scored at UCLA is 30 or 32 points. He is usually around 18 or 20." Bartow concluded, "We feel the more Walton shoots, unless he is just shooting a fantastic percentage, the better chance we have of winning."

Some didn't understand that logic because Walton was ranked in the top five in the nation in field goal percentage each of the last two years.

Looking back at these quotes and the way the game turned out, one has to wonder how Bartow was offered the opportunity to replace Wooden two years later.

That is written tongue-in-cheek, of course. The man had done wonders with the Memphis State program. They had not won an NCAA tournament game previous to Bartow's arrival.

The first UCLA game young Bill Walton watched on television was the 1965 NCAA championship game between UCLA and Michigan. That night UCLA guard Gail Goodrich scored 42 points in a 91–80 Bruins victory. The 42 points stood as the NCAA championship game record entering the 1973 Final Four.

Walton and Kenon matched baskets early in the first half, but Kenon drew a third foul. He also got a technical. In those days a technical was not a personal. In today's rules he would have had four fouls in the first half because today a technical is also a personal.

When he went out, Walton continued to score, many on turnaround bank shots, a patented shot for Wooden players over the years.

Walton missed his first shot of the game at the 7:04 mark of the first half, but he then tipped in the miss to give UCLA a 31–24 lead. But Finch knocked down some shots, and even with Kenon out, Memphis State tied the game at intermission, 39–39.

With the foul trouble on Kenon, Bartow went to a 1-2-2 zone in the second half. The game was still tied at 45, but Walton kept making shots, many on lob passes from Greg Lee. He did not miss in the second half. UCLA did not take a double-digit lead until six minutes to go, but dominated the closing minutes to win, 87–66.

Walton finished with 44 points, two more than the previous championship game record of 42 set by Goodrich in the first UCLA game Walton had watched in 1965. Walton made an incredible 21 of 22 field goal attempts and that .955 percentage still stands as the best field goal percentage in any NCAA tournament game, never mind the championship game.

What is even more remarkable is that Walton played just 33 minutes and played the final 9:27 with four fouls. He left the game with a twisted ankle with under three minutes left, and in the postgame ceremony he limped to the stage to receive his NCAA Tournament Most Outstanding Player award.

Walton was not the only star for the Bruins as Lee had 14 assists, most ever in a championship game, and Wilkes added 16 points.

Larry Finch and Larry Kenon kept Memphis close in the first half and finished with 29 and 20 points, respectively.

Shortly after the game, Walton met with the Philadelphia 76ers about a $2 million contract if he left for the NBA, but he decided to stay and finish his degree.

UCLA fans breathed easy. The streak would continue for at least another year.

Later in the year, Walton won the Sullivan Award as the top amateur athlete regardless of the sport. The award dates to 1930 and Walton is joined by Bill Bradley, Charlie Ward, and J. J. Redick as the only male basketball players to win it.

John Wooden on the 1972–73 Season

"How can I ever forget—the magnificent performance of Bill Walton in the championship game against Memphis State, the inspirational and effective play of Tommy Curtis on many occasions and especially in the NCAA Tournament games against San Francisco and Indiana, the always smooth and often brilliant play of Keith Wilkes, the fine all-around and consistent performances of Larry Farmer, the many brilliant steals and outstanding play of Larry Hollyfield, the beautiful lob passes of Greg Lee to Walton and Farmer, the steady improvement and productive play of David Meyers, the good humor and fine touch of Swen Nater, and although their game time was limited, the often overlooked, but extremely important daily practice contributions of Vince Carson, Casey Corliss, Ralph Drollinger, Gary Franklin, Pete Trgovich and Bobby Webb, the efficient managerial staff headed by Les Friedman, and the loyalty and intelligent cooperation of my assistants, Gary Cunningham and Frank Arnold."

UCLA's 61st Straight Win
UCLA 82, Notre Dame 63
January 27, 1973
at Notre Dame, Indiana
Athletic and Convocation Center

UCLA (82)

Name	FG-A	FT-A	Reb	Ast-TO	F	Pts
Keith Wilkes	10-16	0-0	9	0-4	1	20
Larry Farmer	8-19	0-1	7	2-2	0	16
Bill Walton	8-12	0-0	15	4-2	2	16
Greg Lee	2-7	3-3	1	9-4	0	7

Larry Hollyfield	4-10	0-0	4	3-3	2	8
Pete Trgovich	1-4	1-2	3	2-3	0	3
Dave Meyers	3-3	0-0	3	0-1	2	6
Bob Webb	0-1	0-0	0	0-0	0	0
Swen Nater	1-3	0-0	3	0-1	0	2
Vince Carson	1-1	0–0	0	0-0	1	2
Gary Franklin	0-0	2-2	0	0-0	0	2
Team			6			
Totals	38-76	6-8	51	20-20	8	82
	(.500)	(.750)				

Notre Dame (63)

Name	FG-A	FT-A	Reb	Ast-TO	F	Pts
John Shumate	8-20	5-5	12	6-4	3	21
Gary Novak	0-4	0-0	1	1-0	1	0
Peter Crotty	3-6	1-4	5	1-3	1	7
Gary Brokaw	8-18	0-0	6	1-2	3	16
Dwight Clay	5-17	0-0	3	5-2	2	10
Don Silinski	2-3	1-1	0	0-0	0	5
Willie Townsend	1-2	0-0	1	0-1	1	2
Mike Townsend	0-0	0-0	1	0-0	0	0
Chris Stevens	0-2	0-0	0	0-1	1	0
Tom Hansen	0-0	0-0	0	0-0	1	0
Ken Wolbeck	1-3	0-0	2	0-0	0	2
Team			8			
Totals	28-75	7-10	39	14-13	13	63
	(.373)	(.700)				

Score by Half

UCLA	38	44	82
Notre Dame	25	38	63

OFFICIALS: GEORGE STRAUTHERS, BOB BRODBECK

ATTENDANCE: 11,343 (CAPACITY)

1973 NCAA CHAMPIONSHIP GAME
UCLA 87, Memphis 66
March 26, 1973
at St. Louis, Missouri
The Arena

UCLA (87)

Name	Min	FG-A	FT-A	Reb	Ast	F	Pts
Keith Wilkes	39	8-14	0-0	7	1	2	16
Larry Farmer	33	1-4	0-0	2	0	2	2
Bill Walton	33	21-22	2-5	13	2	4	44
Greg Lee	34	1-1	3-3	3	14	2	5
Larry Hollyfield	30	4-7	0-0	3	9	4	8
Tommy Curtis	11	1-4	2-2	3	0	1	4
Dave Meyers	10	2-7	0-0	3	0	1	4
Sven Nater	7	1-1	0-0	3	0	2	2
Gary Franklin	1	1-2	0-1	1	0	0	2
Vince Carson	1	0-0	0-0	0	0	0	0
Bob Webb	1	0-0	0-0	0	0	0	0
Team				2			
Totals	200	40-62 (.645)	7-11 (.636)	40	26	18	87

Memphis State (66)

Name	Min	FG-A	FT-A	Reb	Ast	F	Pts
Bill Buford	38	3-7	1-2	3	1	1	7
Larry Kenon	34	8-16	4-4	8	3	3	20
Ron Robinson	33	3-6	0-1	7	1	4	6
Bill Laurie	21	0-1	0-0	0	2	0	0
Larry Finch	38	9-21	11-13	1	2	2	29
Bill Cook	18	1-4	2-2	0	2	1	4
Wes Westfall	10	0-1	0-0	0	0	5	0
Clarence Jones	4	0-0	0-0	0	0	0	0
Jerry Tetzlaff	1	0-0	0-2	0	0	1	0
Jim Liss	1	0-1	0-0	0	0	0	0

Ken Andrews	1	0-0	0-0	0	0	0	0
Doug McKinney	1	0-0	0-0	0	0	0	0
Teams				2			
Totals	200	24-57 (.421)	18-24 (.750)	21	11	17	66

Score by Half

UCLA	39	48	87
Memphis State	39	27	66

OFFICIALS: JIM HOWELL, JOE SHOSID

ATTENDANCE: 19,301

CHAPTER 6

1972–73: Notre Dame Makes Significant Progress

EVEN WITH THE RETURN OF JOHN SHUMATE AND THE ADDITION OF Gary Brokaw, Dwight Clay, and Peter Crotty from the freshman team, Notre Dame started the 1972–73 season with a 1–6 record. That meant Digger Phelps was 7–26 in his first 33 games as Notre Dame head coach.

But Digger's second team was much more competitive. There were no 65 or 58-point blowouts. In fact, just about all the games were close. There was an overtime loss to Ohio State, a two-point loss to St. Louis, a two-point loss to Kentucky and first year head coach Joe B. Hall at that "neutral site" in Louisville's Freedom Hall, and a two-point loss to an Indiana team that would advance to the Final Four at season's end.

There was obvious improvement, but Phelps's team needed a big win over a well-known program and coach to move the Irish in the right direction.

That victory came on January 7, 1973, at Notre Dame, a nationally televised Sunday afternoon game against Ted Owens and the Kansas Jayhawks.

"This was a game where Shumate, Brokaw, and Clay clicked together for the first time," recalled Phelps.

The Irish were down two, 61–59 in the final seconds when Brokaw missed a jumper, but Shumate tipped it in at the buzzer sending the game into overtime.

Notre Dame took a five-point lead with just 47 seconds left in the overtime. The three-point shot was still 15 years away in college basketball, but Wilson Barrow scored an "and one" three-point play to cut the margin to two with just 26 seconds left.

Then Brokaw got tied up at midcourt with 19 seconds left and Kansas got possession on the ensuing jump ball. Kansas had the ball with a chance to tie, but they turned it over on an errant pass, and the Irish had a meaningful win for the first time under their new coach, 66–64.

Brokaw led the Irish with 20 points, while Shumate had 18 and Clay had 15, giving the three "newcomers" 53 of Notre Dame's 66 points.

That was the start of a five-game winning streak and the first three wins were by five points or less. "It is amazing how winning one close game can give you confidence and have a carry-over effect," said Phelps.

The Irish were 0–6 in games decided by five or less under Phelps before the Kansas win.

The third game of the five-game streak made the Kansas win look like an average victory.

Marquette was a firmly established national power under Al McGuire. The Warriors (their nickname in those days, now Golden Eagles) would go on to a 25–4 record in 1972–73 and a berth in the Sweet 16 of the NCAA Tournament.

Most impressively they entered this January 13, 1973, game in Milwaukee with an 81-game home winning streak. They had not lost at home since December 16, 1967, a 70–62 loss to Wisconsin.

Phelps and McGuire first met in February of 1971 when Digger's upstart Fordham team faced McGuire's undefeated and second-ranked Marquette squad in Madison Square Garden. The previous Thursday night Phelps and the Rams had upset Austin Carr and Notre Dame. That was the first of consecutive Thursday night sellouts (19,500) at the Garden for Fordham and at the time the two largest crowds for a college basketball game at the Garden.

It was quite a show, but Marquette got the best of Fordham that night in an overtime thriller to keep its winning streak alive, a streak that would reach 28 in a row before Marquette lost to Indiana in the Sweet 16 of the NCAA Tournament.

Phelps remembers that first meeting with McGuire vividly. "Al got a technical foul early and controlled the latter stages of the game (and the officials), while I sat on the bench and watched. I learned a lesson that night. I wasn't going to let that happen again, so [in future games against McGuire] I knew I had to counteract his technical with one of my own. I just had to find the right time to do it."

But this Saturday afternoon at Marquette, Phelps got the best of McGuire thanks to the birth of the legend of "The Iceman."

Marquette had the lead at the half 33–29 and kept it for most of the second half. But the margin was close throughout, which was typical of the 10–0 and second-ranked Warriors, who had already won six games by five points or less.

But Clay hit two free throws with 1:08 left to put the Irish up, 69–67. Marquette's Larry McNeil then hit a jumper with 34 seconds left to tie the score at 69. Phelps had his team run the clock down to 10 seconds then call timeout.

"We were going to Brokaw or Clay, one-on-one in hopes they could draw a foul. The other three were to crash the boards," said Phelps. Brokaw had scored a game-high 28 points and McGuire was not going to let him beat his team, so he double-teamed him. That left Clay open in the right corner.

With just a few seconds left, Clay faked to the foul line, then darted to the baseline to get open. He made the shot with just two seconds on the clock to give the Irish a 71–69 lead. Unlike today, the clock did not stop on a made field goal inside the last minute, so the game ended.

It was just Clay's second made field goal of the game and his sixth and seventh points. He actually scored four of his seven points inside the last 1:08 of the game.

Phelps was euphoric after the game. "We said there was no pressure on us. I like to keep the kids loose."

He followed with one of the more interesting quotes of his young coaching career. "What I didn't want to do was get a lead on them in the first half and irritate their players. I just felt we had to get behind and then somehow pull it out in the end."

That was one of the first times a coach has told the media a key to the game was getting behind early, but that is exactly how the game played out, the first of Phelps's many streak-breaking wins over highly ranked teams in his 21-year head coaching career.

As is the case many times in the game after a thrilling victory, Notre Dame came out flat in its next game at home against Pittsburgh. Behind 22 points from future NBA star Billy Knight, the Panthers had a 46–33 lead at intermission.

The Irish made a second-half comeback behind Brokaw (26) and Shumate (24), who each had at least 20 points for the second straight game. But Pittsburgh still had an eight-point lead with 5:10 left and a five-point lead with just 32 seconds left in regulation.

With 12 seconds left, Shumate cut the margin to two points. On the ensuing possession, Peter Crotty tied up Pittsburgh's Bill Sulkowski at midcourt. There was no possession arrow in those days. Crotty got the tip against the smaller Sulkowski. Shumate then retrieved the ball and fed Clay, who hit a 25-footer with four seconds left. As stated earlier in the rundown of the Marquette game, the clock did not stop and the game went to overtime.

This shot was the longest of Clay's legendary game winners. Once again he had not done a lot of scoring in the first 39 minutes of the game, as the shot that tied the game resulted in his seventh and eight points, and he had been just 3–10 from the field to that point.

Notre Dame dominated the overtime period by an 11–2 score and Digger had his second overtime victory over the season, 85–76.

The Irish went on a three-game losing streak between January 22 and 29, including the 82–63 loss to UCLA documented in the previous chapter.

Phelps handled the loss to the Bruins very well and that carried over to his team. The Irish went on a five-game winning streak, with victories over Villanova, Xavier, Butler, Michigan State, and LaSalle.

The streak was stopped by Digger's former team, the Fordham Rams, at Madison Square Garden, where just two years earlier Phelps had upset Notre Dame in front of a sellout crowd. This time there were just a little over 10,000 in attendance to see two .500 teams. "To say the least this was a payback game for Fordham," said Phelps.

Hal Wissel's team came away with a 70–69 victory, the only win over their last 13 games of the season.

A dejected Irish team then flew straight to Durham, North Carolina, to face Duke and there was a hangover, and the Blue Devils won by 12, 86–74. The loss made Notre Dame 11–11 on the season with four games left.

"I kept a positive attitude after the Duke game and told the guys we could still get in the NIT if we won our last four games," said Phelps.

They did just that.

"The key game down the stretch was winning over St. John's in the Nassau Coliseum." St. John's was an NCAA Tournament team with future pro players Bill Schaeffer and Ed Searcy. Schaeffer scored 30 in the game, but Shumate showed why he was a future NBA player as well and scored 31.

All five Notre Dame starters played the entire game, believed to be the only time this has happened in Notre Dame's modern history. Phelps was big on conditioning and junior Gary Novak came through late. With the Irish up two and St. John's looking for a tying field goal, Novak stole the ball and fed Shumate, who made his 30th and 31st points of the game to give Notre Dame the insurance it needed in the four-point victory.

Notre Dame entered the final regular season game against 19th ranked South Carolina with a 14–11 record. While Digger felt the win over 11th ranked St. John's got the Irish in the NIT, some felt they needed another big win to assure a spot at the 16-team postseason gathering at Madison Square Garden.

The Gamecocks were coached by Frank McGuire, an Irish Catholic from New York who had a strong relationship with Phelps. Phelps had grown up in New York when McGuire was at St. John's. McGuire coached the baseball team and the basketball team at St. John's. He led the Redmen to the College World Series in 1949 and the Final Four of college basketball in 1952. He then continued to recruit the New York area when he led North Carolina to the national championship in 1957.

"I was fortunate to face Frank McGuire after South Carolina left the ACC for independence," said Phelps. "That hurt their program and we were able to beat South Carolina seven out of nine times when he was the coach." Ironically, one of the losses came in 1977–78 when Notre Dame went to the Final Four.

South Carolina hammered Phelps's young first team 109–83 in Columbia, but the Irish came back in 1972–73 to win 73–69 in South Bend behind 25 from Shumate and 20 from Brokaw, two Phelps players who grew up in New Jersey, not far from what used to be McGuire's top recruiting area.

This gave Notre Dame a four-game winning streak to close the season, including two wins over top 20 teams. Two Sundays later, March 11, 1973, the Irish received their bid to the NIT.

Young fans reading this book today may be wondering, "The NIT, what was the big deal?"

The NIT was a big deal in the early 1970s. The 1973 NCAA Tournament had a field of just 25 teams. Only conference champions were invited and independents with a deserving record according to the committee.

That left a lot of good teams available for the NIT. The NIT selected just 16 teams and all 16 went to New York to play in the famed Madison Square Garden.

The field for the 1973 NIT included 10th ranked Minnesota, 11th ranked North Carolina, and 15th ranked Missouri. It also included a 23–7 Louisville team that had been ranked in the top 20 earlier in the year. Eleven of the 16 teams finished the year with at least 20 wins and fewer than 10 losses. Hall of Fame coaches Dean Smith (North Carolina), Denny Crum (Louisville), and C. M. Newton (Alabama) were all in the field.

Basically, every game in the tournament would be an NCAA Tournament game by today's standards.

Notre Dame's first round NIT game was against Southern California, the first meeting in basketball between the football powers. Southern California had just won the 1972 football championship and Notre Dame would go on to win the 1973 title just nine months later.

It was the perfect made for TV matchup and CBS took advantage and showed the game on national TV on St. Patrick's Day. "We had really matured over the second half of the year, having won nine of our last 11, so we had confidence heading to New York," said Phelps. "And it was Notre Dame on St. Patrick's Day in New York City."

While Notre Dame had all those intangibles going for it, it was a close game throughout. Southern California might have accused both referees of being Notre Dame grads, or at least of Irish decent, as Notre Dame had an incredible 33–2 advantage in free throw attempts for the game.

Shumate had his way inside and finished with 24 points, while Brokaw had 17.

The biggest play of the game was turned in by Peter Crotty. The 6–8 sophomore, who was from nearby New Rochelle, New York, made a rare four-point play with 10:15 left to tie the game at 50.

Crotty went to the line and made the front end of a one-and-one, but he missed the second. He was able to follow his shot and get the rebound. He then took a short jumper and converted, and was fouled on the play. The 58 percent career free throw shooter then made the free throw to complete the four-point play.

The game remained close over the last 10 minutes. Brokaw made two free throws with five seconds left to give Notre Dame a 69–65 lead and the victory.

Once again Phelps substituted sparingly. The only sub in the game was Notre Dame football player Willie Townsend, who had joined the team after the Orange Bowl loss to Nebraska.

The victory gave Notre Dame consecutive wins over USC teams in consecutive games. And a football win over Southern California in October of 1973 made it consecutive wins over USC in two different major sports.

That sent the Irish to a Tuesday night meeting against Louisville and head coach Denny Crum, who had taken the Cards to the Final Four the previous year. And he would take them again in 1975 before winning two NCAA championships in the 1980s, a strong factor in his selection to the Naismith Hall of Fame.

Louisville was 23–6 entering the game, but they were not ranked in the final regular season AP poll. Only 20 teams were ranked in those days. They might have been in the 21–25 range had the poll gone that deep in 1973.

While they had not made the NCAA Tournament, Louisville was a typical deep and athletic team with future professionals Junior Bridgeman, Allen Murphy, and Philip Bond.

Shumate had been coming on strong with five consecutive 20-point games going into the Louisville game. He didn't make it six in a row, but he couldn't have played much better, as he made all nine of his field goal attempts and scored 19 points. It is still the Notre Dame record for most made field goals without a miss in a game.

The 79–71 victory was one of most balanced performances by the Irish all year, as all five starters scored in double figures. Clay had made just 12 of his last 36 shots over three games, but he was on his game in the Garden this March 20 evening, as he hit 6 of 12 and scored 18 to provide strong support for Shumate. Most importantly, Clay made three straight field goals at one point in the second half, allowing the Irish to keep up with the athletic Louisville team.

"We didn't want to run with Louisville," said Phelps after the game. "We started in a 1-2-2 zone to try and control the tempo." Notre Dame jumped out to a 6–0 lead and had a 25–16 advantage at one point in the first half.

Thanks to Shumate's perfect game, Notre Dame made 34 of 59 field goals for the game, 57 percent.

The victory over Louisville moved the Irish into the NIT semifinals and a second straight game against a future Hall of Fame coach. The Irish met Dean Smith and North Carolina in the semifinals of the NIT, the first meeting between Phelps and Smith.

Phelps always had respect for Smith because of his impact on the game for many years. "When it comes to innovation, Dean Smith was the master," said Phelps. "He was the first to use the Four Corners, and was outstanding when using his timeouts to milk the clock at the end of games.

"Defensively, his run-and-jump rotation defense forced many turn-overs, especially in late games situations when he stole a lot of victories. He was also the master at making substitutions and incorporating his bench. Often he substituted five at a time. In 1976–77 when we used the S.W.A.T. team the inspiration for that was Dean's Tall Blue team."

Entering this March 24, 1973, game, Phelps was concerned about those substitutions because the Tar Heels definitely had a depth advantage. North Carolina played 10 men or more in its run to the semifinals, Phelps was only using six men and the sixth was Willie Townsend, a wide receiver on loan from Ara Parseghian's football team.

Ironically, that one Notre Dame sub would be a difference maker in Notre Dame's 78–71 victory. Townsend finished with eight points on 4-for-4 field goal shooting, more points and rebounds than any North Carolina sub.

But overall credit for the victory must go to Shumate, who made an incredible 11 of 12 from the field and scored 24 points. He made his first 11 attempts before missing his last one, giving him 20 consecutive made field goals over two games, still the Notre Dame record.

It was quite an accomplishment for Shumate, whose brand (they didn't use that term in 1973) was rising quickly nationally. Shumate had shot 11-for-12 against a North Carolina defense that featured Bobby Jones, regarded as the top defensive player in the nation then and during his NBA career. He is in the Naismith Hall of Fame.

Shumate finished the NIT with a 23.8 scoring average and he made 38 of 51 shots from the field, an incredible 75 percent. He is one of the few players in the history of the tournament to be named its MVP even though he was on the losing team.

The victory over the 11th ranked Tar Heels was their fourth win of the season over a top 20 team and certainly gave the program some national credibility heading into the next season, regardless of the outcome of the NIT Championship the next day.

The NIT Championship game pitted Notre Dame and head coach Digger Phelps against Virginia Tech and head coach Don Devoe.

Both teams were Cinderella stories entering the championship. Notre Dame had reached the championship game after a 1–6 start to its season. Virginia Tech had reached the championship game by winning close games. Devoe's team won all four of its NIT games by a total of five points and had 10 wins by five or less among its 22 victories over the season.

With Shumate as on fire as he was, the Irish continued to feed him in the post. Shumate actually missed a few shots early, but still finished with 28 points on 10-for-19 shooting. That approach led to an advantage in free throw attempts (22–13). Notre Dame attempted 96 free throws to just 24 for the opposition in their four tournament games.

With 6:13 left in the game, Notre Dame had a 70–58 lead. Then the Hokies, in particular point guard Bobby Stevens, got hot. His three baskets over the final six minutes brought Virginia Tech back.

A rare lane violation helped Virginia Tech send the game into overtime. Brokaw was on the line and made a pair of free throws to give the Irish an 80–77 lead. But on the second free throw, referee Hal Grossman wiped out the made shot, saying that Crotty had stepped in the lane too soon. We didn't have video replay back then, and the score went back to 79–77.

It was a tough situation for Crotty, who had grown up in New York and had originally committed to Phelps when he was the coach at Fordham. When Digger went to Notre Dame, Crotty got a release to join him in South Bend.

On the next possession, Stevens found an open Craig Lieder, the Hokies' leading scorer on the day with 26 points, and he buried a jumper to tie the game with five seconds left, sending the game into overtime tied at 79–79.

The two teams continued to play outstanding basketball in the overtime. The game came down to the final possession. Notre Dame had a 91–90 lead with Brokaw on the line for a one-and-one. In those days all non-shooting fouls after the sixth foul were one-and-one situations. Brokaw, who had been 4-for-4 from the line in overtime, missed the front end and Virginia Tech got the rebound with under 20 seconds left.

Virginia Tech called a timeout with 10 seconds left to set up winning play. "The play was supposed to go to Lieder again," said Stevens. "But

Digger Phelps was carried on the shoulders of Notre Dame students upon return-ing to campus after the 1973 NIT. *Notre Dame Archives*

he was not open. So I drove to the right and put up a shot with about five seconds left."

Stevens's shot missed, just his third miss of the game. But the basketball gods were in Virginia Tech's corner this Sunday afternoon. The ball hit the back rim and, incredibly, bounced right back to Stevens, who caught the ball and shot again. The ball was launched, the distinctive Madison Square Garden buzzer went off, and the ball swished.

Virginia Tech 92, Notre Dame 91.

The 13,303 in attendance went wild as Stevens had scored the winning points for Virginia Tech in a game decided by one or two points for the fourth time in nine days.

One had to wonder if fatigue had been a factor on the last play. Four of Notre Dame's five starters had played all 45 minutes. Virginia Tech had substituted more liberally.

"Once I missed I knew there was still time left," said Stevens, who had lost two high school state championship games and a junior college national championship game earlier in his career.

"Notre Dame didn't go for the ball, so I just ran and grabbed it and shot again."

It was a heartbreaking way to end the season, but Phelps and his young team had captured the hearts of Notre Dame fans everywhere. That was especially the case on campus.

The team had come back for classes on Wednesday after beating Louisville in the second round and a thousand students and fans were at The Circle to greet them. How many would be there after a loss?

There was triple the amount to greet the team when it arrived during the lunch hour on Monday, March 26. Shumate and Phelps spoke to the crowd. Notre Dame students put Phelps on their shoulders.

It was the beginning of a tradition when the team came back to campus after a big win whether it be 3 p.m. or 3 a.m. Over three thousand would turn out at 3 a.m. in December 1976 when Notre Dame ended UCLA's 115 home non-conference game winning streak.

With all five starters back, plus the addition of one of the top recruiting classes in the nation for next year, Notre Dame fans couldn't wait for the 1973–74 season.

CHAPTER 7

Buildup to a Historic Game

NOTRE DAME'S FIRST 11 WEEKS OF THE 1973–74 SEASON

There was a lot of excitement on the Notre Dame campus when the 1973–74 Irish basketball season began on December 1 with a home game versus Valparaiso. The Notre Dame football team was ranked second in the nation and was preparing for a New Year's Eve Sugar Bowl game against top-ranked Alabama that would decide the national championship.

Digger Phelps's basketball team won 12 of its last 14 games of the previous season and all five starters from that team returned for 1973–74, including John Shumate, who had been the MVP of the NIT even though the Irish did not win the tournament.

On top of that positive energy, Phelps had recruited his best freshman class with the addition of future Hall of Fame player Adrian Dantley, future NBA player Toby Knight, and four other freshmen who were highly regarded and would be great fits for Phelps's third Notre Dame team.

The third season of a coach's tenure has a great heritage at Notre Dame. Frank Leahy, Ara Parseghian, Dan Devine, and Lou Holtz all won the national championship of college football in their third season running the Notre Dame program.

There was also positive mojo when the preseason AP basketball poll came out and Notre Dame was eighth. Back in August of 1973, Notre

Dame was eighth in the preseason AP football poll. Now Parseghian's team was playing for the national title (and would win it).

Many felt the addition of talented freshmen Luther Bradley and Ross Browner had a big impact on the success of the football team, and the same would be true for the Irish basketball team. Most thought Dantley could do for the basketball team what Browner had done for the football team. (Both would go on to be inducted into the respective sports' Hall of Fame.)

According to all news services at the time, Dantley was a high school All-American as a junior and senior at famed DeMatha High School in Washington, DC. He had been well known nationally since he became the first freshman to start for Hall of Fame coach Morgan Wooten.

Dantley was just the second player at any school to earn All-Metro honors in Washington, DC, three times and was named the most valuable player of six tournaments, including the Dapper Dan, the best-known high school tournament before McDonald's decided to sponsor an All-America game in 1979.

Dantley narrowed his college choices to Notre Dame, Maryland, NC State, and Minnesota. In interviews, Dantley said that Notre Dame was the only school where the staff did not criticize the other schools and the staffs "didn't bug me."

In Digger Phelps's book *A Coach's World*, written with Larry Keith and published after the 1973–74 season, Dantley was quoted as saying, "I eliminated Maryland because Lefty Driesell made everything such a hassle. He would call about every night and wouldn't let me off the phone." Looking back, you can see why Driesell was so enamored with Dantley. It was obvious Dantley was going to be a difference maker no matter where he went. And he lived virtually just down the street from the Maryland campus.

Dantley was also influenced by the success of recent Notre Dame players from Washington, DC. He had played against Austin Carr, Collis Jones, and Sid Catlett in pickup games and knew of Bob Whitmore, who had also been a star at Notre Dame in the 1960s.

Carr and Jones were well aware of the difference Dantley could make in their alma mater's program. When Dantley visited campus in May

1973, Carr and Jones drove all night from the East Coast to be there during his visit.

Much of the preseason talk was whether Phelps would start Dantley from day one over returning starter Peter Crotty. There was no doubt who the better player was, but Crotty and Phelps had a special relationship. When Phelps took the Notre Dame job, Crotty had already committed to play for him at Fordham. But Crotty soon determined he wanted to play for Phelps more than he wanted to attend Fordham.

So, Phelps took the 6'9" Crotty with him when he went to South Bend.

In a public scrimmage that raised money for food for the poor during the Thanksgiving season, Phelps had the freshmen play the veterans. The veterans won, but by just an 87–84 score. Dantley had 24 points and 15 rebounds. Crotty had three points.

When the season opened against Valparaiso, Dantley was in the starting lineup and was Notre Dame's top scorer in the 112–62 victory. He never left the starting lineup the rest of his career.

The following Monday night, the Irish traveled to Ohio State for the first of four December games against teams who defeated the Irish in close games the previous year. These four games, all played prior to the UCLA game, would be great barometers as to how improved this Notre Dame team was and whether or not they deserved a top 10 ranking.

This would be another close game with the Buckeyes. The Irish were down 39–35 at the half. Shumate kept the Irish in it and would finish the game with 25 points and 17 rebounds.

With just 16 seconds left Brokaw fouled out when he was charged while guarding Wardell Jackson. With Ohio State leading 67–65, Jackson went to the line and could have iced the game by hitting the front end of the one-and-one (remember, no three-point shot in this era), but he missed.

Phelps wanted to go inside to Shumate, but he was covered. Clay had the ball and with just seven seconds left, nailed a 21-footer to send the game into overtime. Clay had made just 2 of 10 shots prior to that important shot. "I just prayed the ball would go in," said Clay, who once again lived up to his nickname, "Iceman."

Notre Dame then outscored Ohio State 9–5 in overtime to win, 76–72.

It was a joyous trip back to South Bend. Phelps retired to bed at his home in the wee hours of the morning. But shortly after he had gone to sleep his home phone rang. It was two Notre Dame fans calling from a bar in Hazelton, Pennsylvania. They wanted to know who won the game. "After I hung up my wife mumbled something about getting an unlisted number."

After wins over Northwestern on the road and St. Louis at home, the Irish were holding a Sunday afternoon practice in preparation for a Tuesday night, December 11 game at Indiana.

The Hoosiers had embarrassed Notre Dame two years earlier, 94–29, the worst margin of defeat in Notre Dame history. In 1972–73, Notre Dame had improved dramatically, but lost by two points.

Now, Indiana, who had gone to the Final Four and won the Big Ten the previous year, was ranked third in the nation. Notre Dame had moved from eighth in the preseason poll to sixth.

During the Sunday practice, Notre Dame's fortunes took a downturn. In a collision between two players hustling after a loose ball, reserve forward Roger Anderson crashed into Brokaw, causing him to suffer a leg injury. It put Brokaw in the infirmary and out for the Indiana game.

Thank goodness for the freshman class. Phelps moved Clay from point guard to shooting guard and inserted Ray Martin in the starting lineup at point guard. Dantley was already in the starting lineup and Billy Paterno would see increased playing time at forward.

In his pregame talk to the team, Phelps was very positive and gave a glimpse into what he thought this team could accomplish. "When you go out there, forget about the crowd and the referees and everything else," said Phelps. "Just beat them with your talent.

"Ray [Martin], if you can play with people like Nate Archibald in the [New York] playground, you shouldn't have any trouble with a bunch of college kids.

"Indiana is third in the country and we are sixth. After we beat them tonight, and if UCLA beats NC State on Saturday, we'll move up to number two. And that's how it will stay until we play UCLA in January. Then we'll be number one."

Pretty brazen stuff for the 32-year-old Phelps, but he would prove to be a soothsayer on every statement.

The confidence Phelps showed his team in the locker room continued on to the court. It was important that the Irish get off to a good start with a hostile record crowd of 17,463 in attendance. Five minutes in, the Irish took a 9–4 lead and Bobby Knight called timeout. The Irish led 33–30 at the half.

It was more of the same in the second half, as Paterno had his best game to date hitting from the outside. Time and again Indiana made a run to get within a single possession, but they never took the lead. With 24 seconds left Clay was fouled and hit two clutch free throws to give the Irish a 72–67 lead. Shumate made a late free throw and the Irish won, 73–67.

The story of the game was Notre Dame's freshman class. Dantley finished with 15 points, 13 rebounds, and six assists. Paterno had 16 points in 33 minutes and Ray Martin ran the offense and played terrific defense. Shumate had dominated Indiana freshman Kent Benson.

"After reflecting on where we were after the 1971 game in Bloomington, I couldn't believe we beat them in Bloomington without Gary Brokaw," recalled Phelps.

With exam week coming up, the Irish did not have a game until December 20 and had just one game over the next 16 days.

Phelps watched with interest from his home on Saturday night, December 15, the game between UCLA and NC State. It was top-ranked UCLA vs. second-ranked NC State and Phelps took extensive notes to see what he could learn in preparation for his two upcoming games with the Bruins.

According to *A Coach's World*, here are the notes Phelps took from that 18-point UCLA win at the neutral site in St. Louis:

The keys to the game were Keith Wilkes defensive job on David Thompson, and his ability to turn on offensively after Bill Walton got in foul trouble. Wilkes, not Walton, will be our toughest defensive assignment. (I write Walton off as unstoppable.)

UCLA stayed close in the first half because of its rebounding. They are big and aggressive.

NC State led early because it was willing to attack Walton. This is my philosophy exactly.

UCLA has tremendous depth at center with Drollinger and Washington playing behind Walton. We don't.

UCLA's press forced NC State to hurry down the floor and rush its shots. We should not be forced into that unless we can find a high percentage shot.

NC State stayed in contention as long as it showed poise and patience. It lost both and the game when Walton returned. Poise and patience will be a key for us.

After a 40-point win over Denver on December 20, the Notre Dame players headed home for a holiday break. They didn't have to return to campus until December 26 when preparations begin for Kentucky, a game that will be played at "that neutral site" in Louisville, Kentucky.

Kentucky had beaten Notre Dame the year before and it was the fourth game in December that was a "revenge game" for the Irish. Kentucky was ranked 10th in the preseason poll under second year coach Joe B. Hall, but had a three-game losing streak earlier in the month, losses to Kansas, third-ranked Indiana, and fifth-ranked North Carolina.

Notre Dame had won just two of the 12 previous games in the series with Kentucky, all games in the Bluegrass State. One of them took place three years earlier when Austin Carr scored 50 for the Irish.

Balance won this game, as Shumate (25), Dantley (22), and Brokaw (22) all went for at least 20 points. The Irish shot 58 percent from the field and won the rebounding by 17.

After the game Kentucky's Jimmy Dan Conner said he thought Notre Dame was "about the same as Indiana and North Carolina . . . but I think they have a shot at UCLA. I really do."

When you are an independent, even as prominent as Notre Dame, there are gaps in the schedule because your slate is not tied to a conference schedule. After the win over Kentucky, Notre Dame didn't have another game until January 12 against Xavier, then January 15 against Georgetown.

The break allowed Phelps and many of his players to go to New Orleans to watch Notre Dame beat Alabama by a point, 24–23 to win the national championship of college football. It was one of the great games in college football history and was not decided until the final minute when Tom Clements completed a 35-yard pass from his own end zone to reserve tight end Robin Weber.

For the first time since December 20, the Irish had a home game against Xavier on January 12. Despite the long lay-off there was no rust . . . at all. The Irish jumped out 12–0 and 28–8 on the way to an 87–44 victory. Senior Gary Novak, who was the top scorer as a sophomore on Digger's first team, had his best game of the year with 12 points, nine rebounds, and seven blocks in just 19 minutes. Defensively he held Xavier's leading scorer, Mike Plunkett, to two points.

The final game before the epic with UCLA was against John Thompson's Georgetown Hoyas. Georgetown was still many years away from the Thompson teams of Patrick Ewing and the Irish won, 104–77. It was a big game for Washington, DC, native Adrian Dantley who scored 22 and pulled down 10 rebounds.

The Georgetown players wanted to do everything they could to hold Dantley out of the scoring column as much as possible. Shumate, who scored 26 points, was quoted as saying, "Those guys acted like they didn't even care I was out there. They only person they tried to stop was Adrian."

The Irish were 9–0 and ranked second in the nation after NC State beat second-ranked Maryland the previous weekend. Phelps began his psychological preparation for UCLA in the locker room after the Georgetown game.

As recorded in *A Coaches World*, Phelps addressed the team this way, "For the life of me, I can't understand what's wrong with some of you guys. We gave our bench a lot of action tonight, and it was outplayed and outscored. You're not giving 100 percent. If we call on you and you can't do the job we'll lose, it's that simple.

"We're playing to win the national championship."

He then went around the room and asked each player, "Are you ready to play UCLA? Don't think about Bill Walton [who was injured and his playing status was questionable]. We're playing UCLA."

UCLA's First 11 Weeks of 1973–74 Season

Before the start of each season UCLA head coach John Wooden met with the team and talked about starting the year strong. He had a speech that involved a lucky penny. Walton told an interesting story in a first-person account of his UCLA career in a 1994 *Sports Illustrated* article that previewed that year's Final Four.

> Coach Wooden would always come into the locker room and talk about the importance of a good start to ensure that (potential) for an undefeated season. Then he would glance toward the corner of the room, as if he had spied something out of place. We would follow his eye until we saw a penny sitting on its edge.
>
> "Men," John Wooden would say, holding the coin up for all the see, "this penny means good luck."
>
> The first time I heard the speech we finished 30–0 and won the national title. The second time I heard the speech we finished 30–0 and won the national title.
>
> The third time (preseason of 1973–74) was different. By now we knew the speech by heart. We also knew that John Wooden had instructed an assistant to place the penny in a corner of the room before we entered.
>
> Before Coach Wooden entered the locker room, I snatched the lucky penny, put it in my pocket and watched as he tried to find the coin on the ground. Something was obviously wrong.
>
> "Coach," I said, as I stood up in the center of the room, "we're a great basketball team. We don't need luck. We know what to do."

Walton continued with his narration of the story, "We learned the hard way. We usually do. . . . Never discount the power of luck. Never fool with John Wooden's penny."

The Bruins opened the season with their traditional Friday–Saturday home games on November 30 and December 1. But this was a different opening weekend because the second game of the set was against Maryland and head coach Lefty Driesell.

Wooden did not back down from playing a tough non-conference schedule. In his career at UCLA he played 27 games against Associated Press Top 10 teams in the pre-conference portion of the schedule. But this Saturday evening game at Pauley was against the fourth-ranked team in the nation, the highest ranked non-conference team to come to Pauley since December 17, 1966, when fourth-ranked Kansas came to Los Angeles for just the third game in the history of Pauley Pavilion.

UCLA opened the season on Friday with an easy victory over Arkansas. The Razorbacks had been a respectable 16–10 the year before, so Wooden thought he would get a good test as a warmup before playing Maryland. But Arkansas struggled from the outset of this game and the season. UCLA won the contest 101–79, Arkansas's first loss of a 1–9 start.

It was a good start for seniors Walton and Wilkes, as Walton had 23 points and 17 rebounds, while Wilkes had 16 points.

These were different times when it came to the promotion of games. On Friday afternoon, the day of the opener against Arkansas, a press luncheon was held in Los Angeles for the UCLA vs. Maryland game. That's right, a press luncheon was held on the day when UCLA was playing another team just eight hours later. There are only a handful of coaches who would do that today.

At that luncheon, Driesell was his usual colorful self and was complimentary of the UCLA program, but at the same time made it clear his team would not back down. "You don't have to worry about us holding the ball and slowing down the game," he said.

Driesell had a strong team that had reached the Elite Eight of the NCAA Tournament the previous year and featured three future NBA players in guard John Lucas, and frontcourt players Tom McMillen and Len Elmore.

This game had added buzz because of the attention Driesell had gotten when he accepted the Maryland job in the spring of 1969. During his opening press conference, he said he thought the Maryland program "could be the UCLA of the East."

After going 13–13 his first year in 1969–70, then 14–12 his second year, members of the media were using that quote to mock Driesell. In fact, they edited it a bit and claimed he said, "We will be the UCLA of the East."

Of course, he was asked about it at the November 30 press conference in Los Angeles and he made it clear he was talking about the program's "PO-TENTIAL."

But that changed in 1971–72 when Tom McMillen and Len Elmore joined the varsity team, and the program changed for the better for a long time. The Terps went 27–5 and finished 14th in the final AP poll

The following year when true freshmen became eligible, allowing point guard John Lucas to play right away, Maryland had a worse overall record (23–7), but had a better AP final ranking and went to the NCAA Tournament. NC State won the ACC Tournament with a close win over Maryland, but they were on probation and could not represent the conference in postseason.

Maryland reached the Elite Eight, but lost in the regional final to Providence and Ernie DiGregorio, 103–89. It was an unusual game in that Maryland had a 51–50 lead at the half. In the second half DeGregorio was killing Maryland with floaters and outside shots, but he got in foul trouble. He was called for charging five times and fouled out with 10 minutes left. He had scored 30 points and had five assists in just 27 minutes.

Most in attendance thought Maryland would take over and go to the Final Four, but a substitute named Nehru King hit 7 of 9 shots and scored 15 points for Providence, many down the stretch, and the Friars advanced to St. Louis for the Final Four. It would be the closest Driesell and Maryland got to the Final Four in his 17 years with the program.

With the return of McMillen, Elmore, and Lucas for 1973–74, expectations for the Maryland program were high. Eventually, those three would be selected within the first 13 picks of the NBA draft. McMillen was the No. 9 selection and Elmore No. 13 in the 1974 draft, and Lucas was the top overall pick in 1976.

Everyone was looking forward to what would be three games between Maryland and NC State, but Coach Driesell was focused on playing at UCLA with the opportunity to end the Bruins' winning streak, which was 76 by the time the two teams met on December 1.

In a *Sports Illustrated* story by Curry Kirkpatrick, Driesell said after the 1973 NCAA Tournament game against Providence, Driesell sat with McMillen at the team hotel and said, "Let's forget this. Our next game is UCLA." That was a pretty good indication of what the game meant to Lefty.

Another story was related to Kirkpatrick by an assistant coach. The assistant and Driesell were going over UCLA film just a few days before they were to leave for UCLA. It was 2 a.m. and Lefty was about to leave the office. The assistant coach told him there were just 100 hours left until the UCLA game. Lefty turned around and went back to his office to look at more film.

When the athletic directors at the two schools agreed to the game, Driesell thought it would be the season opener for both teams. But UCLA added the Friday night game against Arkansas to open the season. It should not have been a surprise because UCLA always played Friday and Saturday night games back-to-back to simulate their conference schedule later in the season.

Today we would say it was a disadvantage for UCLA in that they could be lacking energy for the Maryland game after playing the night before. But Driesell looked at it as Wooden having a chance to work out some last-minute bugs for an early season game.

Regardless of your point of view, the Saturday night game would be epic and one that attracted the interest of the nation thanks to the TVS network. It was must-see TV even though it had an 11 p.m. Eastern tip off.

It couldn't have been a worse start for the Terps as the Pauley Pavilion crowd was into it from the get-go and the Bruins took a 9–0 lead. But Maryland came back to take a 17–15 advantage. Walton was incredible on the boards and he had 20 rebounds *at the half*, more than the entire Maryland team. It was amazing to think Walton could dominate the boards to that extent against McMillen and Elmore, who both averaged double-doubles for the course of the 1973–74 season.

But Maryland's defense was stout and the Bruins would shoot just 34 percent for the game. UCLA led by eight points at 65–57 with 3:37 left.

Similar to what we would see in the Notre Dame game seven weeks later, UCLA's offense went cold and had some key turnovers, allowing the Terps to come back. Lucas made a steal at half court and drove in for a layup with less than two minutes left to bring Maryland to within a point at 65–64.

Wooden decided to freeze the ball, something he had done with success in 1970–71 in close games. With 30 seconds remaining, Wooden shouted to his team to keep the ball away from Richard Washington, a freshman in just his second career game, who was playing because Wilkes had fouled out.

But in the heat of the battle and with the crowd in a frenzy, those commands were not heard, and Mo Howard fouled Washington with 22 seconds left. Washington would shoot just 17-for-34 from the line that year and one of those misses came at the front end of this one-and-one situation and McMillen grabbed his ninth rebound of the game

Maryland called timeout with 10 seconds left. Driesell drew up a play for Lucas to go down low to McMillen for a possible game-winner. But, with just four seconds left, sophomore Dave Meyers deflected the ball and tipped it to Tommy Curtis, who dribbled out the clock.

Curtis was actually fouled by Howard just as the buzzer sounded. Today, they would have looked at a replay, put more time on the clock, and given Curtis a free throw attempt. But Driesell signaled to the referees that the game was over. UCLA was not going to argue.

It was clear Driesell didn't want Curtis to have the opportunity to make it a three-point decision. He wanted it known that they had taken the Bruins to the brink, losing by just a single point. It would be the closest victory margin the Bruins would have in the 88-game winning streak, one of just two games decided by two points or less.

A closer look to the box score revealed the Bruins had made just 25 of 74 shots from the field, just above 33 percent. Walton finished with 18 points and a career high 27 rebounds, but he had missed his first eight shots and finished 8-for-23.

Those who witnessed the game, including the national media, came away feeling Maryland was a really good team and could challenge the Bruins, NC State, and Notre Dame for the national championship. It might be the all-time example of a program gaining credibility from a close loss. With UCLA having now won 77 games in a row with so many veteran players back, it could not be that UCLA had some problems.

While many major college coaches will disagree, there are moral victories, and this might be the all-time example in college basketball.

As was usually the case with John Wooden–coached teams, he had his team's attention after a close game or loss. His teams lost back-to-back games just once over his last nine years as UCLA coach.

He certainly had Bill Walton's attention after the Maryland game. In the Bruins' next game the following Saturday night at Pauley Pavilion, Walton had the only official triple double of his career as he scored 25, pulled in 16 rebounds, and had a career high 11 assists in the 77–60 win over SMU.

Unfortunately assists were not included in all box scores until the 1973–74 season. We call the 11 assists against SMU his career high and it was his high his senior year when assists were kept on all games, but we don't have assist totals for all his games as a sophomore and junior.

According to basketball-reference.com, Walton had 148 assists in 1973–74 in 27 games, 5.5 per game. It is not listed in the UCLA press guide, but that has to be a record for a Bruins center. It might be a national record for a center.

Walton's career high in assists in an NBA game came his rookie year on February 1, 1975, when he had 14 against Seattle. But that was the only game in his professional career he had more than the 11 he had as a senior at UCLA against SMU.

That SMU game was the only game for the Bruins between the Maryland game of December 1 and the December 15 game versus NC State in St. Louis.

While the game versus fourth-ranked Maryland was big, the contest with second-ranked NC State was bigger on a national scale. The contest drew national television coverage from ABC Sports with Keith Jackson and Bill Russell providing the commentary. It was the only college game ABC did that year and it was in prime time on a Saturday night.

It is a rare occasion in college basketball when both teams have long winning streaks entering a game. It is usually impossible because of the NCAA Tournament. The Bruins had won 78 in a row dating to the January 23, 1971, loss at Notre Dame, and NC State had won 29 in a row dating to a March 9, 1972, loss by a 73–60 count to Duke in the ACC tournament.

What brought a lot of interest to the game was NC State's 27–0 record the previous year. The ACC let NC State compete for the league championship, but the NCAA would not allow them to participate in a national tournament due to recruiting violations.

For the first time in many years, at least dating to the 1950s when the NIT and the NCAA Tournaments were on equal footing, there were two schools who claimed to be the best in the land. The passion of the media in the Atlantic Coast Conference only added to the interest in the topic in March 1973, and it carried over all summer and early fall when it was announced the two teams would play.

Neither team wanted to play on the other team's home court, so a neutral site in St. Louis at The Arena was proposed. It was a neutral site in terms of mileage, but UCLA did have a bit of an advantage in that they had played the national semifinals and finals in the same coliseum the previous March in victories over Indiana and Memphis.

Walton had to like the idea of meeting NC State in this facility, because he had shot 28-for-34 from the field in the two Final Four games, including the still record 21-for-22 against Memphis State in the championship.

The matchups were very intriguing, especially at center where Walton would go against 7-foot-4 NC State center Tom Burleson who was coming off a season where he averaged 18 points and 12 rebounds a game. David Thompson was in his junior year with the NC State varsity after averaging 24.7 points and eight rebounds a game as a sophomore. He would be matched up with All-American Keith Wilkes.

The game also brought national attention because it was No. 1 UCLA vs. No. 2 NC State, the first time the top two teams in the AP poll had faced each other since the March 22, 1968, NCAA Tournament game in Los Angeles between No. 1 Houston and No. 2 UCLA.

Games between the top two teams in the AP poll have been much more commonplace in recent years, but between 1948–49 when the poll began, and this game of December 15, 1973, there had been just 12 No. 1 vs. No. 2 games. This game was the first of 13 over the next 12 years, the first of four in 1973–74.

NC State fans flocked to St. Louis with an estimated 4–1 advantage. They had in fact proposed the game by getting ABC to guarantee each team $125,000, making it at the time the most profitable regular-season college basketball game in history. One must wonder if the network provided some other benefits to UCLA, who was making the trip during exam week.

Tickets were priced at $10 apiece with an attendance of 18,461, so that also made the game profitable. You can wonder what the ticket price would be today for such a matchup.

Curry Kirkpatrick said in his *Sports Illustrated* article on the game, "Indeed, the game may be the catalyst for a series of regular season network telecasts of college basketball in the future." Combined with the UCLA at Notre Dame game a month later, that statement proved to be prophetic.

The game was a high-level affair that featured great athleticism on the offensive and defensive end, powerful and physical inside play, and at times terrific outside shooting . . . for 30 minutes.

Walton got into foul trouble and was charged with his fourth in the first 11 minutes of the game. That was a key reason NC State held a 33–32 lead at intermission. Even with Walton on the bench, the Bruins took an eight-point lead early in the second half.

But NC State battled back to tie at 54 with 9:37 left. Wooden had waited long enough and brought Walton back in at that point. He scored the first basket of a 9–0 run that put UCLA up, 63–54. Later in the half, he keyed a 10–0 run and the game was just about over. UCLA outscored NC State 30–12 over the last 9:37 of the game, and won 84–66.

In his postgame press conference NC State Coach Norm Sloan indicated his strategy against this talented team, that would have eight players on the roster play in the NBA, as too simple. "We wanted to play them straight-up vanilla," said Sloan. "But they just did more good things than we did."

What was most impressive was UCLA winning without Walton playing half the game. He was productive, certainly the difference maker over the last quarter of the game when he had most of his 11 points and 10 rebounds, but he played just 18:53 of the 40 minutes.

Wilkes came through with his best game to date with a career-high 27 points, and Meyers had his most important contribution with 15 points and 11 rebounds. Combined with his defensive play to win the Maryland game, the sophomore had been a big difference in two wins over top four teams before Christmas.

Thompson finished with 17 points and 13 rebounds from his wing guard position, but he made just 3 of 10 shots in the first half when the Pack should have been taking advantage of Walton's absence. He finished just 7 of 20 from the field.

One of the more unusual quotes of the game was attributed to UCLA point guard Greg Lee. When asked about Thompson he was complimentary of his athletic ability, but not of the other NC State players. "Nobody lobs us ever, let alone complete them four feet above the rim. I can't believe this cat [Thompson]. If they hadn't had him, we'd have won by 50."

I am sure that made an NC State locker room bulletin board later in the season.

After the game, Wooden spoke of his strategy when Walton got into foul trouble in the first half. "I had my mind to bring him back in the game with 10 minutes left if the score was close. If they had gone way ahead I would have had to bring him in earlier."

UCLA's 18-point win was the largest by a number-one team against a number-two team in college history to that point in time and it gave the Bruins confidence and momentum. Not that they needed the confidence, but there might have been some doubters outside the UCLA locker room after the one-point win over Maryland. The Bruins' success only made Maryland look better. State dropped to No. 5 in the polls and

Maryland went to No. 2, where they stayed until they lost to NC State in early January.

UCLA won its next nine games by an average of 32 points. There were some stunning accomplishments in that run:

- The very next game Walton made 11 of 11 from the field on the way to a near triple double (25 points, 15 rebounds, nine assists) in a 110–63 rout of Ohio University.

- Three days before Christmas, UCLA won its 80th straight, as Andre McCarter made a 50-foot shot at the halftime buzzer to give UCLA a 43-point lead at intermission, in a 52-point win (111–59) win over a St. Bonaventure program that had been to the Final Four just four years earlier.

- One of the more impressive wins of the season took place on December 29 in the finals of the Bruin Classic when UCLA beat Michigan, 90–70. The Wolverines had lost to Dick Vitale's University of Detroit team earlier in the season and that kept Johnny Orr's team from being ranked at the time of the UCLA game. But Michigan would finish the season ranked sixth in the AP poll and won the Big Ten championship thanks to the play of Campy Russell.

  Walton had another 20–20 in this game (20 points, 21 rebounds), while an ever-improving Dave Meyers added 16.

- On January 5, 1974, UCLA handed Washington and legendary coach Marv Harshman its worst loss in history, 100–48 on the Huskies' home court.

- The only relatively close game in the stretch took place at Washington State, where the Bruins won by 10 points, 55–45. UCLA had a comfortable 49–33 lead with 10 minutes left when Walton landed awkwardly on his back while going for a rebound. He left the game and did not return.

Walton missed the next three games with the injury, but sophomore seven-footer Ralph Drollinger moved into the center position in

Walton's absence and contributed eight points and seven rebounds in a 92–56 victory against California. It was UCLA's 46th straight conference win, a Pac-8 record.

On January 12, UCLA defeated Stanford as Wooden gave more playing time to freshman Richard Washington, who was improving since missing the late free throw against Maryland in the second game of the year. He had seven points and Drollinger nine in a 66–44 win that would be UCLA's last home game for 13 days. For a second straight game Wilkes paced Bruins scorers with 21 points.

For the fourth year in a row, Wooden took his team to the Midwest for back-to-back games in mid-January. This time UCLA played Iowa at Chicago Stadium the Thursday before what had become an annual game at Notre Dame.

Walton did not play as he nursed his back at the Bismarck Hotel in downtown Chicago, UCLA's headquarters. It did not matter much as UCLA won, 68–44. It was Drollinger's best game with 13 points and 17 rebounds and his defense was outstanding on the inside. UCLA held its fourth opponent in the last five games to under 50 points.

It was UCLA's 88th consecutive win. Despite the 24-point victory, Wooden was quoted as saying after the game, "I thought we were lackadaisical and I have never had that trouble with my teams."

Forty-eight hours later the Bruins would face an undefeated and now second-ranked Notre Dame team in South Bend. Many members of the media who were covering that game had come to Chicago to cover this game versus Iowa and all they wanted to know was an update on Walton's status.

Wooden said, "I think Bill will play. The streak is important to him." It was one of the few times Wooden had referred to the streak as a motivating factor since it had been broken in South Bend two Januarys earlier.

CHAPTER 8

71–70

UCLA (13–0) and Notre Dame (9–0) were both undefeated and ranked 1–2 in the polls, but they also ranked 1–2 nationally in terms of scoring margin, a barometer of the teams' dominance. Notre Dame was first with an average victory margin of 26.4 and UCLA was second at 26.23.

But just about all of the more than 100 media members in attendance for the game looked at UCLA as being the clear favorite. The Bruins had won 88 in a row, won the last seven national championships, and won 218 of their last 223 games dating to the 1966–67 season.

It had been 1,092 days since UCLA had lost. Of course, that loss had come in South Bend to Notre Dame, an 89–82 Irish victory when Austin Carr scored 46 points, including 15 of Notre Dame's last 17 (see chapter 1).

UCLA had won 72 of the 88 games in the streak by double digits and the average margin of victory for the 88 games was 23.5 points a game. They had entered 86 of those 88 games as the number-one ranked team, as they had been ranked No. 1 in each of the last 46 polls, still a record for consecutive polls ranked number one in the nation. Twenty of the wins had come on the opponent's home court. Eighteen of the 88 wins were over top 20 teams.

The campus was in good spirits entering the January 19 contest. The second semester began on Wednesday the 16th, so no one was behind in classes yet and everyone was focused on the first 1 vs. 2 matchup in Notre Dame basketball history.

The senior class felt all the stars were aligning to repeat the athletic accomplishments of their freshman year. On January 1, 1971, Notre Dame upset top-ranked Texas in the Cotton Bowl. Then on January 23, Austin Carr and the Irish defeated No. 1 UCLA in basketball. Then on February 6, 1971, Notre Dame beat top-ranked Denver in hockey in what was the greatest upset of the three because the hockey program was just in its third year.

On New Year's Eve, 1973, the Irish football team beat No. 1 Alabama in the Sugar Bowl, 24–23 to win the national championship, a game Phelps and his family attended. Now, No. 1 ranked Michigan Tech was in town for a hockey weekend series that started Friday night, just hours before the top ranked Bruins would face the Irish in basketball.

With all the articles written about UCLA's dominance over the Irish (last four wins by a total of 128 points) and the Bruins' accomplishments over the last seven years, Phelps did everything he could to put his team in a positive mindset.

Phelps had a picture of Carr cutting down the nets after the 1971 win over UCLA in his office. He had always imagined what that would be like.

"I was always big on visualizing everything, whether it be strategy through practice or any mental intangible," said Phelps. "At the end of practice on Wednesday, I called the team together and said, all right, when we win, Gary [Novak], you go to the far basket and cut down the nets and John [Shumate], you go to the near basket. I even had specific assignments as to whom would lift Novak and Shumate to cut down the nets. Practice had gone well that day and it really didn't come to me until the end of practice."

That was on Wednesday. He had the team do it again on Friday.

Phelps was hoping it would be a moment of déjà vu for Shumate, who as a freshman in 1971, had lifted Carr on his shoulders to cut down the nets after the win over the Bruins.

"It had an impact, no doubt," recalled Ray Martin years later, who went on to be a member of Jim Valvano's national championship staff at NC State in 1983. "Digger was the master of getting you ready mentally.

Have you ever seen a better big game coach in college? When he did that we knew he believed in us. We were ready to play."

Phelps defeated seven top-ranked teams (in either AP or UPI polls entering the game) in his Notre Dame career, at the time a national record.

On Friday night, over 3,000 fans, mostly Notre Dame students, attended a pep rally in Stepan Center. It was set up like a classic Notre Dame football rally with all players and coaches in attendance seated on a stage. One of the speakers was Sid Catlett, starting center during the Austin Carr era who had started the 1971 UCLA game. It was the first time he had been back for a game since he graduated.

Digger Phelps had his team practice cutting down the nets the week of the January 19, 1974, UCLA game. *Rich Clarkson/*Sports Illustrated *via Getty Images*

Catlett addressed the crowd and referred to Walton's back injury. "I have a telegram. It says, 'Sorry Coach Wooden, I won't be able to play tomorrow. I've got a yellow streak coming on. Signed, Bill Walton.'"

The players returned to their dorm rooms for the night. One of the most important contributions of the weekend might have taken place in Fisher Hall where Shumate assigned fellow students to be hall monitors with instructions to keep the noise down as much as possible so he could get some sleep for the game that had a noon local start (1 p.m. on East Coast).

Meanwhile the Irish hockey team did its part to keep the mojo going by upsetting top-ranked Michigan Tech on Friday night at the North Dome of the Athletic and Convocation Center. The final score was 7–1, a result that was a foreshadowing of the key number that would take place the following day.

Phelps asked Rev. Edmund P. Joyce, Notre Dame's Executive Vice President at the time, to celebrate the pregame Mass on Saturday morning. The Athletic and Convocation Center would be named in Joyce's honor 13 years later.

"This is not just an ordinary day," said Fr. Joyce in his homily. "The chances are good that years from now you will look back on this day as one of the most memorable in your life. Is this melodramatic? I don't think so."

Phelps did everything he could in terms of preparation from a game strategy standpoint as well. In those days no video exchange between schools existed and games were rarely on television in the regular season. UCLA had its home games on local television, but the VCR had not been invented yet. There was no way for a Notre Dame fan in Los Angeles to tape the game and get it to the Irish coaching staff. That would change four years later.

But Phelps did see the Bruins up close. He had gone to Chicago on Thursday night (January 17) to see UCLA play Iowa in its last game before coming to South Bend.

He did not learn much from that game, however, as Walton did not play due to his back injury. It was the third straight game Walton missed after an awkward fall against Washington State 10 days earlier.

But Phelps and the Irish coaches prepared as if he would be ready for Notre Dame.

As a high school player in California, Walton had watched on TV as Carr and Notre Dame handed his Bruins their previous loss.

In the book *A Coaches World*, Phelps discussed his pregame strategy for the Bruins. "Our objective is to take away the lob pass and not worry if Walton gets 25 points. I'm more concerned about Wilkes, anyway. Shumate can't let this become a crusade, him against Walton. If Walton beats us with 10 hook shots, let him."

When the players arrived for practice on Wednesday, January 16, they each found a 3 x 5 card taped to their lockers. Novak's read, "Stop Wilkes." Brokaw's said, "Good Shots." Clay's said, "No turnovers." Dantley's said, "Boards." Shumate's said, "Defense-Boards."

Gameday started for John Shumate at 6:30 a.m. when his parents called his dorm room in Fisher Hall and they prayed over the phone. "We prayed so that I would have faith in myself, my coach and my team, praying for confidence to accomplish what 88 other teams had failed to do," recalled Shumate. "My mother told me, no matter what the situation, don't lose faith in yourself."

Those words certainly came in handy in the game's final stages.

Shumate had quite a personality and he knew exactly how to break up the tense mood.

"John loosened up the entire team while we were dressing," said Martin. "He started singing in a Gospel preacher voice, 'I had a dream last night, my brothers

"'And what was that dream, brother Shumate,' the team responded.

"'I had a dream I was being chased by a Big Bear, a Bruin. And he was mean and angry, but I got away from that Bear.'

"'Tell us more, brother Shumate.'

"His story went on and on while we were dressing," said Martin. "He had the entire team in stitches and we were now ready to play the biggest game of our lives. It was just what we all needed."

The two coaches met before the game on the court for a TV interview in something you rarely see today before a big game. Dick Enberg interviewed Wooden about the streak. "No, I didn't think any team could win 88 games in a row." He then said he would not decide if Walton would start the game until after the warmups.

Enberg then handed the microphone to his color commentator, Hot Rod Hundley, who interviewed Phelps. After ribbing each other about their respective suits, Hundley asked him about the keys to the game.

"I think everyone will be a key in this game, there are too many good players," said Phelps. "We need to show improvement on the offensive boards and our outside shooting."

"Keith Wilkes fouled out with 3:51 left against Maryland and that is when they [Maryland] came back. He stopped David Thompson in the NC State game and scored 27 points."

Just prior to the player introductions, two Notre Dame students circled the court with a bedsheet that read,

Dear John Wooden,
God DID make Notre Dame #1.
Sincerely,
Paul "Bear" Bryant

Between 1964 and 1996 Jack Lloyd was the public address announcer at Notre Dame basketball games, but for national TV games of this era, Enberg announced the lineups live on television. Enberg liked to add a note or two on star players and he referred to Wilkes and Walton as All-Americans during his announcement of the starters, which only enhanced the boos from the Notre Dame student body.

The Bruins also started Dave Meyers a forward, with Tommy Curtis and Pete Trgovich, a native of East Chicago, Indiana, at the guards. The Notre Dame starters were Brokaw and Clay at the guards, Shumate at center with Gary Novak and Adrian Dantley at the forwards.

Unlike Notre Dame's victory in 1971 when the Irish ran to a 9–2 lead to open the game, this game started on an even score for the first four minutes. The game was tied four times with the last being 8–8.

Two plays set a tone in the first minute. UCLA scored on its first possession on a jumper by Meyers just 16 seconds in, then the Irish tied it at 2–2, when Dantley scored on Notre Dame's third shot of its first possession. Phelps had said in that pregame interview with Hundley that offensive rebounding would be a key and that is how his team scored on its first possession.

During that rebound action on the first Irish possession, Walton received an elbow to the mouth from Dantley, leading to a considerable flow of blood and a timeout was called to stop the bleeding just 57 seconds into the game. Notre Dame would not back down from the mighty Bruins this afternoon.

The game was still close with UCLA leading by just 14–11 with 13:25 left in the first half. But UCLA went on a 19–5 run over the next 6:44 to take a 33–16 lead. It was a very balanced run, as Trgovich scored five, Meyers four, Walton four, Curtis four, and Wilkes two. Walton also had two brilliant passes that led to field goals.

At this point, it could have developed into another 20-point victory for UCLA. But the Irish came back with a streak of their own, much to the delight of the 11,343 fans in attendance. From the 17-point deficit, the Irish went on an 18–6 run to cut the margin to 39–34 with 49 seconds left in the half. Notre Dame's "spurt time" also included balanced scoring, as six different players scored (Brokaw five, Clay four, Dantley three, Shumate two, Martin two, and Paterno two).

Note that three of the players who scored during the run were freshmen Dantley, Paterno, and Martin. Martin played 22 minutes in the game and was in for his ball handling and defense. His 20 footer at the 5:15 mark was big and quite frankly a surprise.

While he was just one year removed from becoming the all-time leading scorer at Mater Christi High School in New York, Martin was not a great outside shooter. In fact, Digger used to kiddingly call him "Arthur," which was short for Arthur-Ritis . . . as in he shot like he had arthritis. But Martin was smart in his shot selection and finished his freshman year shooting a solid 47 percent from the field and finished his career as a 44 percent shooter.

UCLA scored the last four points of the first half to take a 43–34 lead at intermission. The Irish found themselves down nine at the half against a team that had not blown a halftime lead in four years.

The Bruins had shot 19-for-27 from the field in the first half, 70 percent, compared to Notre Dame's 14-for-32, 44 percent. Walton had made 6 of 7 shots in the first half and pulled down six rebounds. He was wearing a corset to help support his back and it certainly appeared to be helping. Defensively, he held Shumate to 4 of 11 shooting for eight points and intimidated him into two traveling calls in the opening 20 minutes.

In the ESPN documentary on Bill Walton's life released in the summer of 2023, *The Luckiest Guy in the World*, Walton makes a point of saying that Greg Lee played the entire first half and then didn't play at all in the second half. In part 2 of the film, he and Lee tell a story about John Wooden confronting Lee about his use of marijuana. His playing time became sporadic.

In watching the film you could come away with the impression that Wooden benched Lee in the second half because he had an ongoing issue with Lee's drug use. But according to the final boxscore on file in the Notre Dame Sports Information office, Lee only played five minutes in the first half, none in the second half, and had little impact on the game with just two points and no assists. In fact Wooden played just two players off the bench in the game, five minutes for Lee and four minutes for Marques Johnson.

There is a theory of basketball that says, a team should be in the lead at intermission by a margin that is at least half the difference in field goal percentage between the two teams. If they aren't, they might be in trouble in the second half. UCLA had a 26-point margin in field goal percentage and according to the theory needed to have a 13-point lead at the half to feel comfortable. It was only nine.

During halftime the Football Writers Association of America presented its national championship trophy to head coach Ara Parseghian. The ovation was thunderous. It was perfect timing and made the crowd even more boisterous heading into the second half.

And the Irish responded with a 9–2 run to pull within two points. Brokaw and Shumate scored all nine points.

But that spurt appeared to be wiped out when the Bruins put together their own 9–0 run to go back up 54–43 with 10:58 remaining.

The Irish cut the margin to 60–54 with 5:43 left on a jumper by Brokaw, who was working his magic on Wilkes, something All-American David Thompson wasn't able to do a month earlier.

On the next possession, while guarding Wilkes, Brokaw was whistled for his fourth foul at the 5:24 mark. Brokaw then complained about the call and got a technical foul. In 1992–93 the NCAA adopted a rule whereby a technical foul counted as a personal foul. Brokaw would have been disqualified from the game if today's rules were in effect. But in 1974, that was not the case and he remained on the court, and had a significant impact on the outcome of the game.

Wilkes hit two of the three free throws to put UCLA up 62–54, but the Bruins did not capitalize on the next possession. They scored just two of a possible five points on the possession.

Shumate later scored five straight points for the Irish and made the score 64–59 with 4:17 left and the last "television timeout" of the game was called. The Bruins then took advantage of some Notre Dame fouls and made four straight free throws on their next two possessions. It was a rare occurrence in the game, as only 22 fouls were called, 11 on each team. When Curtis made a drive and a jumper on the run from the right corner at the 3:32 mark, the Bruins had an 11-point lead, 70–59.

Curtis, who came to UCLA from Tallahassee, Florida, celebrated as he came up the court. Notre Dame players and courtside media reported after the game that Curtis led the game in trash talking.

Ten seconds later Digger Phelps called timeout.

"The first thing we needed to do was put our pressing team in the game, and that meant freshman 'Dice' Martin," said Phelps. Martin replaced 6–6 freshman forward Billy Paterno, which meant Phelps was going to "roll the dice" with a three-guard lineup against the already taller Bruins lineup.

Phelps had started this lineup to begin the second half and the Irish went on a 9–2 run.

"It was time to go for broke. We had to force some turnovers because in a half court game we were in trouble if they were able to post up.

"The second thing I did was change the press. We had been pressing with Gary Brokaw at the top with Shumate back. All UCLA was doing was bringing Walton into the front court and throwing the ball up high, which meant Brokaw was trying to steal the ball off the inbounds from a player eight inches taller. So, during the timeout, I moved Shumate to the front of the press and put Brokaw deep."

Shumate recalled what Phelps said to the team at the timeout. "I can still see the snarl, the passion in his eyes, his belief and his love for Notre Dame. He pointed to each and every one of us and said, 'If you don't believe we can do this then leave and go to the locker room right now. If you stay here and believe, then we can do this.'"

During the timeout, Walton sat on the press table near the UCLA bench and in front of the television broadcast position. Coming out of the commercial break Enberg documented the incredible streak of personal victories Walton had accumulated.

"Time is running out on the Irish and there is Bill Walton. Twice he has been named college basketball's top player. He won his last 49 games in high school, counting his freshman year at UCLA he won 80 in a row [in college] coming into this year, plus 14 with today would be 143 consecutive games without knowing what it is to lose."

(Technically, Walton's personal streak would have been 140 games instead of 143 if UCLA had won this game. Enberg forgot that Walton had missed three games with a back injury. So, his personal streak ended that day at 139.)

This might have been the original announcer jinx!

Notre Dame had the ball coming out of the timeout and Martin worked the ball down low to Shumate, who hit a turnaround jumper over Walton. The made field goal out of the offense allowed the Irish to set up their press, this time with Shumate on Walton.

It worked to perfection. Expecting Brokaw to be there, Wilkes made a lackadaisical lob pass to Walton, but Shumate intercepted and scored immediately. The lead was now down to seven just 20 seconds after the timeout.

In 1974, there was no shot clock, so UCLA tried to stop Notre Dame's momentum, but it appeared they were just dribbling around without a purpose and playing tentatively. With 2:22 left Dantley stole a pass intended for David Meyers at midcourt and drove in for an uncontested layup (dunking was still against the rules in 1974).

"Now the crowd was really into it, they were getting closer and closer to the court, which was to our advantage," recalled Phelps. "It made our defense even more effective."

Now it is 70–65, and as Enberg said on the broadcast, "Pandemonium now!"

With 2:16 left, Wilkes tried a long inbounds pass for Curtis, who was guarded by Martin. "I fell down and Curtis was all alone for a layup," recalled Martin. "All I could think of was, this is embarrassing. All my family and buddies back in New York just watched me blow the UCLA game. But, fortunately, Curtis was called for traveling."

It was tough to tell. It was one of those plays where UCLA fans say he didn't travel and Notre Dame fans say he did. Coach Wooden didn't think it was traveling, which he addressed in his postgame press conference.

Down five, Martin brought the ball up court, just the second possession for Notre Dame in a set offense during the final three minutes. He passed to Brokaw who took Wilkes one-on-one to the middle and hit a 17-foot jumper to cut the margin to 70–67 with 1:49 left.

On UCLA's next possession the Bruins worked a shot for Meyers from the left side. When he made his initial move from near the 28-foot marker, the crowd thought he traveled on his first steps, but there was no call. Was it an uncalled makeup for the Curtis traveling call?

But Meyers missed, his fourth straight missed shot of the second half after going 5-for-5 in the first half. With 1:25 remaining Shumate got the rebound.

Even though he gave up four inches, Brokaw was a matchup problem for Wilkes one-one-one. He took another jumper from the middle of the court from 15 feet and it hit nothing but net. It was now 70–69.

Walton made a timeout sign to Wooden, but he said no. "Wooden never liked to call timeout, because he thought you were giving in to your opponent and showing a lack of confidence in your own team," said Phelps.

He talked about that in his book *They Call Me Coach*.

Phelps had read Wooden's book over the summer.

So play continued.

UCLA worked the ball to Wilkes and Martin, who was five inches shorter, was caught guarding him after a switch. From the right side, Wilkes decided to fake baseline and go to the middle and in for a layup.

"As he drove by me, he hooked me with his right arm," said Martin, who once again was involved in a key turnover. "I went down and we got the call."

It was the fourth turnover for UCLA in the last three minutes and 18th of the game. The Irish finished with 14, none inside the last four minutes.

The call was made by Richard Weiler, who just happened to be the lead official in Notre Dame's win over UCLA in 1971. That's right, Weiler worked both games that bracketed the 88-game winning streak. Some of his friends in the business referred to him as "Bookend" in later years.

At the end of the season, Weiler was rated as one of the top officials in the nation and was selected to work his first career Final Four. You guessed it, he was assigned to work the UCLA vs. NC State, the semifinal in Greensboro that NC State won to end UCLA's 38-game NCAA Tournament winning streak.

"He never said a word," Weiler recalled years later when asked about Wooden. "I just had wonderful dealings with Coach Wooden, always had a good relationship with him. Even today [in his retirement after 23 years as an official], I'll see him at a tournament or something and we'll say hello."

Believe it or not, Weiler was also on the court for another UCLA streak breaker in 1980. He worked the national championship game against Louisville, a game the Cards won by five. It was UCLA's first loss in a national championship game after 10 straight wins in title games.

After the foul on Wilkes, the Irish gained possession down just a point, 70–69 with just 45 seconds left. "For a third straight possession it was our intention to go to Brokaw," said Phelps. "But this time Curtis left Clay to help Wilkes guard Brokaw. Gary saw that Dwight was all alone in the right corner so he passed the ball."

While Phelps thought the practices leading up to this historic game were good, his team did struggle in one area. In the last three practices leading up to the game, Irish players had been 1-for-15 in converting game-winning shots.

But when it counted most, with 29 seconds left on game day, Clay took the shot from the deep right corner and it went through. It was Clay's only field goal of the second half and just his second field goal of the game. He finished 2-for-5 from the field with seven points in playing 39 of the 40 minutes.

It was the fourth time in his career he had made a shot to win or tie a game inside the last 30 seconds.

"After that shot went in, Walton called time," said Phelps with a smile when reflecting. "I still don't think Wooden called the timeout, but Walton had had enough."

After the game, Clay said, "I didn't think I had won the game, there were still 29 seconds left." His basket had given Notre Dame a 71–70 lead, its first lead of the game.

"With 21 seconds left, we were in the huddle and one of my assistants, Dick DiBiasso, said 'Let's foul Walton and put him on the line so we have the last shot. Let's put the game in our hands offensively because they can't stop us.'"

Notre Dame had converted on six consecutive possessions and was 6-for-6 from the field after making just 24 of its first 56.

"It was a consideration because Walton was shooting 43 percent from the line entering the game and he had not taken a free throw yet in the game, but I decided to play tough defense and rebound."

Twice during UCLA's final possession Notre Dame looked like it had let the victory slip from its grasp. Early in the possession, Shumate jumped in front of Walton and intercepted a Curtis pass near the sideline, but as he was falling out of bounds in trying to get the ball to Martin, he flipped the ball over Martin's head back into play to Curtis. He probably should have just thrown the ball toward the other basket and killed almost the rest of the time.

Curtis now had the ball 25 feet from the hoop with 10 seconds left and he panicked. He just hoisted it toward the hoop from what would be

NBA three-point range today. Brokaw had the rebound. But in his effort, he lost his balance and the ball went out of bounds with six seconds remaining. It appeared that Wilkes might have knocked the ball off of Brokaw's foot. It would have been interesting what would have happened had officials been allowed to look at replays in 1974.

UCLA had the ball out of bounds to the right of its hoop (as you face the basket) with six seconds left. Both teams had timeouts left, but neither coach decided to call one.

"The location of the ball was important because it put Walton on the wrong side of the hoop," said Phelps. "He liked to take the ball from the left (as you face the basket) and turn toward the lane and shoot his little jumper or hook shot. This time he was on the other side."

Curtis threw the ball into Walton, who was guarded by Shumate. Walton immediately turned toward the middle of the lane, and shot. Being a right-handed player, it was easier for Shumate to contest his attempt at a 10-foot bank shot. The attempt was short and fell off the rim, just Walton's second miss in 14 attempts the entire game, his only miss of the second half.

But with Shumate away from the hoop guarding Walton, it opened offensive rebounding opportunities for UCLA. Trgovich missed the first attempt, then Meyers had a tap at the basket from three feet. Finally, Shumate got back to the basket, caught the ball, and threw it straight up in the air, knowing the laws of physics would exhaust the remaining seconds.

The horn went off and Notre Dame students rushed the court. Student manager Ernie Torriero, who would later become a student worker in the Notre Dame sports information office, and eventually a news writer for the *Miami Herald*, caught the ball and secured it, knowing this would be a precious keepsake for Notre Dame sports history.

When the game ended and the students rushed the floor, assistant coach Dick DiBiaso and Tony Villani, a friend of Digger's from New Jersey, picked up Phelps and carried him into the crowd. "I still remember how hot it was," said Phelps. "I was wearing a three-piece suit.

"When I went to the postgame interview room, I walked on the baseline of the court because the room was on the opposite side of the

Notre Dame had converted just 1 of 15 game-winning attempts in practice leading up to the UCLA game. Then Dwight Clay hit the game-winner when it counted.
Notre Dame Archives

Convocation Center. There must of been 1,000 fans, mostly students still in the arena."

The Notre Dame fans didn't want to leave and many stayed until the UCLA team walked through the arena to their bus. Walton walked through wearing a hooded UCLA sweatshirt that all but covered his face. Reportedly, he was humming the Notre Dame Victory March as he left the arena.

For just the second time in college sports history, the same school was number one in football and number one in basketball. The only other time it had happened previously was on November 13, 1967, when UCLA accomplished the feat. UCLA had gone 30–0 behind sophomore Lew Alcindor the previous winter to close as the No. 1 team in college basketball, then started 7-0-1 in football the next fall.

When UCLA defeated Washington 48–0 on the gridiron on November 11, 1967, the Bruins jumped from No. 4 to No. 1. That reign as double No. 1 lasted just one week, as No. 4 Southern California beat the Bruins the next week, 21–20, and UCLA dropped back to No. 4. They didn't rise to No. 1 again in football until 1988.

Notre Dame's reign as double No. 1 would last just one week also, as you will see in chapter 9.

A check of the final boxscore showed that the Bruins made just 10 of 29 shots in the second half after that 19-for-27 first half. Wilkes, who Digger had said repeatedly before the game would be a key for his Irish to stop, made just 2 of 9 field goals in the second half. Meanwhile, Brokaw made 6 of 8 shots from the field in the second half and finished 10-for-16 for the game with a team best 25 points. Shumate, who was just 4-for-11 in the first half, was 7-for-11 in the second half to finish with 24 points and 11 rebounds. Brokaw and Shumate both played all 40 minutes.

They were the only players in double figures for the Irish. Dantley finished with nine points and eight rebounds, while Clay had seven. Ray Martin was an unsung hero in his 22 minutes. He made his only shot and did not commit a turnover against UCLA's press.

The Irish won the rebounding battle 31–27, one of the few games UCLA lost the rebound margin in the Walton era.

Walton finished with 24 points on 12-for-14 shooting. He did not shoot a free throw and had nine rebounds. Wilkes scored 18 points, but shot just 6-for-16. Meyers was the only other double-figure scorer with 10, all in the first half, and had seven rebounds. He shot 5-for-5 in the first half and 0-for-5 in the second. Curtis finished with nine points, but he shot just 3-for-11 and had five turnovers. Both teams shot exactly 16 free throws; UCLA made 12 and the Irish 11.

In evaluating the game, Phelps kiddingly said, "The only thing we messed up the entire day was cutting down the nets.

"We had rehearsed Novak and Shumate cutting down the nets. Novak did his part, but Shumate was nowhere to be found. After he got that rebound, he was knocked down in the crush of the fans and was on the floor." He actually required smelling salts when he got to the locker room.

"Dwight Clay, Adrian, and I seized the moment," said Martin. "We were all under the basket as the game ended, and students were putting us on their shoulders. So, we started taking the net down at the basket where Shumate was supposed to be. Since the photographers were at that end of the court to shoot the last play, Dwight, Adrian, and I got in all the pictures that ran around the country. I've never seen a picture of Novak cutting down the nets at the other end."

POSTGAME QUOTES

Here are the postgame quotes as provided to the media by the Notre Dame sports information office. There were no quotes provided from the

The only thing that went wrong for Notre Dame on January 19, 1974: Ray Martin and Adrian Dantley cut down the nets and John Shumate was nowhere to be seen. *Notre Dame Archives*

UCLA locker room. Coach Wooden closed the locker room to the press, but usually provided a player after games outside the locker room.

In this case he told his team, "Only the winners talk today."

But Wilkes did give one short quote to a couple of reporters as he left the locker room. "They played a good game and they won. That's all I can say."

Curtis added, "The streak had to end sometime."

NOTRE DAME HEAD COACH DIGGER PHELPS

We never quit. We were down 11 points when I called time out and we had to make some changes. We went with our press, putting Ray Martin back in for Billy Paterno. The kids never quit, and it happened.

For 88 other coaches including myself, it was a great win.

We can't stop now though . . . we start preparation tomorrow for Kansas.

Our goal is for an NCAA bid. We're an independent school with no conference affiliation, so we don't have to worry about three or four losses. All we're looking for is the bid.

It was a special win for Notre Dame . . . for everyone involved from the coaches, team, school, alumni and everyone else. It was a great win for college basketball. I'm sure a lot of people around the country were rooting for Notre Dame today. It's only human nature to see the Bruins beaten.

At the time out [with 21 seconds left], we knew they were going to Walton. We installed our normal man-to-man press. If they scored, we would have called another time out.

We played three defenses today and they were effective at the end. At the time out, I just told our boys to play solid defense. Dick DiBiaso mentioned fouling Walton, but I decided against it.

There's nothing you can do about UCLA shooting 70 percent from the field in the first half.

We have great respect for them; now we have to go out there next Saturday and it will be tough.

After the game I told our players that it was a great win and it will be tough going out there next weekend. Now we have to start preparation tomorrow for Kansas and our game in Lawrence on Tuesday.

The team never quit. When we were down 11, our defense held us in there just as it has all year.

This was the fourth game Dwight Clay has made a last second deciding basket [to win a game]. He broke Marquette's 81-game home winning streak last year.

As Phelps left the interview room he crossed paths with Wooden, who went second in the interview room, a crowded converted dressing room used for concerts. The two coaches had not met after the game due to the crush of the Notre Dame student body running on the court.

The two coaches were cordial. "I am waiting on President Nixon to cancel our trip to Los Angeles next week because of the energy shortage," said Phelps with a smile. "You better be there," said Wooden.

UCLA Head Coach John Wooden

If I said it once, I have said it 100 times, once we broke the record last year, the streak was meaningless. I am fairly certain my players felt the same way. I am not mad or glad about the streak, and my players are acting like they should, like men.

Obviously, Bill wasn't as mobile as he was in the past. He was reluctant to take his hook shot, and his injury hurt his board play. He had the option to take himself out at any time of the game. (He played all 40 minutes.)

We certainly didn't figure to lose with three minutes to go and up by 11 points. Of course, if you don't play your own ball game, you're going to lose. They kept coming at us, and they deserve a tremendous amount of credit for their play.

In the last three minutes, there were some tough calls. The traveling call on Curtis really hurt us, and Brokaw and Shumate hurt us with their big baskets. We lost a little of our drive and played a little too conservative at the end. Notre Dame's man-to-man defense hurt us. We learned a lot today, which we will use next Saturday.

Notre Dame's players really hurt us, and the crowd really inspired them.

We will know a lot more about the two ball clubs after next Saturday's game.

I am going to vote [in the UPI poll] for Notre Dame this week, but I think Maryland is a better team. They rallied on our court, and Notre Dame rallied on their court. If you ask Coach Phelps, he will tell you it is tougher to come from behind on the road.

If they win on the West Coast, that will prove they are a better ball club. If we win on the West Coast, that will prove we will have a better chance on a neutral court. I hope we will find out.

NOTRE DAME PLAYER QUOTES
Gary Brokaw
"We're number one. I still can't believe it. In the first half I don't think I was executing. Coach told us at halftime to play our game in the second half, and that is what we did."

John Shumate
"I think that rebound [at the end] was the greatest rebound I ever got. We still were trying in the first half even when we were down. We knew if we stuck with it, we would do all right. This is the greatest feeling I have ever had in my life."

Adrian Dantley
"It feels good to beat UCLA as a freshman. I had a bad day offensively [4-for-12 from field] and I knew I had to play good defense and grab rebounds if we were going to win. That was the key." Dantley, eight rebounds, just one less than Walton's nine.

Dwight Clay
"It feels real great, unbelievable. In the second half Coach wanted Shue to work on Walton, so that is why he put Ray (Martin) in. I was to relieve some of the pressure from Shue's side by going to the opposite side.

"I didn't have time to think about being worried [on the last shot]. When the ball came to me, I was open and I knew we had to have it. So, I just concentrated on the shot, and thankfully I made it."

Gary Novak

"This is nothing like anything I have ever experienced. It was a team effort. The whole team worked hard all week. It has been one great season so far, and we have to keep it together the rest of the way. Boy, this sure does make up for all those things [a 6–20 record his sophomore year] in the past."

Ray Martin

"We were pressing in the second half. Dwight, Gary, and I were to put pressure on them to hopefully force turnovers. And that's what happened. I can't describe how great it feels to beat UCLA."

The Final 3:32

Time	ND-UCLA	Description of the Play
3:32	59-70	Curtis right corner jumper
3:22		Timeout Notre Dame (third)
3:07	61-70	Shumate with short jumper over Walton
2:57	63-70	Shumate steals inbounds pass and lays it in
2:22	65-70	Dantley steal at midcourt, drives and lays it in
2:16		Curtis travels after receiving long inbound pass
2:01	67-70	Brokaw with 20-footer from left corner over Wilkes
1:25		Meyers misses short jumper
1:11	69-70	Brokaw with pull-up jumper from foul line
:45		Wilkes driven and scores but hooked Martin on the drive
:29	71-70	Clay with right corner jumper on pass from Brokaw
:21		Timeout UCLA (second)
:08		Curtis misses long jumper, but Brokaw loses the ball out of bounds after Wilkes knocks the ball off his leg with six seconds left.
:06		Walton misses, Trgovich misses, Meyers misses
:00		Shumate gets final rebound, Irish win

NOTRE DAME ENDS UCLA'S 88-GAME WINNING STREAK
Notre Dame 71, UCLA 70
January 19, 1974
at Notre Dame, Indiana
Athletic and Convocation Center

UCLA (70)

Name	FG-A	FT-A	Reb	Ast-TO	F	Min	Pts
Keith Wilkes	6-16	6-7	5	1-2	2	40	18
Dave Meyers	5-10	0-2	7	3-5	2	36	10
Bill Walton	12-14	0-0	9	2-2	3	40	24
Pete Trgovich	3-5	1-1	0	1-2	4	40	7
Tommy Curtis	3-11	3-4	1	4-5	3	35	9
Greg Lee	0-0	2-2	0	0-1	1	5	2
Marques Johnson	0-0	0-0	0	0-1	0	4	0
Team			5				
Totals	29-56 (.518)	12-16 (.750)	27	11-18	15	200	70

Notre Dame (71)

Name	FG-A	FT-A	Reb	Ast-TO	F	Min	Pts
Gary Novak	0-2	0-0	0	2-0	0	11	0
Adrian Dantley	4-12	1-1	8	2-3	3	37	9
John Shumate	11-22	2-4	11	1-5	1	40	24
Gary Brokaw	10-16	5-7	3	3-2	4	40	25
Dwight Clay	2-5	3-4	6	2-3	3	39	7
Bill Paterno	2-4	0-0	1	0-1	4	11	4
Ray Martin	1-1	0-0	2	1-0	2	22	2
Team			1				
Totals	30-62 (.484)	11-16 (.687)	32	11-14	17	200	11

Score by Half

UCLA	43	27	70
Notre Dame	34	37	71

OFFICIALS: RICHARD WEILER, GEORGE SOLOMON

ATTENDANCE: 11,343 (CAPACITY)

NOTRE DAME RANKED #1 FOR THE FIRST TIME

Associated Press Poll, January 22, 1974

Rk	School (First place)	W-L	Pts	Head Coach
1.	Notre Dame (31)	10-0	990	Digger Phelps
2.	UCLA (15)	13-1	944	John Wooden
3.	N.C. State	11-1	782	Norm Sloan
4.	North Carolina	12-1	651	Dean Smith
5.	Maryland	10-2	649	Lefty Driesell
6.	Marquette	14-1	510	Al McGuire
7.	Vanderbilt	12-1	423	Roy Skinner
8.	Providence	13-2	375	Dave Gavitt
9.	Alabama	10-2	334	C. M. Newton
10.	Long Beach State	12-1	285	Lute Olson
11.	Indiana	11-3	176	Bob Knight
12.	Southern Cal	12-2	150	Bob Boyd
13.	South Carolina	10-3	105	Frank McGuire
14.	Louisville	10-3	104	Denny Crum
15.	Michigan	11-2	99	Johnny Orr
16.	Pittsburgh	13-1	88	Buzz Ridl
17.	Wisconsin	10-2	69	John Powless
18.	Centenary	12-0	41	Larry Little
19.	New Mexico	12-3	23	Norm Ellenberger
20.	Arizona State	11-4	16	Ned Wulk

United Press International Coaches Poll, January 22, 1974

Rk	School (First place)	Record	Pts	Head Coach
1.	Notre Dame (21)	10-0	334	Digger Phelps
2.	UCLA (14)	13-1	329	John Wooden
3.	NC State	11-1	272	Norm Sloan
4.	Maryland	11-2	212	Lefty Driesell
5.	North Carolina	12-1	198	Dean Smith
6.	Marquette	14-1	178	Al McGuire
7.	Providence	13-2	85	Dave Gavitt
8.	Vanderbilt	12-1	76	Roy Skinner
9.	Long Beach State	12-1	37	Lute Olson
10.	Alabama	10-2	31	C. M. Newton
11.	Southern California	12-2	30	Bob Boyd
12.	Pittsburgh	14-1	26	Buzz Ridl
13.	Indiana	11-3	22	Bobby Knight
14.	South Carolina	10-2	21	Frank McGuire
15.	Louisville	10-3	20	Denny Crum
16.	Wisconsin	10-2	11	John Powless
17.	Kansas	11-3	10	Ted Owens
18.	Arizona State	11-4	9	Ned Wulk
19.	UTEP	12-3	7	Don Haskins
20.	Michigan	11-2	6	Johnny Orr

CHAPTER 9

Party at Digger's, Winning at Kansas, UCLA's Revenge

DIGGER PHELPS HAD PLANNED ON HAVING A MAJOR PARTY AT HIS house after the UCLA game, win or lose. Ara Parseghian had parties after big Notre Dame football games, so Digger thought he would do the same after big basketball games. He actually had four during this 1973–74 season.

The party that celebrated the ending of the longest winning streak in college basketball history was an all-timer. The game was over at 2 p.m. local time, so friends of Digger didn't wait until the evening. He estimated more than 500 people showed up at various times at his home on Peashway Street between 3 p.m. and 1 a.m.

"People just kept calling the house and I just said come on over and bring your friends," said Phelps.

"Dick Harter, my mentor at Pennsylvania, who was the head coach at Oregon at the time, took the red-eye and came in for the game. It was also a scouting trip for him." (His Oregon team would also beat UCLA later in the season.)

"I had a lot of guests staying at the house as it was. There were friends I grew up with in Beacon, New York. Our priest from St. Gabriel's where I got my start in coaching, Father Deviney, also came in, as did my parents, my sister . . . the house was packed. Even Otis Bowen, the Governor of Indiana, came to the house after the game.

"I spent half the time on the phone and half the time greeting people at the front door.

"I remember everyone taking a break at 6:30 p.m. to watch the *CBS Evening News*. Heywood Hale Broun had come in earlier in the week to do a feature on our program."

In the days before ESPN and CNN, Broun did a five-minute sports feature each Saturday night. It was must-see TV.

"He had finished the piece on Friday, leaving a little time to review the game. We made him do a major edit on Saturday afternoon."

Digger went to bed around 2:30 a.m. and got up at 7 a.m. At that time, Father Deviney said Mass at the house. "Some of the 'parishioners' hadn't been to bed yet," recalled Phelps with a laugh.

Downtown South Bend was up for grabs. There were no arrests or violence, but all five bars ran out of beer before midnight. It was an all-night party on campus as well.

Shumate went out on a date and got home at 5 a.m. His phone was still ringing from friends from back home in New Jersey.

For Ray Martin and many of the players one of the great memories of the day took place on campus at dinner. "We walked into the South Dining Hall [eating area] with our trays and when we sat down, the entire dining hall gave us a standing ovation that lasted about five minutes," said Martin, who went on to a long career in coaching.

"Whenever someone asks me what it was like to play basketball at Notre Dame in the seventies and what Notre Dame spirit is all about, that image comes to my mind."

It was a busy day for Phelps on Sunday, January 20. With less than five hours of sleep, he had to get his staff together to prepare for the game at Kansas, which was just two days away. They would be leaving on a commercial flight on Monday afternoon. There would be practice late Sunday as well.

Early Sunday afternoon there was a celebration for Notre Dame's national championship football victory over Alabama, which had taken place just 20 days earlier on New Year's Eve. Phelps had earlier declined an invitation to sit up front, but after the win over UCLA, everyone in the athletic department wanted to celebrate both accomplishments, so he accepted. Two blue and gold Notre Dame banners hung over the stage to signify both number-one ranked teams.

There was a great relationship between the football and basketball programs at that time. Part of the reason was the leadership of Athletic Director Moose Krause, who was an All-American in both sports at Notre Dame in the early 1930s.

But most of it had to do with the big brother, little brother relationship between Parseghian and Phelps. They were always willing to help each other. Their relationship had started in 1965 when Phelps wrote Parseghian about his goal to become Notre Dame's head basketball coach someday.

Their desire to help each other, especially in the recruiting process, was never more evident than at the 1974 UCLA game. Recruits Joe Montana and Ken MacAfee both made their official visits to Notre Dame that weekend and the excitement surrounding the game and the game itself were certainly positives when it came time for them to make a decision. They were both big reasons Notre Dame won the national championship in 1977. Montana of course went on to a Pro Football Hall of Fame career and MacAfee was inducted into the College Football Hall of Fame before starting a career as a dentist.

When Phelps came to Notre Dame, Parseghian was in his seventh year. He was the coach Phelps went to for advice. But they were also friends away from the office, playing in golf tournaments and attending Notre Dame alumni events together.

In 1974, Notre Dame opened the football season on a Monday night in Atlanta against Georgia Tech. Phelps worked it out that he had a recruiting trip in the area so he could go to the game. These were simpler times as the following story from Phelps shows.

> I saw Ara and asked him if there were any extra rooms at the team hotel because I hadn't made a reservation yet. He said he had an extra bed in his room and that I could stay with him.
>
> Notre Dame won the game, 31–7 and the team did not fly back until the next day. Late night charter flights after night games were years in the future.

So, we went back to his room after the game and turned on the TV set and one of the stations was playing the movie, *Blazing Saddles*. I had seen it in the theatre, but Ara had not.

So there we were laying in our respective beds watching that movie. At one point I said to Ara, "Wait until you see this next scene, you won't believe what Alex Karras does to the horse."

Of course, that was the scene where Karras [former Detroit Lions All-Pro lineman] punches the horse and knocks him out.

I have never seen Ara laugh like that. He fell out of his bed he was laughing so hard.

It is funny how you remember some things from your younger days of coaching. Watching *Blazing Saddles* in an Atlanta hotel room with Ara Parseghian is one of those memories.

KANSAS GAME

After meeting with his staff to review the UCLA game and work on the plan for Kansas, the team held a two-hour practice Sunday night that did not conclude until 10 p.m. At the end of practice Phelps brought the team into a huddle.

At the end of each practice as Notre Dame head coach, even during the 6–20 season, Phelps would end his practices with, "Notre Dame, No. 1," a cheer the team said with him in unison.

This time he brought the team together and said,

"The first time ever . . . Number One?"
"Notre Dame!"
"Number One!"

The team left on Monday for Lawrence, Kansas. This was an era before team charters, so the team flew commercially from South Bend to Chicago, then from Chicago to Kansas City.

The trip did not start well because the flight from Chicago to Kansas City was canceled and the team was delayed six hours getting to Lawrence.

When the team got to the hotel there were messages telling Phelps that Notre Dame was officially ranked number one in the nation with

36 first place votes and 990 poll points. UCLA still had 15 first-place votes and 944 poll points.

While Notre Dame had not won a championship by beating UCLA, it was a landmark accomplishment in the school's basketball history, for January 21, 1974, was the first time the program had ever been No. 1 in the AP poll. It also had the No. 1 ranking by the UPI Coaches poll.

Phelps had the AP poll blown up to poster size and it was framed and displayed in the outer office of the basketball complex at the Athletic and Convocation Center.

UCLA had been ranked No. 1 in 46 consecutive polls dating to February 8, 1971, two weeks after their previous loss to Notre Dame. The streak of 46 straight #1 rankings is still first by 19 polls. Ohio State had a streak of 27 in a row during the 1960–61 and 1961–62 seasons.

UCLA ranked second in the January 21, 1974, poll, thus allowing their incredible streak of top five rankings to continue. Wooden would run that top five streak through the end of his career, an incredible run of 146 consecutive top five rankings. It lasted just three polls into the Gene Bartow era, giving UCLA a streak of 149 consecutive top five rankings, still the all-time record in that category as well.

Kansas was the preseason No. 13 team in the AP poll, but they had gotten off to 4–3 start to drop out of the top 20. But Phelps and his staff knew they were still very good. Two of the losses were to a No. 3 Indiana team and a No. 17 Vanderbilt team. They had beaten Kentucky when the Wildcats were No. 10.

This was a balanced Kansas team that had five players averaging between 11 and 12 points, and they were big with three 6-foot-10 players who were part of their rotation.

Phelps was worried about this game for many weeks because it would be natural for a team to let down after such an emotional win and after an entire student body spent the last two days slapping the players on the back and telling them how great they were. He told the team a few times on Tuesday, "We don't want to be number one for just one day."

Fears of a letdown at the beginning of the game were wiped away by one of the best first halves of the season. Notre Dame led 49–35 at intermission, as it hit 59 percent from the field and 15 of 15 from the foul line. Defensively they allowed Kansas to shoot just 36 percent and forced 10 turnovers.

Rick Suttle was a 6'10" backup center for Kansas who had the game of his life, especially in the second half. He scored time and again over Shumate and forced him into foul trouble. He scored five baskets in the first nine minutes of the second half to bring Kansas to within 61–59.

On top of that, Shumate picked up a fourth foul just a few possessions later. The 17,100 Kansas fans were going wild.

Somehow with Shumate out, the Irish hung in and actually increased the lead.

With a 71–67 lead and Shumate now back in the game, assistant coach Frank McLaughlin suggested to Digger that the team go into a "four corners offense," a strategy Dean Smith had made famous the last few years at North Carolina. The shot clock was still 10 years away.

Kanas could not steal the ball and the Irish made free throws and came away with a 76–74 win.

Shumate had struggled, but was still Notre Dame's leading scorer with 23 points, thanks to making 11 of 14 free throws. Dantley added 17 and Brokaw 14. Suttle finished with 27 points off 13 field goals and one free throw in a head-to-head meeting with Shumate. Notre Dame won the game at the free throw line, making 20 of 27, while the home team Jayhawks made just 4 of 7.

Shumate was dejected after the game because Suttle had done so well against him. And Kansas had won the rebounding 42–23, by far the worst rebounding performance of the season.

At the time it appeared Notre Dame had escaped with a road win over a team that was considered, at the time, to be middle of the road. But Kansas would go on a run after this loss, qualify for the NCAA Tournament by winning the Big Eight, finishing seventh in the final AP poll and reaching the Final Four.

Considering the circumstances, it has to be regarded as one of the top wins of Phelps's career.

The team had a 5:45 a.m. wake-up call on Wednesday, January 23, for a bus ride to Kansas City to catch a plane to Chicago and another flight to South Bend.

In those days, most subscribers received their copy of *Sports Illustrated* in the mail on Thursday or Friday. But some advance copies were first shipped to big city airports around the country for sale on Wednesday. When the Notre Dame team got to O'Hare, they saw the cover of the new *Sports Illustrated* dated January 28, 1974.

Much to their disappointment, it was not Dwight Clay's shot to beat UCLA on the cover. It was not Gary Novak or Adrian Dantley, Gary Brokaw or Ray Martin cutting down the nets. It was not even a closeup picture of Digger Phelps being carried off the court by Dick DiBiaso.

The cover was a picture of model Ann Simonton. You have to Google the magazine to actually determine it is Simonton on the cover. Incredibly, the cover and table of contents page never identified the then 22-year-old. (She is identified inside the magazine, but it never documents that it is her on the cover.)

Back on campus five thousand Notre Dame male students were the most disappointed they have ever been to see the *Sports Illustrated* swimsuit issue in their dorm mailbox. They had to settle for a four-page lead story with four pictures on their team's historic win.

What was even more disappointing to the Notre Dame males, there were only seven pages of bathing suit–clad models inside the publication. *We lost the cover for only seven pages of models?* everyone thought. At least a young Cheryl Tiegs was the subject in three of the pictures.

(Cover girl Simonton went on to be the founder of Media Watch, a watchdog group that teaches media literacy and challenges exploitative images. She has long protested advertisers whose images she calls hurtful and degrading, particularly to women and minorities. She once picketed Miss America contests and dressed herself as a slab of meat during demonstrations. Her efforts landed her in jail 11 times.)

For Shumate, it was more disappointing than the other Notre Dame players to see someone other than a Notre Dame basketball player on the *Sports Illustrated* cover. Twice previously he had been on the cover of *Sports Illustrated* as a defender in a loss. First, on December 11, 1972, he was the defender in a picture of Michigan's Campy Russell for a feature on Big Ten basketball, then in the February 5, 1973, issue he was in the foreground of a battle for a rebound with Walton when the magazine featured the Bruins breaking of San Francisco's streak at Notre Dame.

The Irish arrived back on the Notre Dame campus at midday on Wednesday. That night at 6:30 p.m. local NBC affiliate WNDU, whose station was on campus, rebroadcast the UCLA game. Today we wish someone at that station had saved a tape of the complete game. There are sections of the game on YouTube, but not the full game. Fortunately, the last four minutes of the game are posted.

Phelps never would have said it 50 years ago, and he might not say it now, but he did not think much of St. Francis (PA), whom he squeezed into the schedule on Thursday, January 24. The team had to be exhausted after the emotions of beating UCLA on Saturday, followed by the road trip and narrow win over Kansas on Tuesday.

The Irish led by just nine at the half and Digger read the team the riot act. This was the first time Notre Dame entered a game at the Convocation Center as the nation's number-one team and he was embarrassed. But he got their attention and Notre Dame won by 20, 78–58. Dantley led the way with 22 points and 11 rebounds, while Shumate had 19 and 11.

It was now time to refocus on UCLA.

THE REMATCH IN LOS ANGELES

While Notre Dame had two games to prepare for prior to heading to California for the rematch with UCLA, the Bruins had just about all week to review what had happened and how to correct it.

Coach Wooden spoke to a Southern California writers' group on Monday, January 21. With the plane ride from Chicago to Los Angeles, and all day Sunday to think about it, he was much more forthcoming about the last 3:22 of the game that ended his program's 88-game winning streak.

"All of us, and especially the coach, must recognize our mistakes, admit them, learn from them and forget them," Wooden told the group. "In retrospect I feel that I personally fell victim to the complacency that I was afraid might victimize my team. I failed to make the proper adjustments in the waning minutes of the game."

He continued, "Our play lacked something in the last few minutes that we've always credited ourselves with keeping—our poise."

Wooden also said he was looking forward to the rematch with Notre Dame. "I'm pleased we have the opportunity of playing them again—not in the sense of a grudge game for we'll try to keep free of such thoughts—but for the opportunity to shore up our weaknesses."

There were some other interesting quotes during the week. When asked about Notre Dame's victory to end the streak, Al McGuire said, "All Notre Dame did by winning was guarantee UCLA its eighth straight national championship." When asked about that quote from his friend, Phelps responded, "What are we supposed to do, apologize for winning?"

Former UCLA forward Curtis Rowe, who was with the Detroit Pistons and had started in UCLA's loss to Notre Dame in 1971, was asked about the ending of the streak. "Notre Dame better take some more players to UCLA next Saturday, because the ones they have won't be enough. I think the defeat just insured the national championship for UCLA."

There was some history to back up the quotes by Rowe and McGuire.

- In 1964–65, UCLA lost to Iowa on January 29, then won its last 15 games to win the national championship.
- In 1967–68, UCLA lost to Houston on January 20, then won its last 16 to win the national championship, a run that included a 101–69 win over Houston in a rematch in the national semifinals.
- In 1968–69, UCLA lost to Southern California on March 8 in the final regular season game, then won its four games in the NCAA Tournament.
- In 1970–71, UCLA lost to Notre Dame on January 23, then won its last 15 games to win the national championship.

It seemed the people in Las Vegas who do point spreads had the same feeling and the Bruins were made a 14-point favorite in the rematch. Digger had to wonder if a number-one team had ever been such an underdog.

Additionally, the rematch was in Pauley Pavilion, where UCLA had won 127 of 129 games, including 59 in a row in the nine years they had played in the facility. They had never lost to a non-conference opponent, and in fact wouldn't until Notre Dame turned the trick in December 1976.

As he always did to simulate the Pac-8 schedule, UCLA played a game on Friday night against Santa Clara while Notre Dame players rested in their Century Plaza Hotel rooms. The Bruins won easily, 96–54. At the end of the game, the Bruin students started chanting, "Beat Notre Dame! Beat Notre Dame!"

Some of those same UCLA students left Pauley after the game only to camp out for the night at the facility's front door so they could get the best student seats for the Notre Dame game the next night. The UCLA student section was first-come first-served, so the closer you were to the front door when the facility was opened at 5:30 p.m., the better your seat.

It was obvious everyone at UCLA was stoked for this game. While Wooden had tried to downplay it all week, revenge was a factor.

Phelps, on the other hand, felt it was all about the revenge factor. He thought Wooden had decided against opening his locker room to the media because he knew he had that revenge factor advantage and he didn't want one of his players to say something that would give Notre Dame motivation.

As detailed in *A Coach's World*, Phelps said this to the team at the hotel in Los Angeles Saturday after watching tape of the first half of the previous Saturday's game:

"Don't get discouraged about the officials, I will take care of them. You just keep your poise and show your class, no matter what happens on the court. UCLA and their fans want revenge, so the pressure is on them. If you can accept the crowd and UCLA's intensity, we will win again."

The crowd was already in a frenzy during the entire pregame, but when the starting lineups were introduced it reached another level. Bruins fans felt Pete Trgovich had played solid to that point in the season, but many felt freshman Marques Johnson should see more playing time.

Johnson was a highly recruited player from Crenshaw High School in Los Angeles and UCLA fans thought he could do for UCLA what Dantley was doing to Notre Dame, but he had not played that much to this point in the season. The previous Saturday he played just four minutes and didn't score in Notre Dame's victory.

Dick Enberg announced the starting lineups over the public address system live on television for the game at Notre Dame the previous Saturday, and Al Michaels had the honor for the game in Los Angeles. When Michaels announced the lineups and said, "a 6–6 freshman from Los Angeles," the Pauley crowd knew they were getting their man in the starting lineup. Those in attendance could not hear Johnson's name when introduced.

Johnson's insertion in the starting lineup was part of a change that Wooden had been considering for this game all week. He put Johnson into the lineup at guard, and had him work on Meyers's normal spot on the right side of the offense. It also meant that the six-foot Dwight Clay would be guarding him in a man-to-man situation.

The enthusiasm generated from the starting lineups continued at the start of the game. UCLA jumped out to a 9–0 lead. Notre Dame missed its first eight shots from the field until Dantley made a field goal six minutes into the game. The lead got up to 16 at 33–17, almost an identical score and time as UCLA's 33–16 lead in South Bend the previous week.

And Notre Dame did make a comeback, cutting the margin to seven. It was 39–30 in the final minute of the half when Lee made two free throws and Meyers had a follow up field goal to make the margin 13 points at intermission, 43–30. Wilkes, the player Phelps worried about the most in both games against UCLA, had scored 18 points in the first half.

The first half had gone very similarly to the first half in South Bend the week before when the Bruins shot 70 percent from the field in scoring 43 points. It was a 13-point lead instead of a nine-point lead, but this time it was in the Bruins' home.

While the margin was 13, some felt the Irish still had a chance because Walton had three fouls in the first half. But unlike the game in South Bend, Notre Dame did not start the second half on a 9–2 run.

UCLA only increased its lead with balanced scoring. The margin moved from 13 to 17 back to 13, but a 53–40 score with 15:25 left was as close as Notre Dame could get.

UCLA grew the lead to as many 27 points in the final 10 minutes. With 5:39 to play, Walton fouled out with his team up by 26. He had scored 32 points on 16-for-19 shooting, giving him a 28-for-33 stat line in the two games against Notre Dame.

Instead of returning to the Bruins bench, Walton waved to his team, which was at the opposite end of the floor and went straight to the locker room as the crowd gave him a thunderous ovation.

Notre Dame won the last five minutes by seven points against the UCLA reserves, giving the Bruins a 94–75 victory. It wasn't that close, proving all the experts were right. UCLA had even beaten the spread.

The Bruins shot 59 percent for the game to just 46 percent for the Irish. Another key statistic was rebounding as UCLA won that data point, 43–29. It was the second time in three games Notre Dame had been blitzed on the boards by at least 14 rebounds.

As stated, Walton was terrific with 32 points, but he also had 11 rebounds and a team-high seven assists. Wilkes had just two points in the second half, but finished with 20 for the game and Johnson had 16 points and four rebounds. Meyers had 10 points and seven rebounds, while Curtis, who shot 3-for-11 in South Bend, was 4-for-4 in Pauley and had 10 points and five assists.

Shumate had 25 points, but he had just five rebounds. Brokaw had 14 points, but shot just 5-for-16. Paterno (11) and Martin (10 on 4-for-5 shooting) were the other double-figure scorers for the Irish. Dantley was held to seven points on just 3-for-9 shooting.

Wilkes summed up the feeling of his team when he told the media, "I guess we played with a little more intensity than usual. We were motivated."

Wooden said after looking at what had transpired over the two games, "I think there are times when a loss really can help a team." That obviously had happened again for UCLA, who ran its streak of games without consecutive losses to 230 going back to the 1965–66 season.

Bill Walton scored a season-high 32 points and led UCLA back to the No. 1 ranking with a 94–75 win over Notre Dame one week after the end of the streak. *Associated Students of the University of California at Los Angeles, Public domain, via Wikimedia Commons*

UCLA RETURNS TO NO. 1 ONE WEEK LATER
UCLA 94, Notre Dame 75
January 26, 1974
at Los Angeles, California
Pauley Pavilion

Notre Dame (75)

Name	FG-A	FT-A	Reb	Ast-TO	F	Pts
Gary Novak	2-3	0-0	4	0	3	4
Adrian Dantley	3-9	1-2	5	2	3	7
John Shumate	8-15	9-12	5	1	3	25
Gary Brokaw	5-16	4-4	6	2	3	14
Dwight Clay	2-6	0-0	2	3	1	4
Ray Martin	4-5	2-2	0	2	2	10
Bill Paterno	5-9	1-2	1	1	2	11
Peter Crotty	0-0	0-0	0	0	1	0
Team			6			
Totals	29-63	17-22	29	11-15	18	75
	(.460)	(.773)				

UCLA (94)

Name	FG-A	FT-A	Reb	Ast-TO	F	Pts
Keith Wilkes	8-18	4-5	11	1	3	20
Dave Meyers	5-10	0-0	7	6	4	10
Bill Walton	16-19	0-0	11	7	5	32
Tommy Curtis	4-4	2-3	1	5	4	10
Marques Johnson	8-11	0-0	4	2	3	16
Greg Lee	1-3	2-2	1	1	0	4
Pete Trgovich	0-2	0-0	0	0	1	0
Ralph Drollinger	1-2	0-0	2	1	2	2
Andre McCarter	0-1	0-0	1	0	0	0
Gary Franklin	0-2	0-0	2	0	0	0
Richard Washington	0-1	0-1	1	0	0	0
Team			2			
Totals	43-73	8-11	43	23-16	22	94
	(.589)	(.727)				

Score by Half

Notre Dame	30	45	75
UCLA	43	51	94

OFFICIALS: LOUIS SORIANO, CHARLES MOFFETT

ATTENDANCE: 12,874 (CAPACITY)

CHAPTER 10

Digger's Best Team

THE REST OF 1973–74 FOR NOTRE DAME

Notre Dame's challenging schedule continued the Tuesday after the decisive Saturday night loss to UCLA against fifth-ranked Marquette. The Irish had dropped from No. 1 to No. 3 with the 19-point loss at UCLA. UCLA received 51 of the 52 first-place votes from the Associated Press media. Notre Dame received the other. David Israel of the *Chicago Daily News* still voted Notre Dame first.

NC State also moved ahead of Notre Dame into the second spot. The Wolfpack had not lost since their 18-point defeat to UCLA in St. Louis on December 15. The Irish had beaten UCLA and lost by 19 at UCLA, but as has been the case with AP poll voters for 50 years, it is all about "what have you done for me lately."

Dating to their first meeting in Madison Square Garden in 1971 when Phelps was in his only year at Fordham, the Digger Phelps vs. Al McGuire games were great theatre. As we discussed in chapter 6, Phelps didn't want to let McGuire control the officials by getting a technical. If Al got one, Digger was going to get one at some point when he needed a change in momentum.

The two coaches had totally different approaches to game day preparation. Phelps was always in the locker room prior to the game writing diagrams on a blackboard. On this night, McGuire was on campus at the Morris Inn bar, having a drink with, among others, Notre Dame priests. He stayed there until 7:15 p.m., just 45 minutes before tipoff.

Phelps tells a story that in January 1971 when he went to Milwaukee to scout the Notre Dame vs. Marquette game as the Fordham coach, McGuire brought Phelps into the locker room to meet some of his players . . . before the game. Phelps felt a little strange since he would be playing this team a month later, and asked, "Al, don't you need to get ready for the game." McGuire responded that Hank Raymonds, his top assistant, had everything set up.

McGuire would come to the locker room just minutes before the game, give his inspirational talk to the team and they were off. His unique approach worked, for he finished his career with a .787 winning percentage (295–80), still 10th in Division I history. He led the Warriors to a top 15 final AP ranking in each of his last nine years, including the national championship in his final year, 1976–77.

The atmosphere was electric at the ACC in the pregame with two top five teams and two of the most charismatic coaches in the country set to do battle. Prior to the game, veteran official Art White came to Phelps and said, "Remember, the fight was last night." He was referring to the Muhammad Ali vs. Joe Frazier fight that had taken place in Madison Square Garden the night before.

McGuire seemed to love playing at Notre Dame and quite frankly the Notre Dame crowd loved it when Marquette came to Notre Dame. McGuire interacted with the crowd. On this night when Notre Dame students threw rolls of toilet paper on the court during pregame, McGuire picked up a couple of rolls and threw them back at them.

Whenever Notre Dame and Marquette met in this era, the sportswriters covering the game had a pool to predict who would get the first technical and how far into the game it took. On this night it didn't take long to determine the winner.

With the score tied at 2–2, a foul was called on Marquette's Marcus Washington. McGuire disagreed with the call to the point that he got a technical. It was just a minute into the game. It was a little surprising in that McGuire usually got a technical when he felt the momentum, or a number of officiating decisions, were going against him.

Digger did not retaliate initially, because the Irish were playing one of their best first halves of the year, one that rivaled the performance at

Kansas the previous Tuesday night. Notre Dame made 14 of 23 shots from the field in the first half and held Marquette to 38 percent on 11-for-29 shooting, leading to a 33–25 Notre Dame advantage at intermission. The only area the Irish were poor was free throw shooting. They hit just 5 of 11.

Marquette turned the game around in the first five minutes of the second half and eventually took the lead, 45–43 with under 11 minutes left.

It was time to change the momentum.

It was time for Phelps to get a technical.

With 10:19 left in the game and Marquette still up 45–43, Ray Martin was called for a foul. Digger became demonstrative, stomped a few times, and got a technical. Marquette freshman Bo Ellis made the one technical free throw (only one in those days, would have been two today), to put the Warriors up by three.

Notre Dame got a stop on Marquette's ensuing possession and then ran off nine consecutive points. During the run, Ellis, who was Marquette's top player on the night, picked up his fourth foul.

Amazing how that happens after a technical.

Two minutes later Ellis fouled out, and by the two-minute mark, Marquette starters Washington, Lloyd Walton, and Earl Tatum all had four fouls.

Amazing how that happens after a technical.

The Irish struggled from the line throughout, hitting just 13 of 24 for the game, but made enough down the stretch to win, 69–63.

Shumate, who had one of his worst games of the year the previous Tuesday at Kansas, was brilliant in this game with 27 points on 11-for-14 shooting. At the other end of the court, he held Marquette star center Maurice Lucas to 3-for-16 shooting, five turnovers, and just eight points. Lucas would go on to a productive NBA career and in 1976–77 teamed with Bill Walton to lead Portland to the NBA championship.

Ellis won the battle of the freshman forwards with 21 points on 10-for-13 shooting. Dantley had just seven points and committed four turnovers in 26 minutes.

It was always a night to remember when Digger Phelps and Al McGuire were on opposing benches in the 1970s. *Notre Dame Archives*

It was another freshman who saved the day for Notre Dame. Billy Paterno had one of his better shooting games from the perimeter and scored 14 points on 6-for-8 shooting. Clay added 10 points. Brokaw struggled with just nine points, but he didn't have a turnover in 38 minutes. The Irish shot 28-for-46 from the field, 14-for-23 in each half, and won the turnover margin by seven, 14–21.

McGuire singled out Paterno in his postgame press conference. "In the first half, we ran our triangle-and-two defense, which leaves someone free and Billy Paterno really hurt us," said McGuire, who wore a plaid suit for the game. "We were able to hold Brokaw and Clay, but Paterno dropped some real bombs on us."

Notre Dame's NBA-like schedule continued on Thursday night with an eighth game in the last 19 days against DePaul, a school that was a few years away from being a Final Four team. The Irish won, 101–72, after leading by just three at the half. Brokaw returned to form with 25 points on 12-for-16 shooting and won his second straight Wendell Smith Award as the MVP of the Notre Dame vs. DePaul game.

But the story of the night was Adrian Dantley, not for his 23 points and 15 rebounds, but for what happened when he was on the bench in the final minutes.

With less than four minutes left the last media timeout was called. While Phelps was talking to the team, Dantley, who had come out of the game at a previous dead ball, collapsed and was unconscious. Doctors raced to him, but he was unresponsive.

A stretcher was brought to the court and he was carried off motionless. It was a dramatic scene and the Convocation Center was in total silence. Dantley was brought by ambulance to the Notre Dame infirmary where he remained for the night. It was determined that he was suffering from exhaustion.

On top of the pressures of the season and a schedule with eight games in 19 days, and his academic responsibilities, Dantley was trying to lose weight. While he was having a terrific year averaging 17 points and nine rebounds a game, there had been some criticism that he was overweight. He was not one to talk about such things with Phelps or the trainers or even his teammates. He was trying to cut down on his eating to lose the weight and it came to head at the end of the DePaul game.

Phelps had been outspoken against the freshman eligibility rule. He felt freshmen needed that transition year. He was playing three freshmen (Dantley, Paterno, and Martin) in every game with great success on the court, but he was aware of the pressure it put on those players. In the first semester he had given Dantley time off to work on his studies.

Dantley would recover and sit out the next game against Davidson. He returned to more sensible eating habits, got more sleep, and was fine the rest of the season.

After a Saturday afternoon victory over a Davidson team that had won six straight games and had defeated South Carolina earlier, the Irish traveled to Michigan State for their fourth game of the year against a Big Ten foe.

Playing on the road on Monday night after a Saturday game is not a recipe for success, in 1974 or today. But as an independent, Phelps had to do what he could to put together a challenging national schedule and this Monday night was the only time he could get a game with the Spartans.

The February 4 game was the fifth for the Irish with just one day to prepare in the last two weeks. There would be 11 such games with just one day to prepare during the 1973–74 regular season. Earlier in the season between December 11 and January 11, Notre Dame had just three games.

Would the hectic schedule catch up to the Irish against a Michigan State team that was 10–6, but had just won four in a row, including an impressive win over Purdue?

The Spartans jumped out to a 10-point lead at 12–2 in the first four minutes, but the Irish had a 43–39 lead at intermission. A highlight of the first half took place when Shumate and Novak both recorded their 1,000th career points to become the 16th and 17th players in Notre Dame history, respectively, to accomplish the feat. Shumate was just the fourth to do it as a junior.

The second half was more outstanding offensive basketball. With 2:42 left Michigan State had a four-point lead after sophomore Terry Furlow made a hook shot. But Brokaw and Shumate both made field goals to tie the game at 89.

Michigan State called a timeout with 21 seconds left. Most felt they would hold the ball for a game winning shot. They had been in this same situation the previous game against Purdue and guard Mike Robinson, who had 31 points at this point against the Irish, hit the game winner. Surely coach Gus Ganakas would set up a play for the senior guard who was averaging over 20 points a game.

The Spartans started to run a play, but with 12 seconds left, Furlow, who had great confidence after making 10 of his first 13 shots from the field, shot an air ball from the top of the key and the ball went out of bounds.

Phelps passed on taking a timeout, and Paterno took the ball up floor. It was his intention to go to Shumate or Clay, who had made four game winners to that point in his career.

But both players were covered, so with three seconds left, Paterno, who had taken just two shots all night, hoisted his third from just inside the top of the key. The ball went in and Notre Dame had a 91–89 victory.

Robinson was the star all season for the Spartans and he would be on this night with 31 points on 12-for-16 shooting. Furlow finished with 22 and the following year made up for his late air ball by leading Michigan State to an upset victory at Notre Dame.

Shumate finished with 27 points on 12-for-16 shooting and Brokaw had 21 on 9-for-15 shooting. Dantley was back to almost full strength and scored 15 and had a team best nine rebounds in 36 minutes. Novak shot 5-for-5 from the field in scoring 10 points and he grabbed six rebounds.

Both teams were efficient when it came to shooting in both halves. In fact, both teams made 20 of 31 shots from the field in the second half, 64.5 percent. The odd stat was that while the two teams were so proficient shooting the ball, they committed a combined 45 turnovers, 23 by Notre Dame and 22 by Michigan State.

After double digit wins over LaSalle, Duke, and Fordham, the Irish traveled to South Carolina to meet a Gamecocks team that was headed to the NCAA Tournament. Frank McGuire's team had won 34 in a row at home in the Carolina Coliseum, which had opened in 1968, the same year as Notre Dame's Athletic and Convocation Center.

The Gamecocks were 17–3 and ranked No.14 in the nation, while the Irish had still lost just one game at UCLA and ranked third in the AP poll with a 19–1 record.

Carolina Coliseum featured a tartan floor, which Phelps did not mind because the arena they might play to start the NCAA Tournament in Terre Haute, Indiana, had a tartan surface.

There were many intangible aspects to this game, circumstances that took place before the tipoff.

First, South Carolina coach Frank McGuire had been ill and missed each of the last five South Carolina games. The team carried on, however, and actually had won eight in a row entering this game televised by TVS on a regional basis.

Second, McGuire's longtime head coach when he was a player at St. John's, Buck Freeman, and his assistant coach for many years, passed away on Thursday, two days prior to the game. Many were sure there would be a "Win one for Buck" speech in McGuire's pregame.

Third, late Friday night, Oregon State upset UCLA by a 61–57 score. The Irish now had a shot to move back to No. 1 with a victory in this game.

Both teams played strong defense in the first half, Notre Dame with a man-to-man and South Carolina with McGuire's experienced zone. It was 31–26 Irish at the half.

The second half was much more up-tempo with both teams scoring over 40 points.

The Irish had a 62–54 lead with 4:45 left and Phelps called for the four corners offense. This must have been a nightmare for McGuire, who had coached in the ACC for many years against Dean Smith, who used the approach often with considerable success.

While Notre Dame had some games with poor free throw shooting in 1973–74, this was not one of them. The Irish made 10 free throws after going to the four corners and 19 of 24 for the game, leading to a 72–68 win.

Shumate had another outstanding game with 26 points and 13 rebounds, while Dantley had 17 points thanks to a school record 11-for-11 from the foul line. Brokaw had an unusual stat line in that he had 15 points and a career-high 15 rebounds, but he was just 5-for-13 from the field and an even more unusual 5-for-11 from the line.

South Carolina had three future NBA players in its starting lineup, led by Alex English, who went on to score over 25,000 points in the NBA. He had 30 points on 13-for-20 shooting from the field in playing all 40 minutes. Guards Brian Winters and Mike Dunleavy also went on to long NBA careers and had double-figure scoring in this game, but they combined to shoot just 13-for-41 from the field. Notre Dame made 22 free throws to just 12 attempts for South Carolina, much to the disappointment of the sellout crowd of 12,576.

That result improved Notre Dame to 7–0 for the season in games decided by six points or less. The win over South Carolina's Frank McGuire was the fifth of the season against a coach who would eventually be inducted into the Basketball Hall of Fame.

This was a key game in what proved to be a key season in South Carolina's history. They had left the ACC after the 1970–71 season for many reasons. It was theorized that one of them was the success of independent teams and their inclusion in the NCAA Tournament. Many times, South Carolina had a team worthy of an NCAA bid, but in those days only the conference champion could be chosen.

McGuire had watched many NCAA Tournaments sitting on his couch while independents Notre Dame and Marquette were in the field.

South Carolina made the NCAA Tournament as an independent in 1971–72, 1972–73, and 1973–74. But 1973–74 was the last season they made the "dance" in McGuire's career that lasted until 1979–80. The South Carolina program could not recruit against the other ACC teams without the league's status, which only grew as the years went on.

For those wondering if Adrian Dantley had "hit the wall" at this point of the season, those questions were eliminated in the West Virginia game on February 23. With five days in between the Western Michigan victory and the West Virginia game, Dantley was well rested and had a game for the record books.

The freshman from Washington, DC, scored 41 points going 18-for-23 on shots from the field and 5-for-5 from the foul line, pulled down 12 rebounds and had three steals, all in just 29 minutes. Scoring at least 40 in less than 30 minutes was Austin Carr stuff. Combined with 25 points from Shumate, the Irish easily disposed of the Mountaineers, 108–80.

Dantley's 41 points still ranked as the Notre Dame freshman record entering the 2023–24 season.

The victory over Villanova on March 2 was another noteworthy offensive performance as the Irish won 115–85 on Senior Day. Senior Days were starting to be a bit confusing because it was in the second year of the "Hardship Rule," which allowed underclassmen to enter the NBA draft. The rule had started in September of 1971 when a special draft was held and Phil Chenier, an underclassman from the University of California, was taken by the Washington franchise.

By 1973–74 speculation began about underclassmen turning professional with a year to play. Shumate was in his fourth year at Notre Dame, but due to his physical problems that forced him to miss the entire 1971–72 season, he was eligible to return for 1974–75. Brokaw was in just his third year, his second year on the varsity, but his stock had risen significantly over the course of the year due to his ability to beat his opponent one-on-one, something he demonstrated against Keith Wilkes in the win over UCLA.

It was many months before those decisions would be made, so they were considered juniors on "Senior Day."

The certain seniors were Chris Stevens, Tom Hansen, Ken Wolbeck, Greg Schmelzer, and Gary "Goose" Novak, players who were part of the program during the 6–20 season of 1970–71. In fact, Stevens and Hansen had started Phelps's first game, but now they were bench warmers, or didn't even dress.

The only senior who was in the starting lineup was Novak, who was beloved by the student body. He was a model student-athlete who was studying to be a doctor. He would receive many academic honors in his Notre Dame career.

Novak scored 10 points and had seven rebounds in 25 minutes, but his highlight of the afternoon came during the pregame introductions.

When Novak was introduced, two students carried out a wooden box. Inside the box was a live goose to give an extra acknowledgment to his nickname. When the box was opened, it was a complete surprise to Novak and just about all of the 11,343 in attendance.

As we have said before, these were different times in 1973–74.

Perhaps the biggest example of this was how and when teams found out they were going to the NCAA Tournament.

There was no such thing as a Sunday evening NCAA pairings show on live television.

On Thursday morning, February 28, 1974, Athletic Director Moose Krause received a call from a member of the NCAA Tournament committee extending Notre Dame an invitation. He then called coach Phelps to tell him. That is how Notre Dame got its bid that year.

In 1973–74, only 25 teams were invited to the NCAA Tournament, nine at-large and 16 conference champions. The only conference that had a postseason tournament was the ACC. Most of the 16 conference champions were known by this Thursday, as well, because many regular season championships had been determined.

In those days if a team finished second in a conference and ranked in the top five in the nation, tough luck, you weren't going. That is why the NIT was so strong.

Maryland lost the ACC championship game by three points in 1974, was ranked fourth in the final regular season AP poll, but didn't go to the tournament. That situation led to the expansion of the tournament to include more than one team from a conference the next year.

Notre Dame still had two games remaining after receiving the bid, the aforementioned Villanova Senior Day game, and a Monday night, March 4 road game at Dayton.

Dayton had also received an at-large bid with a 19–7 record. It was a bit surprising to some because the Flyers had not beaten a ranked team all year, had a stretch at midseason when they had lost three of four, and had recently lost to a Western Kentucky team that finished 15–10.

Phelps was concerned about the game at Dayton for many reasons. First, the Irish had beaten Dayton 94–58 the previous year, the biggest victory margin of the 1972–73 season. That could lead to overconfidence.

Second, Dayton would be excited to get into the NCAA Tournament when it was questionable as to whether they would get in.

Third, Dayton was good at home, losing only to Louisville that year. They had a great following and the game was a sellout.

Fourth, Phelps had stressed getting into the NCAA Tournament all year. Now that they had the bid, this game at Dayton appeared to be meaningless toward that goal. Notre Dame's first round and second round opponents were already set, as the committee had announced Notre Dame would play Austin Peay in Terre Haute, Indiana, the following Saturday, March 9, then face the Big Ten champion (who had a bye), the following Thursday in Tuscaloosa, Alabama. Indiana and Michigan were to face off in a playoff game for that bid.

The fifth reason was Dayton's outstanding guard play. Johnny Davis and Donald Smith had been terrific all year, and they would be in this game. Smith finished with 32 points on 12-for-21 shooting and he made 8 of 9 free throws. Davis had 18 on 7-for-11 shooting. Mike Sylvester, whose brother Steve was a starting offensive lineman for Notre Dame in its recent national championship victory over Alabama, added 14 points. Overall, the Flyers made 40 of 69 from the field, 58 percent.

Shumate played well in defeat with 29 points and 16 rebounds on 11-for-18 shooting. But the other starters were just 14-for-47. Dantley had 11 points and 11 rebounds, but he made just 3 of 12 from the field.

After the game, Dayton coach Don Donoher called it Dayton's greatest victory, which was quite a statement for a coach who had led Dayton to the NCAA Championship game just seven years earlier. But Dayton had beaten a 24–1 Notre Dame team ranked third in the nation on a 12-game winning streak with a resounding 97–82 victory.

Notre Dame headed into the NCAA Tournament game against Austin Peay on a downer, but at the same time the Irish were still ranked second. They had moved to second after UCLA lost both games in Oregon on the same weekend in February. And the Dayton game had not been factored into the polls because the votes were cast on Monday afternoon, a few hours before the tipoff of the Dayton contest.

The first game of the tournament in Terre Haute was a contest between Marquette and Ohio University. That meant Digger and Al McGuire were both at the same site, but not playing each other. McGuire had earlier in the year said Notre Dame's victory over UCLA gave the Bruins their eighth straight NCAA title.

Now when he saw Phelps in person in between practices in Terre Haute, he told Digger, "I think the Dayton loss will help you." UCLA had stubbed their toe and gone on to win the national championship four times in recent years, so it was a common theory.

The Irish played that opening game against Austin Peay like the Dayton game had never happened. They jumped out to a 52–34 lead at halftime and never looked back before winning 108–66, at the time the sixth largest victory margin in the history of the NCAA Tournament.

Brokaw (25), Shumate (22), and Dantley (22) all had at least 20 points, and the Irish shot 60 percent from the field, and had 30 assists on 50 baskets. Clay, who had been fighting an ankle injury since early February, had eight points and nine assists.

Austin Peay's top scorer was James "Fly" Williams, who scored 26 points, but he took 31 shots. He was the subject of a great cheer by the Austin Peay fans.

"Fly's open, Let's Go Peay."

The Irish faced Michigan in their second game of the NCAA Tournament on Thursday, March 14, 1974. There wasn't much time for Phelps and his staff to scout the Wolverines because they had to beat Indiana on Monday night in a playoff to determine the Big Ten champion. They had both been 12–2 in the regular season in Big Ten play and had split two regular season games.

Indiana got the home court advantage for the playoff, but Michigan beat the Hoosiers at Assembly Hall, 75–67.

Phelps knew this was a very good Michigan team. They entered with a 21–4 record and No. 12 national ranking. They had lost in the regular season to Detroit and head coach Dick Vitale, by a 70–59 score, UCLA by 20 in Pauley Pavilion, Purdue by just one point, and Indiana, 93–81.

They had a talented team with five double-figure scorers. They were balanced, but had a star player in Campy Russell, a sophomore 6–8 forward who averaged 23.7 points and 11.1 rebounds. C. J. Kupec was a 6–8 center who also averaged a double-double with 13.7 and 11.6 figures. Steve Grote was the freshman point guard, who two years later would take Michigan to the national championship game against Indiana.

The regional was played in Tuscaloosa, Alabama, at the university's basketball facility. The Irish football team had just beaten Alabama to win the football national championship the previous New Year's Eve. Phelps didn't have to wonder who the hometown fans would root for.

It was a pro-Michigan crowd and they were excited for the first 14 minutes of the game because Michigan dominated the Irish with a strong man-to-man defense. Johnny Orr's team jumped out to a 28–8 lead in those first 14 minutes.

The Irish did not give up and cut the margin to five by halftime, 34–29. Back-to-back field goals by Shumate tied the game at 52 at the 10-minute mark and Notre Dame supporters felt better as Notre Dame had now outscored Michigan by 20 over the past 16 minutes.

The Irish then took a two-point lead, but Russell made a 25-footer to tie the game again with 8:24 left. Russell continued to make clutch shots down the stretch. With the score 70–65 with 1:20 left, Joey Johnson made a free throw for the Wolverines, but missed the second. The ball caromed far away from the basket, and Russell got his 18th rebound. He then fired the ball at the basket from long range and scored his 35th and 36th points to put the game out of reach at 73–65.

It was a crushing defeat for Notre Dame who certainly aspired to reach its first Final Four and compete for a national championship. They had showed their capabilities throughout the regular season with three wins over top five teams.

A sullen Digger Phelps sized up the game this way in his postgame press conference. "We can't just rely on Shumate. When the defense sags, we have to score from the outside and we weren't doing that tonight."

Shumate was terrific again with 34 points and 17 rebounds. But a check of the box score verified what Digger said. Brokaw was 4-for-16 and Clay 3-for-10. In fact, Shumate shot 14-for-22 for the game and the rest of the team was just 15-for-53 (.283). The Irish, who came in with a program best 52.5 percent for the year, shot just 39 percent in this game.

Dantley was 1-for-7 and scored just two points in 27 minutes. Perhaps he had hit the wall, which freshmen do, it was just a tough time to see it happen. He said after the game to Larry Keith of *Sports Illustrated*, "My legs felt like log cabins."

That said, Dantley scored 29 points two days later in the regional consolation game against Vanderbilt. Shumate led with 30, in what would be his final college game, in Notre Dame's 118–88 win over the Southeastern Conference champions. It would also be Brokaw's final game in a Notre Dame uniform as he decided to turn pro a couple of months later.

MY BEST TEAM
Certainly the goal of the 1973–74 Notre Dame team was to get to the Final Four. Phelps had a team accomplish that four years later.

But when looking back in 2004 for a book on his career, he said this 1973–74 team was his best.

"Your dream as a head coach is to get to the Final Four and have a chance to win the National Championship. We did that in 1978.

"But the best team I ever had was this 1973–74 club. The accomplishments of that team lose their impact over time because we lost in the Sweet 16 in the tournament to Michigan. But one off night does not diminish the accomplishments of this team in my mind.

"Just look at the results. We beat UCLA, Kansas and Marquette in a 10-day period in January and all three of those teams went to the Final Four. No school has beaten three different Final Four teams in the regular season before or since, never mind in just 10 days. UCLA ended the season ranked second in the final AP poll with a 26–4 record. Marquette finished third at 26–5 and Kansas was seventh at 23–7.

"In addition to those victories there were wins over Indiana, who finished ninth in the AP poll at 23–5, and Vanderbilt who also had a 23–5 record and ranked 13th in the final poll. We beat them by 30 points on a neutral court.

"South Carolina finished 22–5 and 19th in the final poll. We ended their 34-game home winning streak in February. That is six wins over teams that finished in the top 20, including four top 10 teams. No Notre Dame team has done that before or since."

Seven of the coaches Notre Dame beat that year are in the Naismith Basketball Hall of Fame. That list includes Fred Taylor (Ohio State), Bobby Knight (Indiana), John Thompson (Georgetown), John Wooden (UCLA), Al McGuire (Marquette), Ray Meyer (DePaul), and Frank McGuire (South Carolina). Four of those coaches were ranked in the top 15 in the nation when Notre Dame beat them, so it wasn't like Notre Dame caught those coaches on a down cycle.

Statistically, Notre Dame averaged almost 90 points a game and outscored the opposition by 17 points a game, still a Notre Dame record for the modern era. The Irish shot 53 percent from the field even though it was an up-tempo team, and had nearly a +10 rebound margin.

The 26–3 record is a Notre Dame modern record (.897) when it comes to winning percentage. Mike Brey had a team that reached the Elite Eight in 2014–15 that had a 32–6 record and that is the modern mark for total wins, but its .842 winning percentage is still below the

1973–74 team. Brey's 27–7 team of 2010–11 also had more wins, but had a .794 winning percentage.

The road wins by the 1973–74 team were also remarkable. The 1973–74 team won at Ohio State and Indiana, where the 73–67 victory ended a 19-game Indiana home streak. The Irish also won against Kentucky in Louisville, and defeated Kansas in Lawrence, just three days after ending UCLA's 88-game streak.

Then the Irish won at South Carolina in February to end the Gamecocks' 34-game home winning streak.

In Phelps's book *Tales from the Notre Dame Hardwood*, that reviews his 20 years at Notre Dame, he picked his all-time starting five. Three of the five were on this team. Gary Brokaw, Adrian Dantley, and John Shumate combined for nearly 60 points per game and shot a combined 58 percent from the field that year. All three shot at least 56 percent for the year. No team has three 55 percent field goal shooters today.

Shumate became a first-team All-American, while Brokaw was third team that year. Dantley went on to become a first-team All-American as a sophomore and a junior when he was second in the nation in scoring both seasons.

"This might have been my closest team at Notre Dame and they certainly have enjoyed our reunions. When we had our 30-year reunion in 2004, 15 of the 18 players on that team returned to campus.

"What I am most proud about this team is that all 18 of them got their degrees (17 of them from Notre Dame)."

CHAPTER 11

End of Another UCLA Streak

THE REST OF 1973–74 FOR UCLA

After beating Oregon and Oregon State on February 8 and 9 in Los Angeles, the Bruins turned around and made the trip to the Beaver State the next weekend. The second game of that two-game set in Los Angeles against Oregon State was tougher than expected, as the Bruins won by just 80–75.

The way the Pac-8 schedule worked, each team played one other school back-to-back once during the season. Oregon State was that school for UCLA in 1973–74. So the two teams played again just six days later in Corvallis.

While it was a game that got the Bruins' attention, most felt UCLA would come back strong with a better performance. The win over the Beavers on February 9 was the 50th consecutive Pac-8 victory for Wooden's team and its 92nd consecutive win over an unranked team, be it a conference foe or non-conference.

Much to everyone's surprise, they didn't come back with a strong performance and lost, 61–57.

UCLA had a 34–27 lead at the half and it appeared this game would not be much different from all but one of the games so far in the season. But, like the Notre Dame game when UCLA had a 43–34 lead at the half, Oregon State made a charge to start the second half, then held the ball late in the game.

Ralph Miller's team nearly blew a 57–50 lead with three minutes left by taking some bad shots, and it was 57–56 with 33 seconds left. But Oregon State freshman guard George Tucker made four free throws inside the last 25 seconds and the Oregon State team that would finish the season 13–13, had its first win over UCLA since 1966.

UCLA had not lost back-to-back games since 1966, a streak of 233 consecutive games. On Saturday night, February 16, they faced Dick Harter's Ducks team that had lost on Friday night to Southern California, 76–61.

Harter was the head coach at Pennsylvania before he came across the country to Oregon. He had attracted national attention by leading Penn to a 53–3 record his last two years there. His freshman coach in 1969–70 was Digger Phelps. Harter had scouted the Notre Dame vs. UCLA game in South Bend back in January and took a lot of notes.

Harter's approach was similar to Phelps in that he played a physical defense, some said to an excessive extent. After the 1973 game at Oregon, an 11-point UCLA win, Wooden was quoted as saying, "It was the roughest game I've ever been in."

The always quotable Greg Lee said, "Last year was the only time ever I was afraid on the court." An incident contributed to that feeling. During that game a spectator ran out on the court and kicked Walton.

For the second straight night UCLA got off to a good start and led, 11–2. Oregon came back thanks to the play of forward Bruce Coldren, who made 8 of 9 shots from the field in the first half. But despite Coldren's incredible performance, it was 32–26 in favor of the Bruins at halftime.

Oregon took a 52–43 lead with about seven minutes left thanks in part to the play of Ron Lee, an athletic sophomore guard who would go on to become the Ducks' all-time leading scorer (and still is today) with over 2,000 points.

After Walton made a field goal, Oregon went into a stall, which frustrated a Bruins team that was seven points behind. Oregon's ball handling was outstanding and the Ducks won, 56–51.

It was the fewest points by UCLA all season, in fact the fewest in a loss since a 46–44 loss to USC in 1969. Oregon had run a patient offense that hit 61 percent of its shots and Oregon's hometown stat crew credited the Ducks with 23 assists on 25 made baskets. Known for its "kamikaze" defense, the Ducks held UCLA to 45 percent shooting.

"At least I have caught up with my old assistant coach at Penn," Harter said referring to Phelps after the game. "He'll be calling me tonight."

The Bruins had lost both games over the weekend even though they had the lead at the half in both by at least six points. They had trailed at the half in only two games going into the weekend, the win over NC State in December and the first USC game at Pauley.

Most striking was losing consecutive games for the first times since the 1965–66 season when they also lost consecutive games at the two Oregon schools. Plus, both teams were unranked, and under .500 entering the game. Oregon was 8–9 and Oregon State 8–10.

Wooden admitted after the Oregon defeat that he had made some tactical errors in the team's preparation for the games. "I made some changes in our offense the past week to give us more [ball] movement," he said. "I thought it would make us sharper, but instead it made us hesitant. Maybe, in retrospect, I made a mistake."

While the media was upset with Wooden at times because of the limited access he gave to his players, he was honest in his postgame interviews.

One player who was very honest and forthcoming after the Oregon State game was point guard Greg Lee, who didn't really live up to the expectations in 1973–74 he had created when he had 14 assists in the 1973 national championship game against Memphis State. He would finish this year averaging 4.0 points and 2.9 assists per game.

After the Oregon State game he said, "The right people are not playing. I think we were playing better when I was in the lineup, but I don't make those decisions."

After reading that quote in *Sports Illustrated* many felt there were some issues within the UCLA program. If there were, Wooden quelled them quickly because the good Bruins returned the next weekend, and for the last five games of the regular season.

February 22–23 was Senior Weekend with Washington State and Washington coming to Pauley Pavilion. Seniors led the way in a 25-point win over Washington State on Friday and a 34-point win over Washington on Saturday. Wilkes had a season-high 31 points against Washington State, just one point short of Walton's team season high against Notre Dame.

The Bruins dispatched of California on the following Friday night, then struggled to beat Stanford on Saturday night, 62–60. Again, UCLA had an eight-point lead at the half against Stanford, then became complacent in the second half. Walton led the way with 23 points and 14 rebounds.

While the Bruins had won four in in a row since the "Ambush on the Oregon Trail" as *Sports Illustrated* called it, the question was obvious. Which UCLA team was going to show up for the final regular season game against Southern California, a road game in the Los Angeles Sports Arena?

Lose and the Bruins, the 22–3 Bruins who had won seven straight NCAA championships, were not going to the NCAA Tournament. While UCLA was losing back-to-back games in the state of Oregon three weeks earlier, the Trojans were winning two games in the same state playing opposite opponents on consecutive nights.

That weekend allowed Southern California to tie UCLA in the Pac-8 standings and the Trojans had not lost since. Both teams were 11–2 entering the final regular season game. The winner would be 12–2 in the conference and the loser 11–3.

Southern California was 21–3 overall and ranked seventh in the nation. The ACC championship game between NC State and Maryland was a top five matchup and got a lot of the national attention on this March 9 date, but this final regular season game in Los Angeles was just as big and had as much on the line.

Basketball historians today talk about the drama and pressure of the ACC Tournament in 1974 because only one team would go, the winner of the conference championship game. But the pressure involved in this UCLA vs. Southern California game was just as big.

While UCLA had only lost three games to this point in the season, they were the most mercurial John Wooden team in the last decade. The reasons for that inconsistent pattern were unknown, but it didn't stop the media from speculating.

Curry Kirkpatrick wrote in a *Sports Illustrated* article previewing the NCAA Tournament that the media (not him personally) had felt, "The UCLA offense was too predictable, they said. The press was a fraud and didn't work anymore. The guards could not shoot or penetrate. . . . Walton was bothered by a back injury. He had become passive from transcendental meditation, and weak and docile because of his vegetarian diet."

At times Walton would be seen coming into an arena carrying a sack of fruit and vegetables, something that would be applauded today by team nutritionists.

Kirkpatrick wrote the article in a sarcastic tone because he knew the results and statistics of UCLA's victory in this regular season final. The Bruins played their best first half of the year against the Trojans, perhaps their best first half at both ends of the court in any year against a quality opponent.

UCLA held the Trojans to just four baskets in the first half and had a 47–13 lead at the intermission. A 34-point lead against the No. 7 team in the nation on their home court. Walton had 20 points and 16 rebounds at halftime and finished with 26 points and 20 rebounds, his 14th career 20–20 game, and UCLA coasted to an 82–52 victory to clinch the Pac-8 title and more importantly, the NCAA bid, which in those days with just 25 teams in the field, also carried a bye to the NCAA Tournament's Sweet 16.

It was a dominant performance in all phases. UCLA shot 54 percent from the field to just 29 percent for USC and the Bruins dominated the boards, 55–32.

UCLA was back to its old self. Look out NC State, Notre Dame, Marquette, and the other teams viewed as threats to end the dynasty.

THE NCAA TOURNAMENT

UCLA's first game of the 1974 NCAA Tournament was against Dayton in Tucson, Arizona. In reading this today you might think of this as an advantage for UCLA, because they now play at Arizona because of the Wildcats' Pac-8 affiliation. (That will end when UCLA joins the Big Ten in 2024.) But in 1974, Arizona was in the WAC and no UCLA players had ever played in that arena.

Both teams were coming off outstanding performances. UCLA had crushed USC to win the Pac-8 championship and Dayton had beaten No. 3 Notre Dame in its final regular season game, handing the Irish just their second loss of the season. The Flyers then defeated Cal State Los Angeles, 88–80 in their opening round NCAA Tournament game.

Dayton was 20–7 and ranked 20th in the country entering the game thanks to a three-headed monster scoring attack of Mike Sylvester, Donald Smith, and Johnny Davis. In the win over Notre Dame, they had combined for 64 points, but they added 10 onto that against Cal State Los Angeles as Sylvester had 30, and Smith and Davis had 22 apiece.

Davis would go on to play with Walton on the Portland Trail Blazers NBA championship team in 1976–77, but on this night they were opponents.

UCLA jumped out to a 48–36 lead at the half, and it appeared it would be an easy road to a 37th straight NCAA Tournament win.

But Sylvester started hitting shots from the elbow and Dayton closed the gap. The score was tied at 80 and Dayton had the ball. Davis drove to the lane and hit a jump shot with 14 seconds left to put Dayton up by two, but a whistle had blown just prior to the shot. Dayton coach Don Donoher had called a timeout, and it was ruled to have been called before Davis's shot. Donoher then called for a play that would give Davis a shot from the left wing, but his game-winning attempt with five seconds left was a bit long and hit off the back rim. The two teams went to overtime.

The first overtime was tied at 88 with a minute left. UCLA had the ball this time and ran the clock down. On the possession, Donoher had his team double team Walton in the post, daring freshman Marques Johnson to take an unguarded 20-footer from the right wing. But he wouldn't shoot it. After a scramble, a jump ball was called with 10 seconds left, but UCLA got the midcourt tip (no possession arrow in 1974).

Johnson then drove the ball to the lane and missed a guarded jumper, sending the game to a second overtime.

Both teams scored 10 points in the second extra period. Dayton had the last possession this time, but Walton stole the ball on a pass to the post with just five seconds left. He dribbled the ball up court and with time running out, put up a 23-footer from the left wing, a shot that would be just outside the three-point line today. The shot missed and the teams headed to a third overtime period.

This time UCLA dominated, especially on defense. The Bruins allowed just two points in the third session and scored 13, leading to a 111–100 victory.

With the game lasting 55 minutes, the first triple overtime NCAA game since 1957, there were some large numbers. Dave Meyers led UCLA with 28 points on 13-for-25 shooting, just the second time he had led UCLA in scoring all year, the first time since the St. Bonaventure game on December 22. Walton had 27 points and 19 rebounds, while Johnson finished with 14 and Greg Lee 12. It is interesting to note that Lee, who had complained about playing time after the two losses in Oregon, was now playing much more.

Dayton was led by Sylvester's 36 points and 13 rebounds. His 36 points were the fourth most scored by an individual against a Wooden coached team, the most in an NCAA Tournament game. "He was amazing," said John Wooden of Sylvester's performance after the game. "Defensively we didn't play him that bad. He was under great pressure."

With the triple overtime win against Dayton in the books, UCLA needed one more victory to reach the Final Four for the eighth straight year. A San Francisco team that was led by future professionals Kevin Restani and Phil Smith stood in the way.

San Francisco was one of the Cinderella teams of the tournament. Bob Gaillard's team started off the season 1–6, but had won 15 of its last 17 entering this game with UCLA. They won the WCAC to get into the tournament, then defeated 17th ranked New Mexico to advance to the Elite Eight against the Bruins.

UCLA continued to toggle between outstanding and mediocre performances, something that dated to the game at Stanford on March 2 when the Bruins won by just 62–60.

This was a day of efficient play on both ends of the court. UCLA shot 51 percent from the field and Wilkes led the way with 27 points, while Walton had 17 points and nine rebounds in an 83–60 win. Wilkes put up 28 shots because San Francisco was double teaming Walton inside, allowing Wilkes to shoot from the perimeter. Restani (20) and Smith (18) got 38 points but the rest of the Dons scored just 22 and shot just 8-for-27 from the field.

The victory was the Bruins' 38th consecutive NCAA Tournament victory, still a record today by 25. In many ways that streak could be considered more impressive than the overall 88 game-winning streak because every one of those games was a win or go home situation.

NC STATE'S REVENGE

That sent UCLA to Greensboro, North Carolina, where they would face North Carolina State, a team they had beaten by 84–66 back on December 15 at a neutral site in St. Louis. This semifinal game also went in the books as a neutral site contest, but in reality, it was not.

Greensboro, North Carolina, is just 80 miles from Raleigh, the home of the Wolfpack. The geography had never been set up so well for any college basketball team. NC State captured its second straight ACC Tournament championship by winning just two games in Greensboro. Granted one was a heart stopping "best game in ACC history" win over fourth-ranked Maryland.

They started the East Regional at their home arena, Reynolds Coliseum, where they defeated Marvin Barnes and Providence by 14, and then Billy Knight and Pittsburgh by 28.

Only a regular season game at Clemson, which is in South Carolina, just 100 miles from the state line, was out of the Tar Heel state for the Wolfpack out of their last 11 games. It was the most geographically friendly postseason schedule for a team since . . . UCLA played the 1972 Final Four at the LA Sports Arena, then played the 1973 West Regionals at Pauley Pavilion.

When NC State practiced on Thursday at their home court in Raleigh, 6,000 fans showed up. There was so much excitement about the possibility of NC State playing in the Final Four in their home state that there were 88,000 ticket requests for Final Four. The Greensboro Coliseum sat just 15,829 for the semifinals on March 23.

Wooden acknowledged there would be a "home court" advantage for NC State in pregame press briefings, but he also stated that his program had the same advantage in recent years.

Much of the pregame talk centered around the incredible success of both programs in the last two years. NC State had won 55 games and lost just one in the last two years and the Bruins had won 53 of their last 56.

Storyline number two centered around NC State star forward David Thompson who had taken a frightening fall in the regional final against Pittsburgh. He went to the hospital, was bandaged to cover a 15-stitch cut on his head, then heroically returned to the game to sit on the bench and watch his team finish off the Panthers by 28 points.

All knew he had some sort of a concussion and it was not known if he could play in the national semifinal. Protocols were vastly different when it came to concussions in 1974. One must wonder if he would have played in the Final Four at all with today's standards.

The third storyline centered around the rankings of the teams. NC State was ranked No. 1 and UCLA No. 2, which relegated the other semifinal, Marquette vs. Kansas, to "JV" status in the minds of the national media . . . and perhaps the coaches too.

Sports Illustrated's Curry Kirkpatrick attended a Friday evening party before the semifinal games and quoted Al McGuire as saying his game vs. Kansas was the "B Class Division," while Kansas's Ted Owens called it the "preliminary" game. It was in fact the first game of the semifinal Saturday.

Most predicted the winner of the NC State vs. UCLA game would go on to win the national championship on Monday night. Many long-time college basketball fans remember it as the national championship game and can't tell you who NC State beat in the championship game.

It was a similar situation to the United States winning the 1980 Olympic Gold medal in men's hockey. The United States defeated the Russians in its next to last game of the tournament, a game everyone remembers, but beat Finland 4–2 to win the gold medal.

UCLA had won the December 15 game by 18 points, but those who base their livings in Las Vegas on point spreads had UCLA favored by just three points in this game.

The first half was very similar to the first meeting when UCLA had a one point lead at intermission, 33–32. There were four ties and seven lead changes in the first 12 minutes. A key point in the game took place at the 13:35 mark when NC State's 7-foot-4 center Tom Burleson picked up a second foul. Obviously, he was the man charged with guarding Walton.

NC State Coach Norm Sloan went to his bench and 6-foot-8 reserve, two-sport star Tim Stoddard. Stoddard was a star pitcher on the NC State baseball team who went on to pitch 13 years in the major leagues as a relief pitcher. He had 26 saves for the Baltimore Orioles in 1980 to rank fourth in the league. Two of the three ahead of him that year, Dan Quisenberry and Goose Gossage, are in the Hall of Fame.

Stoddard's basketball performance on this Saturday in Greensboro was Hall of Fame quality as well when you consider he was being called on to defend Bill Walton, one of the greatest college players in history.

Stoddard held his own during an important six minutes in the first half. He scored a banker, then forced Walton into a couple of turnovers. He then got a couple of rebounds and another basket from the right corner to give the Pack a 17–14 lead. He actually outscored Walton for the six minutes he was in the game at this point and UCLA trailed by just three when he left the game.

NC State held a 35–31 lead late in the half, but the Bruins scored the last four points. The first bucket came at the one-minute mark by Wilkes on an elbow jumper. NC State went into a spread to hold for one shot, but Mo Rivers was called for traveling with five seconds left.

The Wizard of Westwood lived up to his nickname and put Meyers back in the game for freshman Marques Johnson. Meyers received a pass at midcourt, took a couple of dribbles and banked in a 35-footer from the left wing to send the two teams to the locker room deadlocked at 35.

We have seen many games over the years where a last-second shot at the end of a half can give a team momentum in the early stages of the second half and that was the case in this game.

UCLA went on a 6–0 run to start the second half with two of the made field goals by Walton, giving the Bruins a 10–0 run spanning the end of the first half and the start of the second.

It was 41–36 before Stoddard stopped the streak with a free throw and Thompson cut it back to three points with a steal and layup. (What a dunk it would have been had dunking been allowed in 1974.)

The Bruins continued to play well and had a 49–38 lead on a rebound basket by Walton. At this point you wondered if UCLA would go on to another 18-point victory as it did in the first meeting. NC State had committed five turnovers in the first five minutes of the second half and at a timeout, famed NBC television announcer Curt Gowdy said to his partner Tommy Hawkins, "I wonder if this is going to be another classic Bill Walton performance in an NCAA Tournament game." He had scored 19 points and had 13 rebounds at this point and there were still 15 minutes left.

The two teams traded streaks over the next 10 minutes. NC State cut the Bruins' 11-point lead to five at 51–46 on a long jumper by Monte Towe. UCLA then ran it back up to 11 at 57–46 at the 10:40 mark on a Meyers jump shot.

NC State was a team capable of scoring quickly and they did over the next 1:31, outscoring the Bruins 10–0 to cut the margin to 57–56 when Stoddard picked up a loose ball and scored.

The Pack finally took the lead on a lob pass to Thompson. He was also fouled on the play, but missed the free throw. But a whistle blew after the miss because a UCLA player stepped into the lane. It gave Thompson another free throw attempt and he made it to give NC State a 63–61 lead with 4:50 left.

Obviously in a game that went to overtime, that extra made free throw would prove to be a huge mistake for UCLA.

Meyers tied the game at 63 at the 4:30 mark after a pass from Walton. Norm Sloan then ordered a four corners offense, and this game that included three future Naismith Hall of Fame players ground to a halt for the rest of the half.

NC State held the ball until the 2:40 mark when Thompson was fouled by Greg Lee. Lee was not trying to foul and Thompson was not making a move toward the basket; it happened 30 feet from the basket.

Thompson had a one-and-one opportunity (all non-shooting fouls from the seventh foul on were one-and-one in 1974), but he missed the front end and UCLA had the rebound. Wooden called timeout with 2:36 left and soon after Walton made one of his patented bank shots from the left to give the Bruins a 65–63 lead. Now trailing, NC State was not interested in holding the ball for two minutes for a shot to tie. They went right to Thompson who converted a lob pass at the rim to tie the score at 65.

UCLA was patient with the score tied, but they did not hold for a last shot. Walton took a hook shot with 50 seconds left and it missed.

Now NC State had the ball with a shot to win and called timeout with 23 seconds left.

Wooden changed his defense during the timeout and on that last possession he double-teamed Burleson in the post and left Stoddard open on the wing. Meyers went back and forth between Burleson and Stoddard. You could tell Stoddard was instructed to go to Burleson, but he just wasn't open, so he took an open 18-footer from the right wing with a few seconds left and missed.

So, this thrilling game between the top two teams in the nation went to overtime.

Wooden and the Bruins fans had to feel confident with the game going to extra minutes. They had just beaten Dayton in triple overtime, and Wooden had never lost an overtime game in his UCLA career.

The two teams traded field goals in the first 75 seconds of the overtime, then NC State got the ball after a steal by Stoddard, who was continuing to make big plays. Again Sloan called for his team to hold the ball, at least until UCLA played a more aggressive defense that might open something up for a drive by Thompson.

State held the ball from the three-minute mark until 15 seconds remained when Sloan called another timeout. This time the Pack got the ball into Burleson, but his last-second shot over Walton was contested and it missed sending the game into a second overtime.

UCLA scored the first seven points of the second overtime to take a 74–67 lead. But again, the Bruins let up. A tip-in by Burleson with two minutes left brought NC State back to 75–73.

UCLA was up 75–74 with Meyers on the line for a one-and-one. UCLA was 11-for-11 from the line at this point in the game. Gowdy told the millions watching the game on television that statistic and of course Meyers missed.

NC State came back down court and Thompson banked in a shot with 50 seconds remaining to give them a 76–75 lead. Lee missed a shot and there was a foul on Wilkes in the rebound action, his fifth of the game.

Thompson made both ends of the one-and-one with 32 seconds left. On the trip back up court, Mo Rivers knocked the ball out of bounds at side court about 10 feet from the timeline. Down three with 29 seconds left, and wanting to score quickly, Lee made a long pass attempt up court for Walton, but Burleson stepped in front for the biggest steal of his career. With 12 seconds left Towe was fouled, and was his style, caught the ball from the official and shot the free throws without a dribble or hesitation. Both went through to ice the game.

Walton hit a jumper with two seconds left and the game ended with an 80–77 score.

Walton and Burleson played to a statistical standoff. Walton, who played all 50 minutes, finished with 29 points and 18 rebounds, while Burleson, who played 42 minutes, had 20 points and 14 rebounds.

Thompson had won the battle of future Hall of Fame forwards. In their earlier meeting at St. Louis, Wilkes was clearly the better player, but on this day, Thompson won the battle. The 6'4" NC State forward scored 28 points and added 10 rebounds, while Wilkes had 15 and seven rebounds. Thompson had shot 7-for-20 in the game in St. Louis, and Wilkes shot 5-for-17 in Greensboro.

Both coaches played just seven players. NC State reserves played just 22 total minutes and UCLA's played just 10 minutes. Future NBA players Ralph Drollinger and Richard Washington never appeared in the game for UCLA.

Stoddard finished with nine points, nine rebounds, five assists, and three steals in one of the top unsung hero performances in Final Four history.

Two numbers haunted UCLA in two of its four losses in 1974. Twice they blew 11-point leads in the second half, the first against Notre Dame when the Irish came back from 11 points down with 3:22 left, and twice in the second half of this national semifinal against NC State.

Losing leads was a problem for this UCLA team, and that had not been the case the previous seven seasons. Perhaps it was just natural complacency from a veteran team (they started four seniors) that was so used to winning. Many coaches will tell you it is a positive to have a confident team that expects to win. But there are teams that can become overconfident from long-term success.

And the number 29 was haunting as well for UCLA. Dwight Clay's shot from the corner with 29 seconds left gave Notre Dame its 71–70 lead on January 19. In this game, a UCLA turnover off an inbounds play with 29 seconds left prevented the Bruins from cutting NC State's lead to a point.

All in attendance will tell you, this was the game for the national championship. It is a wonder the NCAA didn't change its rules and reseed teams once they got to the Final Four. Had that been the case, NC State would have played Kansas and UCLA would have played Marquette in the semifinals.

This quote from David Thompson after NC State's championship win over Marquette two nights later certainly told the story: "It's funny, we celebrated more after we beat UCLA than we did after winning the championship. After the semifinals, they tore up Hillsborough Street [which runs alongside campus], but they weren't as wild after we beat Marquette."

UCLA was relegated to the third-place game against Kansas on Monday night. "We were devastated [after losing to NC State]," recalled Bill Walton in a 2004 article by Mike Lopresti in *USA Today*. "I'm not sure I am over it [the loss to NC State] 30 years later. I wish they would have eliminated the consolation game before we had the embarrassment of playing in it." The last consolation game was at the 1981 NCAA Tournament in Philadelphia.

While the seven-time defending NCAA champion was not motivated to play in that game, UCLA still had plenty of talent to beat Kansas. UCLA won 78–61.

UCLA saw its 38-game NCAA Tournament winning streak come to an end at the hands of NC State at the 1974 Final Four. *NC State University*

Kansas seemed plenty motivated in the first half and took a 38–31 lead at intermission. But, UCLA won the second half, 47–23.

Wooden used the game as a prep for the following season, as 10 different players played at least 10 minutes and only Pete Trgovich, who had not played against NC State, played more than anyone with 25 minutes. Trgovich finished the game with 14 points, the team's leading scorer for the only time all season.

Wooden's desire to give returning players experience in a game in this atmosphere would pay off the following season.

As you can imagine, Walton's last college game in a consolation contest was not memorable from an individual standpoint. He scored just six points on 3-for-3 shooting, and missed all three of his free throws, in 20 minutes.

The consolation game did accomplish one thing for Walton, however. He needed five rebounds in that game to break Kareem Abdul-Jabbar's career UCLA record of 1,367. Walton got eight rebounds and finished with 1,370, still the UCLA record today. Even though players today can play four years and many more games, no UCLA player since has come within 300 rebounds of the mark.

UCLA had finished 26–4, nearly the same record as Notre Dame's 26–3. Those were great records, but both teams were disappointed in their respective finishes.

For the first time, and one of just two seasons in history (1975 the other), the Associated Press had a poll after the championship game of the NCAA Tournament. Previously the poll had ended either after the conclusion of the regular season or the first round of games of the NCAA Tournament.

Today the AP final poll is conducted after the conference tournament games.

We don't know why the AP conducted a final poll for only those two years other than someone in charge thought these NCAA Tournament games should be reflected in the final poll.

At some point someone at the AP thought it was ridiculous to have a final poll after the tournament where the winner of the national championship was not No. 1 in their final poll. For instance, Marquette came from nowhere to win the 1977 national championship. But with seven losses, some of the voters didn't think Al McGuire's team should be the poll champion with that many defeats.

The *USA Today* coaches poll still has a final poll after the NCAA Tournament, so the debate rages on.

In the 1974 final poll, NC State was voted first, no controversy there. The Pack lost only one game back in December to UCLA and won the rest.

UCLA was voted second and Marquette third. The number-four team was very interesting in that Maryland, a team that did not play in the postseason, got the nod there. The Terps lost five games, three to NC State.

A look to this final AP poll of March 26, 1974, reveals that Maryland was one of eight final top 20 teams that did not have the opportunity to play in the NCAA Tournament because of the rule that allowed just one team from a conference to participate.

It is amazing that rule stood from 1939 through 1974. The final top 20 teams who did not play in the NCAA Tournament that year were Maryland (No. 4), Indiana (9), Long Beach State (10), Purdue (11), North Carolina (12), Alabama (14), Utah (15), and Southern California (17).

Notre Dame, despite losing two of its last four games, finished fifth thanks to beating three of the Final Four teams. Michigan was sixth, which was a bit of a surprise in that they lost in the regional final to Marquette, and Final Four team Kansas finished seventh.

CHAPTER 12

John Wooden Goes Out a Winner

THE 1974–75 SEASON STARTED A NEW ERA IN COLLEGE BASKETBALL. Bill Walton and his gang had graduated, defending national champion NC State no longer had 7-foot-4 center Tom Burleson, and Notre Dame no longer had John Shumate and Gary Brokaw.

Plus, after seeing a final AP top 20 that included eight teams that did not have the opportunity to play in the 1974 NCAA Tournament, the national governing body made a new rule that allowed more than one team from a conference participate in the now 32 team (up from 25 teams) NCAA Tournament.

Sports Illustrated's preseason issue trumpeted Denny Crum's Louisville Cardinals as the preseason top team in the nation followed by defending national champion NC State and generational player David Thompson in second, Bobby Knight's Indiana Hoosiers were predicted third, and UCLA fourth.

The magazine had South Carolina fifth, Kansas sixth, Alabama seventh, and Pennsylvania (that's right, from the Ivy League) eighth.

The Associated Press had NC State as their preseason No. 1 with UCLA second, Indiana third, Maryland fourth, Marquette fifth, Kansas sixth, South Carolina seventh, and Louisville eighth.

This was just the second time in the last nine years that UCLA was not the preseason No. 1 team by the Associated Press (South Carolina was preseason No. 1 for the 1969–70 season).

During the preseason a reporter asked John Wooden, "Can UCLA come back?" Wooden answered the scribe, "Where have we been?"

Such were the expectations for UCLA during this era. They had won seven straight national championships, then lost in double overtime in the semifinals of the Final Four by just three points to a team that was essentially playing at home.

Looking back, it was absurd to think that some people believed UCLA was done when Walton and Wilkes graduated. They still had John Wooden running the show and a large group of high school All-Americans ready to take on increased roles.

But *Sports Illustrated* wrote in its preseason issue, "Because of past standards, coming back [for UCLA] means all the way, and that will be some task. For the first time since the Bruin reign began, UCLA has neither a dominant force in the middle, nor an experienced leader in the backcourt."

When we look at the roster of that 1974–75 team and the boxscores throughout the season, we laugh today. The team had three centers between 6'11" and 7'2," all of whom went on to play in the NBA, plus two forwards and two guards who were future NBA players. That is seven NBA players on that 1974–75 roster.

One of the more interesting preseason articles for the 1974–75 season was written in the official NCAA record book, a publication that featured UCLA senior Dave Meyers on the cover. In an article by Ed Chay of the *Cleveland Plain Dealer*, Wooden was quoted as saying the 1973–74 season was difficult because he had such a veteran team.

"When you have the same group for three years, they're a little more difficult to work with. They don't mean to be, but they are. I can't find fault with my team, but I failed to motivate them. And I'm not talking about won-lost record. In many games we won, I didn't think we displayed intensity and didn't play up to our potential."

With Walton graduated, Bruins fans looked to see what Ralph Drollinger and Richard Washington could do up front. In the season opening win over Wichita State, Drollinger had 21 points and 17 rebounds on 8-for-11 shooting. Washington added 14 points and seven rebounds on 7-for-10 shooting. The Bruins won 85–74 and there was renewed enthusiasm in Pauley Pavilion.

Four more wins followed before Notre Dame came calling to Pauley for the first of two meetings this season. Adrian Dantley was now the Notre Dame star and he played like it, scoring 30 points on 15-for-23 shooting, one of the few games in his career, college or pro, that he did not go to the free throw line, much to the dismay of Digger Phelps.

Dantley and the Irish threw a scare into UCLA and took a 10-point lead at halftime, but Wooden made some adjustments on Dantley defensively and this time there was no John Shumate or Gary Brokaw to bail out the Fighting Irish team. Richard Washington hit 10 of 12 shots and scored 25 points and Meyers added 16 points and 10 rebounds as UCLA outscored the Irish 48–25 in the second half and won easily, 85–72.

The college basketball world remembered how close Maryland came to ending the Bruins' streak at 76 the previous year when UCLA won by just a single point on a late steal by Meyers in the second game of the year in Pauley Pavilion. Now the return engagement was scheduled for Cole Field House in College Park, Maryland.

There was an odd twist in that UCLA and Maryland were two of four teams playing in the Maryland Invitational, so each had to win a Friday night game before meeting on Saturday, December 28. Both accomplished that detail with UCLA defeating a St. Bonaventure team that did not have anyone resembling Bob Lanier. Maryland beat Georgia Tech, who was an independent at the time, by 35 points.

That set up a Saturday night game between second-ranked UCLA and fifth-ranked Maryland, one of the top December games of the college season. The contest attracted national media attention, but most of the prominent players in the game from the previous year were now in the NBA.

It turned out to be a game that enhanced Dave Meyers's professional stock, as he scored 32 points on 14-for-22 shooting to lead the Bruins to an 81–75 victory. Steve Sheppard and Owen Brown combined for 38 points for Maryland, but they could not rebound like Len Elmore had the previous year. The Bruins were +7 in the rebound margin category and outshot the Terps 57 percent to 43 percent.

Lefty had now lost both of his shots at beating the Wizard of West-wood in his attempt to make Maryland the UCLA of the East.

With that win on the road, people were starting to think the UCLA dynasty might not be dead after all.

The winning continued for two more weeks as victories over David-son, Oklahoma (by 45 points), Washington, and Washington State followed. Meyers, Washington, and Drollinger all took turns leading the team in scoring and rebounding. Marques Johnson, who was rebounding from a summer bout with hepatitis, was just rounding into shape.

On January 17, 1975, the same weekend as the trip to South Bend and the end of the streak the year before, UCLA made a much shorter road trip to Stanford. Shockingly, the result was the same as the previous season.

The Bruins were 12–0 with a victory margin approaching 20 points per game and ranked second in the nation. Stanford was 6–6 and had just ended a four-game losing streak by beating Oregon State.

But Stanford shocked the Bruins with a 37–24 lead at the half, then hung on for a 64–60 victory. Center Rich Kelley, who had battled Walton the previous two years, had 22 points and eight rebounds on 9-for-12 shooting. Junior forward Ed Schweitzer also scored 22 and pulled down 13 rebounds. His defense helped hold UCLA to 38 percent field goal shooting. Stanford lost the turnover margin 20–9, but still found a way to win.

It proved to be one of the great weekends in Stanford basketball his-tory, because they beat sixth-ranked Southern California the next night. The two wins vaulted Coach Howard Dallmar's team into the top 15 in the nation the next Monday. But it didn't last long and Stanford finished with a 12–14 record. At the end of the season Stanford fans and UCLA fans must have wondered, "How in the world did that happen?"

The Bruins were stunned as well, but felt a little better when Stanford also beat Southern California on the same weekend and UCLA came back to best California 102–72 the next night.

While Wooden was a wizard when it came to most of the respon-sibilities of a head coach, figuring out his non-conference schedule was puzzling at times. Perhaps he wanted to give his team a new challenge, or perhaps he was just so confident in his team.

On Thursday night, January 23, UCLA easily defeated UC Santa Barbara in Pauley Pavilion behind 30 points and 11 rebounds from Washington.

The next day they got on a plane and flew multiple time zones eastward to South Bend, Indiana, to face Notre Dame in a nationally televised Saturday afternoon game at the Athletic and Convocation Center. In previous years, Wooden had scheduled a game in Chicago either the Friday night before or the Thursday night before at the Chicago Stadium, leading to a 2 or 3 a.m. arrival at Notre Dame. But at least they were somewhat used to the time zone.

As big as the rivalry had become, one might have thought Wooden would have scheduled the Santa Barbara game earlier in the week or earlier in the season to give his team more rest for the long trip.

As usual, Digger Phelps had the Notre Dame crowd wired and he had that revenge factor going dating to the game at Pauley back in December.

Once again Dantley was terrific and scored 32 points on 13-for-21 shooting, giving him 28-for-46 from the field and 62 points in two games against the Bruins that year. Billy Paterno, who was becoming a star in his own right, had a double-double with 16 points and 10 rebounds, and the 7–6 unranked Irish defeated the No. 4 Bruins, 84–78.

There was no doubt this was a very talented but young UCLA team, but there were some results during 1974–75 that made UCLA fans wonder if Wooden's 27th team would even make the tournament.

Losing to a Stanford team with a 6–6 record, then to a Notre Dame team with a 7–6 record was something his eight previous UCLA teams had done just twice, the two losses on the Oregon trail the previous year.

There was another scare at Oregon on February 8 when UCLA won at McArthur Court, 107–103. UCLA shot 64 percent from the field, 74 percent in the second half, but still won by just four.

At times this UCLA team got lost on defense and it showed in this game. UCLA won the second half, 61–60. Meyers saved the Bruins with

39 points in 39 minutes, and Drollinger scored 18 and made 8 of 10 free throws. Ron Lee, a future pro, and Stu Jackson, a future pro and college coach, both scored 27 for the Ducks.

The two teams met just six days later and it was a completely different game with UCLA winning 96–66 behind a balanced Bruins attack that featured five double-figure scores. They were two UCLA wins, but the back-to-back results brought up more questions than answers.

If John Wooden thought the media and fans were questioning his team after the loss to Notre Dame and other close games, he hadn't seen anything yet.

On February 22, Washington defeated UCLA in Seattle, 103–81. It was the largest margin of defeat for a Wooden-coached team since a 27-point loss (110–83) at Illinois to open the 1964–65 season. Washington had five players in double figures led by Larry Jackson's 27 points and 14 rebounds.

Once again UCLA had some defensive problems and allowed Washington to make 48 field goals and shoot 55 percent from the field, while UCLA shot 37 percent.

The following week in practice the defensive drills intensified and UCLA snapped out of their defensive funk and beat California, 51–47. It was the fewest points a UCLA opponent had scored in 40 games.

That defensive effort carried over the next night in a revenge game (although Wooden would never call it that) against Stanford. Meyers had 21 points and this time UCLA held Stanford to 39 percent shooting, as UCLA clinched the Pac-8 title on senior night, 93–59.

The Bruins wrapped up a 12–2 league schedule with a 72–68 win on the road over Southern California.

UCLA entered the NCAA Tournament on a modest three-game winning streak. They had won nine of their last 10, but four of the wins had been by five points or less and the loss was by 22 points.

The media would not count out a John Wooden–coached team in the NCAA Tournament, a program that had won 39 of its last 40 tournament games. The Bruins were 23–3 overall, but an even more impressive 8–0 versus top 20 teams (at the time of the game). But they had also lost three games to unranked team, the most since the 1965–66 team lost four.

UCLA's NCAA Tournament Run

With the NCAA Tournament at 32 teams for the first time, everyone in the field played a first-round game. When you look at the list of teams UCLA played in the 1975 NCAA Tournament you might think the order of the first two games was backward. UCLA played Michigan first, then met Montana in the second round.

The first-round Michigan game was at the Performing Arts Coliseum in Pullman, Washington, the same facility UCLA had beaten Washington State on February 20, by a 69–61 score.

This game with the Wolverines would be even closer.

Michigan came into the tournament with a 19–7 record, but they were 0–3 against top 20 teams. Many of the same players who had upset third-ranked Notre Dame in the NCAA Tournament the year before in Tuscaloosa were now attempting to upset a second-ranked UCLA team the next year.

Campy Russell, who had torched Notre Dame for 36 points the previous year, was now in the NBA, but Johnny Orr still had C. J. Kupec, a future pro, and point guard Steve Grote, who would lead Michigan to the NCAA championship game the next year.

It was an up-tempo game and the Wolverines led at the half 50–46. But UCLA tied the game and sent it into overtime tied at 87. UCLA then took control in overtime, winning the extra period, 16–4 and the game, 103–91. The high possession game was incredibly well played by both offenses as each team had just 10 turnovers.

Wooden had decided to start a front court of Richard Washington, Marques Johnson, and Dave Meyers and bring Ralph Drollinger off the bench. All three starters scored at least 22 points and combined for 70 of the 103, and the Bruins won the rebounding, 59–41.

Kupec scored 28 for Michigan and Joe Johnson added 24, while Grote added 14 points, nine rebounds, and four assists in playing all 45 minutes.

The win sent UCLA to the West Regional and a Sweet 16 game with Montana, who had won the Big Sky Conference under head coach Jud Heathcote. Heathcote would go on to win the national championship at Michigan State just four years later thanks to his ability to keep Magic Johnson in-state.

Heathcote had another future NBA star on his Montana roster in Michael Ray Richardson, who started this game as a freshman, but he was not the key player that kept the Grizzlies in the game. Eric Hays, a 6'3" forward, lit up UCLA like he was Adrian Dantley and scored 32 points on 13-for-16 shooting, had seven rebounds and six assists in the best all-round game by a UCLA opponent all year.

But the Bruins had too much inside in the end, as Washington and Drollinger combined for 24 points and 20 rebounds, leading to a 67–64 win.

Those two close victories sent UCLA to the West Regional final for the ninth straight year against an Arizona State team that had won the Western Athletic Conference, was ranked seventh in the AP poll, and had lost just three games all year.

This game would be drastically different in pace because Ned Wulk's team averaged 87 points a game in 1974–75, 16th in the nation. They had just defeated Alabama and UNLV, teams coached by C. M. Newton and Jerry Tarkanian, respectively, in two high-scoring games to get to the regional final.

This was a talented Arizona State team with three future NBA players in Lionel Hollins, Rudy White, and Scott Lloyd. Those three combined for 51 points against the Bruins.

Marques Johnson had scored just seven points against Montana, so he was motivated to have a strong game this time around. He responded with his high scoring game of the year, 35 points on 14-for-20 shooting and added 12 rebounds in the 89–75 UCLA victory.

It was on to the Final Four for Wooden and UCLA for the ninth straight year, a record that still stands today for one coach at one program. (It will probably still stand when someone writes the 100-year anniversary of UCLA's 88-game winning streak.)

The 1975 Final Four was held in San Diego at the San Diego Sports Arena, obviously not far from the UCLA campus. One might think that would give UCLA the home court advantage, but two of the other three teams were Kentucky and Louisville, and fans of both teams flooded the city for the games of March 29 and 31, 1975.

The always entertaining Curry Kirkpatrick wrote this in his *Sports Illustrated* article about the Final Four, "Because two teams representing the Commonwealth were there, San Diego was overrun with Kentuckiana.

"Nobody rode Secretariat [who had won the Triple Crown in 1973] across the country, but fans of both Louisville and Kentucky arrived by plane, bus, car and hillbilly wagon. One charter flight ran out of bourbon over Little Rock, Ark., and had to make a refill stop in Amarillo, Texas, less the thirsty mob storm the cockpit with empty Old Grand-Dad bottles."

Kentucky faced Syracuse and UCLA faced Louisville in the semifinals on Saturday, March 29.

Louisville had been the preseason No. 1-ranked team in *Sports Illustrated* and they had lived up to their billing as a national championship contender under Denny Crum. The Cards were 27–2 entering the Final Four and ranked third in the AP poll entering the NCAA Tournament.

Crum was in his fourth year at Louisville and this was already his second Final Four. Both times he had to face UCLA and Coach Wooden. He had played for Wooden at UCLA in the 1950s and coached under him first as freshman coach from 1959 to 1961, then as an assistant on the varsity from 1967 to 1971.

Crum had recruited Allen Murphy and Junior Bridgeman and they were now senior leaders of this Louisville team. He had added athletic players Wesley Cox and Phillip Bond as well.

There was some question about Louisville coming into the tournament because they had dominated the Missouri Valley Conference, but had not played a ranked foe in their last 21 games entering the tournament. But in the NCAAs they had defeated No. 16 Rutgers, No. 12 Cincinnati, and No. 4 Maryland to get to San Diego.

Louisville looked prime for a victory and had a 65–61 lead with 48 seconds left. Cards center Bill Bunton blocked two shots by Meyers, but both times the Bruins got the rebound. Washington was fouled on a third attempt and he made two free throws to cut the margin to two.

Thirteen seconds later Marques Johnson stole a Wesley Cox pass and scored the tying basket with 35 seconds left. Louisville had the ball for a game winner, but Bridgeman's shot from the right wing was long and the teams went to overtime.

For the second straight year, UCLA was in an overtime game in the national semifinals. NC State had ended UCLA's season in that game, the only overtime loss of Wooden's UCLA 27-year career.

Murphy took over for Louisville in the overtime and scored seven of his game-high 33 points. His bucket gave Louisville a 74–73 lead and they had the ball when Coach Crum called for the four corners offense.

Crum had been successful in this situation all year and one of the reasons was the presence of guard Terry Howard who was an outstanding free throw shooter. He averaged just seven points a game, but he was 28-for-28 from the foul line entering this game.

With 20 seconds left in the game, Howard was fouled and went to the line for a one-and-one. With every broadcaster in the building stating he had not missed a free throw all year, the collective announcer jinx was too much to overcome, and he missed the front end. It was the third front end of a one-and-one that Louisville missed in the game and they finished just 16-for-27 from the line.

UCLA took possession and called timeout. On the Bruins' last possession Johnson hit Washington with a pass on the right baseline. The 6-foot-9 sophomore then made a jumper from the baseline with just two seconds left, giving the Bruins a 75–74 lead and the victory. It was the 25th and 26th points of the game for Washington.

It was an incredible game, sending UCLA back to the national championship game against another prominent program from Kentucky.

While they had just witnessed two games, the work of the media covering the day's events was just beginning. After the game, Wooden met with his team, congratulated them on the win, then shocked them by saying that Monday night's game, regardless of the outcome, would be his final game as UCLA head coach. According to Seth Davis, who authored the book *Wooden: A Coach's Life*, he told the team, "I'm bowing out. I don't want to, I have to."

Wooden then went to the postgame interview, said a few things about the game, then said, "I've asked [athletic director] J. D. Morgan to release me from my coaching duties at UCLA. I have done that for a number of reasons I'd rather not go into. I just told my players."

It was a shocking announcement nationally and to most of the media, but there had been a hint from of all people, a fellow Pac-8 head coach earlier in the month.

Washington State Coach George Raveling was one of the most enterprising coaches of the era and he wrote an occasional column for the *Seattle Post-Intelligencer*. In his March 8 column he wrote, "The public announcement won't come until mid-April, but John Wooden won't return as head coach at UCLA next year."

Kirkpatrick mentioned what Raveling had said in his 1975 game story.

According to Seth Davis, Raveling was friends with Gene Bartow and Bartow had told him he was going to leave Illinois and be Wooden's replacement. He gave Raveling permission to go with Wooden's intentions in the column, but not to disclose him as the replacement and not reveal his source.

Bartow had impressed J. D. Morgan when he was the head coach at Memphis State and played the Bruins in the NCAA championship game in 1973. Morgan liked his "Clean Gene" persona.

For many years after in interviews for ESPN and HBO, Wooden claimed he had decided to retire as he was walking off the court after that Louisville game. But interviews in various publications indicate Wooden had told some coaching colleagues he had decided before the season that 1974–75 would be his last.

The Sunday press conference prior to the UCLA vs. Kentucky national championship game was all about Wooden's announcement the previous day. Would it be a distraction or a motivation for the UCLA players?

The national championship game between UCLA and Kentucky was certainly a battle of blue bloods. They were and still are the top two teams in Division I college basketball in terms of national championships.

Kentucky entered the championship game with a 26–4 record and a number-two ranking in the AP poll, so this was a No. 1 vs. No. 2 matchup, the first in the national championship game since 1966 when No. 2 Texas-Western upset No. 1 Kentucky. Entering the 2023–24 season, there has been just one matchup of the top two teams in the AP poll in the championship game since, in 2005 when No. 2 North Carolina beat No. 1 Illinois.

Kentucky and coach Joe B. Hall, who was in his third year after replacing Adolph Rupp, had recorded the win of the year so far in the NCAA Tournament by beating No. 1 ranked Indiana in the Regional Finals. The Hoosiers were 31–0 entering that game and would go on to a 32–0 record and national championship the next year. So it was Indiana's only loss over a 64-game period.

The national championship game was competitive, but not quite as thrilling as the semifinal between Louisville and UCLA. The Bruins took a 43–40 lead at the half and the two teams were separated by just one point, 76–75, with 6:49 left.

At that point, UCLA's Dave Meyers went up for a jumper near the foul line and fell into Kentucky guard Kevin Grevey, who would score a game-high 34 points. Meyers was called for the foul and reacted in an inappropriate manner according to the officiating crew of Hank Nichols and Bob Wortman.

Meyers was hit with a technical, much to the disgust of the normally reserved Wooden. On the NBC video of the game, you can see Wooden call Nichols "a crook."

Grevey went to the foul line and missed both technical free throws. They would be the only free throws he missed in 10 attempts that night. Freshman James Lee, who would be a key player in Kentucky's national championship game win in 1978 as a senior, was then called for an illegal screen.

So Kentucky had the opportunity to score four points on that possession and scored zero.

UCLA took over from there and won, 92–85. The score was somewhat ironic in that Kentucky came into the game averaging 92 points a contest and scored 85. UCLA came in averaging 85 a game and scored 92.

Washington, who had hit the game winner against Louisville, had 28 points and 12 rebounds in the championship and was named the tournament's Most Outstanding Player. Meyers added 24 points and 11 rebounds, and Drollinger was an unsung hero with 10 points and 13 rebounds in just 16 minutes.

Drollinger's role had been important because one of the keys to Kentucky's success in the tournament was the play of 6'10", 260-pound centers Rick Robey and Mike Phillips. They combined for just six points and shot just 2-for-10 from the field.

Team captain Andre McCarter saved his best for last with a career-high 14 assists and just two turnovers. His assist total was the same figure Greg Lee had recorded in the NCAA championship game against Memphis State two seasons back.

Wooden was his typical understated self in postgame interviews. In his live interview on NBC with Jim Simpson he said, "I am extremely happy. I've had such a wonderful year with these youngsters. We have not had a single problem all year. I have never had a finer group. I am happy they could go out this way too."

The Bruins played just six players in the game and he addressed that with Simpson. "We are in good condition. One of my theories is to get our players to believe we are in better shape than anyone we play. Whether we are or not, if you can believe that, I think it will help them. I have always had the philosophy to go with six or seven men until the game is won or lost."

His final comment to Simpson might have been the most revealing. "I'm just glad it is over."

This was an era when coaches worked hard, and many of them had such a desire to win that they put undue pressure on themselves.

In hearing Wooden's interview with Simpson and saying he was glad it was over, it makes us wonder if Wooden had the same feelings as Notre Dame football coach Ara Parseghian had just four months earlier. Parseghian had announced his retirement in December 1974 and said his

John Wooden beat Louisville and Kentucky to go out a winner. *Associated Students of the University of California at Los Angeles, Public domain, via Wikimedia Commons*

final game would be in the Orange Bowl against undefeated Alabama. He was 50 years old and basically said he could not take the pressures of coaching any longer. Like Wooden, Parseghian went out a winner with a 13–11 victory over top ranked Alabama in his final game preventing Bear Bryant from a national championship.

Billy Packer was the color commentator on the UCLA vs. Kentucky game, the first Final Four of his legendary broadcasting career. His final comment on the broadcast put the scene at the San Diego Sports Arena that night in perspective.

"This has been, for all of sport, one of the great moments in college athletics history . . . to have John Wooden go out like he did."

CHAPTER 13

The Irish Get to the Final Four

NOTRE DAME ACCOMPLISHED AN OUTSTANDING RUN UNDER HEAD coach Mike Brey, especially in 2014–15 and 2015–16 when he guided the program to consecutive Elite Eights, but he never had anything close to the run of eight straight top 15 AP poll finishes, including six straight top 10s, that Phelps had between 1973–74 and 1980–81.

Phelps had six straight Sweet 16s from 1973–74 through 1978–79. Since the NCAA Tournament went to a field of at least 32 teams in 1974–75, only five coaches have taken the same program to the Sweet 16 of the tournament at least five consecutive tournaments. Those coaches are Dean Smith (North Carolina), Mike Krzyzewski (Duke), Mark Few (Gonzaga), Roy Williams (Kansas), and Digger Phelps (Notre Dame). Few had a streak of eight in a row entering the 2023–24 season.

The 1973–74 season was filled with significant accomplishments, including the breaking of UCLA's 88-game streak and beating three of the four Final Four teams during a 10-day period in the regular season, but reaching the Final Four in 1978 is the highlight of Phelps's career.

There were some similarities between the 1973–74 and 1977–78 teams. The biggest was the influence of the freshman class on each team. Adrian Dantley, Billy Paterno, and Ray Martin were all starters at one time or another in 1974. Previous chapters of this book document the many times they made huge plays in important wins, including Martin's insertion into the lineup with 3:22 left in the UCLA game that ended the streak.

The same could be said for the 1977–78 team, which included freshmen Kelly Tripucka, Orlando Woolridge, and Tracy Jackson. Tripucka and Jackson were big contributors to this team, while Woolridge was a year away, but did start a couple of contests as a freshman. All three went on to play several seasons in the NBA and were top 25 picks in the 1981 draft.

The seasons were also similar in that the 1973–74 team was ranked eighth in the preseason AP poll, remained in the top 10 all year, and finished fifth. The 1977–78 team was fourth in the preseason poll, stayed in the top 10 all year, and finished fifth.

The big difference between Phelps's 1973–74 and 1977–78 teams was depth. The 1973–74 team averaged 90 points a game and had three star players in Shumate, Brokaw, and Dantley, who all scored over 17 points a game. The 1977–78 team averaged 81 points a game, but had four players average between 11 and 14 points per game.

Phelps was optimistic about his 1977–78 team and when reviewing his Notre Dame career in 2004, called it his "Noah's Ark" team because they had two of everything.

"We had Bruce Flowers and Bill Laimbeer [who both played in the NBA] at center, Kelly Tripucka and Bill Hanzlik at small forward [both went on to play at least 10 years in the NBA], Dave Batton and Orlando Woolridge at power forward [both played in the NBA], Duck Williams and Tracy Jackson at the shooting guards [both played in the NBA], and Rich Branning and Stan Wilcox at point guard.

"We sold them on the team concept and they bought into it."

Batton was the leading scorer at 14 points a game. No player scored more than 25 points in any game, a big change from the 1973–74 team that saw Dantley, Brokaw, and Shumate combine for 27 games of at least 25 points.

Balance was the key in 1977–78. Six different players shot at least 50 percent from the field and the team shot 51.5 for the year, second best in Notre Dame history behind the 1973–74 team.

By the end of their careers, seven different players on the 1977–78 roster had scored at least 1,000 points: Tripucka (1,719), Williams (1,433), Jackson (1,293), Branning (1,232), Batton (1,205), Woolridge (1,160), and Flowers (1,029). Mike Douchant of *The Sporting News* determined this was the first team in college basketball history to have seven different players on the roster finish their careers with at least 1,000 points.

The Irish opened the season ranked fourth in the AP poll and they moved up to No. 3 after winning their first five games. The victories over Mississippi, Baylor, Valparaiso, Lafayette, and Northwestern were by an average of 35.6 points a game.

Game six was at UCLA on Saturday, December 11, 1977. The Bruins were 4–0 and ranked fourth in the nation under first-year coach Gary Cunningham. Gene Bartow had taken over for John Wooden in 1975–76, but he lasted just two seasons. They were 51–10 in those two years, went to a Final Four, had two top five final rankings in the AP poll, but lost in the second round of the 1977 NCAA Tournament to Idaho State by one point, an unpardonable sin.

Cunningham had been one of Wooden's longtime assistants. He saw the pressure Wooden was under and declined to succeed him in 1975. But two years later he was ready.

Even though Wooden was in his third year of retirement, the Notre Dame vs. UCLA rivalry was still one of the best in the nation and it attracted national television (either TVS or NBC) every time they played.

Notre Dame had added to its list of accomplishments in the rivalry the previous year by winning in Pauley Pavilion for the first time, a 66–63 victory that ended UCLA's 115-game home winning streak against non-conference opponents.

Coach Phelps was always looking for a way to get a strategic or psychological edge over his opponent. For his first game against Cunningham, he found a way to get both.

If Phelps was coaching today, he probably would be one of the biggest users of social media or other electronic devices to get an edge in recruiting or scouting.

He found a way to do that in the fall of 1977 thanks to the invention of the Betamax video recorder. It was the first time the general public could put something in their homes to record television programs. They were expensive when they first came out, costing upward of $2,500, and the tapes were $25 apiece as well.

It just so happened that Phelps had a friend named Julian Lobosky who lived in Los Angeles. Lobosky was a Notre Dame grad who had a son at Notre Dame at the time and he was the first on his block in Los Angeles to buy a Betamax. He was talking to Digger during the preseason and told him about his recent purchase.

Instantly, it occurred to Phelps that Lobosky could tape UCLA games that aired locally in Los Angeles, then ship them to him so they could be used to scout the Bruins.

"UCLA had three home games on local TV prior to our first game, so Lobo taped them and shipped them to me," said Phelps.

"The only Betamax in South Bend was at a local electronics store so Frank McLaughlin and I spent Monday morning and early afternoon prior to the Saturday game sitting in this store watching the games and taking notes." As a tradeoff, Phelps told everyone he knew about the Betamax and told them to go to that store.

This was a big scouting advantage because in those days no one traded tapes or film. Coaches, usually assistants, went on scouting trips, which was very costly and time consuming when opponents were located 2,000 miles away.

UCLA scheduled just the Notre Dame game for weekend of December 9–10, so with no Friday night game as Wooden used to schedule, Notre Dame practiced at Pauley Pavilion late in the day immediately after UCLA's Friday practice. Just before his team's practice, Phelps spoke briefly with Cunningham.

Phelps said to him, "That [Kurt] Rambis kid from Santa Clara was something against you guys. How about that move he made on the baseline in the closing minutes? I thought that was a bad call on Roy Hamilton at the end of the Colorado game."

Then Phelps really busted Cunningham by mentioning, "Gary, I don't think your tie matched your suit the other night against Seattle."

Cunningham didn't have a clue how Phelps had seen all these details from the games.

Thanks to a 22-point performance by Dave Batton, and a really good scouting report, the Irish won 69–66, the second straight year Phelps and the Irish had beaten the Bruins by exactly three points in Pauley Pavilion.

It was just the sixth loss in 13 years for UCLA at home and only the second time anyone, conference or non-conference, had beaten them at Pauley in consecutive years (USC had done it in the late 1960s).

Notre Dame spent Saturday night in Los Angeles. Before the Irish left for home Phelps bought one of those Betamax recorders at a store in Los Angeles and had it carried on the plane back to South Bend. "It cost $2,500, but I would have paid $5,000 for it," said Phelps. "I was sold on how much it helped us against UCLA."

The following Wednesday night, Notre Dame was to play at Indiana. The Irish had beaten the Hoosiers the previous year in South Bend for just their second defeat since winning the national championship with an undefeated 32–0 record in 1975–76.

The Notre Dame vs. Indiana game was becoming about as big a rivalry as the UCLA game, but because the two teams met just once a year in December, it did not receive the national attention of the UCLA series.

This December 14, 1977, game was played in an unusual atmosphere because the night before, the entire 26-person Evansville basketball traveling party died in a plane crash. The Evansville team was to fly to Nashville, the closest airport to Middle Tennessee State, their opponent the next night.

The plane went into a tailspin and crashed into a side hill on the Evansville Airport property a mere 90 seconds after takeoff.

What really hit home for the Notre Dame team was the knowledge that the same plane was supposed to first take them to Bloomington that same Tuesday. Notre Dame's use of the plane was scratched because of bad weather in South Bend.

Phelps told his senior manager in charge of travel (no one had an assistant AD for administration in those days) to get a bus to Bloomington and to make sure that plane was at the Bloomington airport after the game to bring Notre Dame back home so the players could get some sleep before 8 a.m. Thursday classes.

There were no cell phones and the bus driver didn't have the radio on during the trip. So the team did not learn of the plane crash until they arrived in Bloomington.

Coaching staffs from Indiana and Notre Dame were friends with Evansville head coach Bobby Watson and his staff, so it was an emotional time for both teams.

The next night there was a moment of silence for the Evansville team.

Notre Dame was lethargic and shot just 39.7 percent from the field, the only game all year they failed to shoot 40 percent from the field. Indiana won by a single point, 67–66.

"It was a long, ambivalent ride home," said Phelps. "We were disappointed we lost, but we were all alive."

In telling this story, Phelps remembered one other nightmarish detail about the Evansville plane crash. "Two weeks later I picked up the newspaper to read about David Furr, who was the only Evansville player who was not killed in the crash. He was out for the season due to an injury so he didn't make the trip. The story said he had been killed in an auto accident just two days after Christmas."

From the first game of the 1977–78 season Phelps was serious about giving a lot of his players' action and some thought it was a mistake. He received a lot of criticism for it when the Irish lost three in a row, the one-pointer to Indiana on December 14, a five-pointer against Kentucky in a game played in Louisville, and a 79–70 loss against San Francisco in a game played in Oakland.

San Francisco was just 9–4 and unranked entering the contest. The Dons were coming off a terrific season, and they had the revenge factor going because Notre Dame had beaten them the previous March to end their 29–0 start. The Dons then lost in the first round of the NCAA Tournament and their season was ruined.

More doubt surfaced after a one-point win, 79–78, at St. Bonaventure, a team that was a mediocre 6–4 at the time, but would go on to make the NCAA Tournament.

That win ended the three-game losing streak and actually got the Irish going in the right direction. It turned out to be the first win of a nine-game winning streak. The fourth victory of the streak was a 75–73 win at home over UCLA, who was again ranked fifth in the nation. Duck Williams scored 19 points off the bench to lead another balanced performance, as six players scored at least eight points. It the first time Notre Dame had ever beaten UCLA twice in the same season.

The winning continued on January 29 when the Irish beat Lefty Driesell's Maryland team that featured freshman Albert King, who had been touted as the top player in the high school class of 1976–77.

This game was played in unusual circumstances as well. The Wednesday night prior to this Sunday game, Notre Dame defeated West Virginia, despite 40 points from Mountaineers guard Lowes Moore, at the time the most points scored by an opponent in the Convocation Center.

During the game it started snowing, which was not unusual for January in South Bend, Indiana, but this was a heavy, fine snow. Over a 48-hour period it snowed 40 inches. West Virginia could not get out and stayed at a hotel in South Bend until Saturday.

The local authorities opened the South Bend airport solely to plow a runway for the Maryland team to fly into on Saturday. A plow led the team bus to the Convocation Center so they could practice on late afternoon Saturday.

Father Edmund Joyce decided the game would be played (much to the relief of NBC Sports who was televising the game nationally), and he announced that anyone who could get to the game could get in. No ticket was needed. All roads leading to South Bend were closed, so basically that meant the public had to walk to the game.

That eliminated a lot of people, but it did not preclude the Notre Dame and St. Mary's student bodies from attending. They had been shut in their dorms for four days, so cabin fever had set in.

Nearly every student in the two schools walked to the Convocation Center for the Sunday afternoon game.

This was a talented Maryland team and the Irish led by just 31–28 at halftime. Roger Valdiserri, Notre Dame's legendary sports information director, was told that the university would still be closed on Monday. This was only the second time Notre Dame had closed school due to weather since 1960.

Valdiserri wisely waited until right before the start of the second half to have public address announcer Jack Lloyd make the announcement.

After hearing the announcement students obviously cheered like they had never cheered before.

Notre Dame went on a run to start the second half and beat the Terps soundly, 69–54.

Notre Dame's winning streak continued until February 12 when 11th-ranked DePaul came to South Bend to face the now fourth-ranked Notre Dame team. DePaul had lost just two games all year to this point. They were led by 6-foot-11 center Dave Corzine and guard Gary Garland, whose nickname was the Music Man. He was the half brother of singer Whitney Houston.

It was a close game, but Corzine scored 23 points against Notre Dame's front line and Garland added 16, and DePaul won in overtime. Garland missed a shot with 12 seconds left in overtime and Notre Dame up one. But Rich Branning, a 79 percent free throw shooter on the season, missed the front end of a one and one. Corzine got the rebound, fed Garland, and the DePaul guard made a 20-footer from the left wing with three seconds left to give DePaul the victory and end Notre Dame's 22-game home winning streak.

Two games later Notre Dame traveled to Columbia, South Carolina, to face a South Carolina program that was going in the wrong direction after being selected to three straight NCAA Tournaments in its first three years after leaving the ACC to go independent. They were 12–11 entering this game with Notre Dame, who had dropped from fourth to seventh in the AP poll with the loss to DePaul.

After the teams were tied at 29 at the half, South Carolina won the second half, 36–31. They committed just nine turnovers the entire game and won the rebounding against the bigger Irish, 31–27. Guard Jackie Gilloon, the closest thing to Pete Maravich in college basketball at the time, led the Gamecocks with 15 points.

South Carolina won 65–60 in front of a sellout crowd of 12,113. It would be the last top 20 win of McGuire's legendary career. While Phelps was disappointed in the loss, he saw McGuire as a fellow New Yorker and as a mentor. On some level he had to be smiling inside that he had been on the other bench in McGuire's last great victory.

Notre Dame had now lost two of three games entering a home game with NC State, a team that by today's standards would have been an NCAA Tournament team. They were led by Hawkeye Whitney, one of the top forwards in the ACC, and guard Clyde "The Glide" Austin.

But Batton had 22 points and 12 rebounds and Tracy Jackson had 11 points and 11 rebounds in a 70–59 win that got the Irish some confidence heading into the following Sunday's game with No.1-ranked Marquette.

Marquette had won the national championship in Al McGuire's last year in 1976–77 and longtime assistant Hank Raymonds had taken his place. The Warriors were ranked third in the preseason and had not been outside the top five all year because of a 21–2 record entering this game.

They had moved to number one the previous Monday with an eighth straight win, a victory over Cincinnati.

Marquette was led by guard Butch Lee, who had burst on the scene at the 1976 Olympics when he scored 35 points against the United States, nearly helping Puerto Rico to an upset.

Phelps and McGuire had a strong relationship, so when McGuire started his broadcasting career with NBC and it was known he would do this game, Phelps asked McGuire to speak at the Saturday night pep rally leading up to the game. "I know it sounds odd today, but Al and I had a special relationship," said Phelps. "He had a lot of respect for Notre Dame. Somewhere inside I always thought he wanted to coach at Notre Dame."

McGuire was his entertaining self at the rally and handled the situation with some great quotes. He started by saying, "OK, quiet down. If you don't let me talk, I'll go back to Marquette and start a football team." Everyone howled at that one.

It was apparent that Phelps put an emphasis on defending Butch Lee, who was on a roll coming into the game. Over the last seven games he had averaged over 20 points per game and shot 64 percent from the field, an amazing percentage for a guard.

Whenever his team got in a tough situation during the Warriors' NCAA championship run the previous year, McGuire said it was "Butch Lee time" and he would bail them out.

At the rally, Phelps encouraged the students to chant, "Butch Lee, no time."

Phelps also had his team wear green socks for this game, a takeoff from the football team's green jerseys for the Southern California game the previous fall. They were ugly, but Digger was always looking for a psychological angle.

An even more important contribution to the Notre Dame mojo might have been the official assignments. One of the officials for this game versus No. 1 Marquette was Richard Weiler, who had worked both games that bracketed UCLA's 88-game winning streak.

So much for all the intangibles being in Notre Dame's favor. Just like the 1974 UCLA game, Notre Dame got behind by 17 points in the first half at 34–17 (it had been 33–16 in the first half of the 1974 UCLA game).

Marquette led at the half, 39–25, thanks to 17-for-28 shooting, 60.7 percent. It was not the 19-for-27 UCLA had in the first half of the 1974 game, but it felt like it.

Phelps had substituted a lot in the first half, because he felt he could wear down Marquette. Coach Raymond was like McGuire in that he did not substitute much, playing just six or seven players. In fact, in this game Marquette subs played just 16 minutes and Notre Dame's played 58.

Bill Hanzlik, Digger's defensive specialist, entered the game with 6:18 left in the first half and Notre Dame down, 28–14. He was the 10th player Phelps used in the first half. He was assigned to Lee when he was in the game and he was to shoot just 3-for-11 from the field when Hanzlik was guarding him. Lee would finish with 14 points on just 6-for-19 shooting overall.

Down 14 at the half, the Irish needed a spark and Phelps got it from freshman Kelly Tripucka, who had not scored in the first 20 minutes. But he scored 11 of Notre Dame's first 17 points of the second half and had 15 on 5-for-6 shooting in the last 20 minutes. He also took two charges at key moments.

Notre Dame shot 15-for-22 from the field and beat the Warriors 40–20 in the second half to win, 65–59. Tripucka was named the game's most valuable player by NBC Sports, but many thought it should have gone to Hanzlik whose defense on Lee was pivotal. Hanzlik had just four points, but dealt out six assists offensively.

As McGuire had said many times previously, "Butch Lee is the brains of the team. You cut off the head and the body dies."

Notre Dame finished the regular season with a loss at Dayton (what else is new?) and a victory over Loyola. The Irish were ranked 10th in the AP poll entering the tournament, but had just a 4–3 record over their last seven games. It was not exactly an end of the year resume that would lead the national media to believe this would be Notre Dame's first team to go to the Final Four.

THE NCAA TOURNAMENT

Notre Dame's NCAA Tournament run began with a first-round game against Guy Lewis and the Houston Cougars. If ever there was a team better than its record, it was Houston in 1977–78. They entered the NCAA Tournament with a 25–7 mark, but the Cougars were on an eight-game winning streak. They had seven losses, but incredibly five were by exactly one point.

Two of their last six wins were against Arkansas, including an 84–75 win in the last game of the regular season when the Razorbacks were ranked No. 1. Then they won four straight in the Southwest Conference Tournament to clinch an automatic bid. They upset Arkansas again in the conference tournament. This was the Arkansas team that featured "The Triplets," Sidney Moncrief, Ron Brewer, and Marvin Delph, who would turn around and make it to the Final Four.

"Our guys took Houston very seriously and we played one of our best games of the season," said Phelps. "Houston played a 1-3-1 trap press against us the entire game and we just sliced right through it."

Houston wanted to play fast and force the Irish into turnovers, but it did not work. The Irish had just 12 turnovers in a high possession game and everyone, especially the big guys, were hitting from the outside.

If you watched this game, you would see what would make Bill Laimbeer a terrific pro. He came off the bench to make 7 of 9 shots from the field, 6 of 6 from the line, and score 20 points. He also had nine rebounds in only 21 minutes. Batton hit 6 of 8 from the field and

Flowers 2 of 3, making the Notre Dame three-headed monster in the post 15-for-20 from the field. Duck Williams added 19 while Tripucka and Branning had 14 apiece.

Notre Dame won 100–77 thanks to shooting at least 56 percent from the field in each half. Lewis, who along with Phelps was part of the coaching fraternity that had beaten UCLA and John Wooden in a monumental upset, didn't know what to say. He was quoted in *Sports Illustrated* the next week as saying the game was not going to hurt them in recruiting. "The only good thing about it was, if there were any recruits looking in [on TV] they know we need help."

With the NCAA Tournament at just 32 teams for the fourth straight year, Notre Dame only had to win one game in Tulsa to move on to the Midwest Regional at Lawrence, Kansas. Allen Fieldhouse had good vibes for Phelps because he had won three straight there, two against the Jayhawks in the regular season and an NCAA Tournament win over Cincinnati in 1976 that was won at the buzzer on a tip-in by Toby Knight.

The first opponent in Lawrence was Jerry Pimm's Utah team. It was just the second meeting ever between the two schools. Like Houston, Utah was on a hot streak, having won eight straight, including a victory over fifth-ranked New Mexico.

But like Houston, who had to win four SWC Tournament games the week before playing the Irish, Utah had to go to double overtime to beat Missouri in the opening round.

The Utes had four future NBA players on their roster in Jeff Judkins, Danny Vranes, Greg Deane, and Tom Chambers. They played a much more defensive approach and Notre Dame led by just 28–26 at the half.

But Tripucka had one of his best games of his freshman year, the first of two great games in Lawrence. He scored 20 points on 8-for-11 shooting in just 29 minutes. Batton continued to play well and scored 15, while Branning (11) and Duck Williams (10) also scored in double figures. The four future NBA players for Utah scored 36 of their 56 points, but they shot just 15-for-36 from the field and the Irish won, 69–56.

There was considerable joy in the Irish locker room because this was the first time Notre Dame had reached the Elite Eight of the NCAA

Tournament under Phelps and the first trip to the Regional Finals for any Notre Dame team since 1958.

Notre Dame's foe for the right to go to the Final Four for the first time was DePaul, coached by former Notre Dame captain Ray Meyer. This was the same DePaul team that had beaten the Irish in South Bend on February 12 by one point on a wing jumper by Gary Garland with just three seconds left, a gut-wrenching defeat.

As we have noted previously, Phelps was big on the motivation of a "payback game," especially when it was against a team that had barely won the previous meeting.

For the third straight NCAA game Notre Dame's opponent was coming off an emotional victory. On the same night the Irish beat Utah, DePaul defeated Louisville, 90–89 in double overtime.

DePaul had continued to win since their exhilarating triumph in South Bend and jumped all the way to No. 3 in AP poll entering the NCAA Tournament. They had won 13 in a row, including NCAA Tournament games against Creighton and ninth-ranked Louisville.

Dave Corzine was having an All-America season and he got a lot more votes for the honor after he scored 46 points against Louisville. The native of Chicago made 18 field goals and was 10-for-10 from the foul line in playing all 50 minutes against the Cards.

The Irish led 37–32 at intermission against the Blue Demons, and it was cut to 56–54 with eight minutes left. At this point, Notre Dame's depth began to make a difference. Tripucka had his way inside, while Laimbeer was hitting the boards. The Irish went on an 11–0 run to take a 67–54 lead just 2:47 after it was a two-point affair.

The Irish went on another 13–2 run over the last three minutes and Notre Dame had a 20-point victory, 84–64.

After four straight years of disappointment in NCAA Tournament games, the Irish had beaten the No. 3 ranked team in the nation by 20 points to reach the Final Four. Tripucka finished with 18 points and 11 rebounds and combined with his 20-point performance against Utah, he was named the Midwest Regional MVP. Laimbeer had a double-double off the bench in 28 minutes. Corzine was held to

17 points as Flowers and Laimbeer used eight of their 10 fouls to keep him away from the basket.

Phelps was very emotional in doing interviews after the game. When he initially spoke to Al McGuire and Dick Enberg, he couldn't talk.

When reflecting on getting to the Final Four Phelps said later, "You go to the Final Four every year and sit in the stands watching the teams and you wonder what it would be like to be on the bench on that side of the court. I am finally going to experience it."

Notre Dame's semifinal opponent at the Checkerdome in St. Louis was Duke, who had beaten Villanova in the East Regional final. The Blue Devils were coached by Bill Foster, one of two Bill Fosters in the ACC at the time.

Duke had surprised many in 1977–78 because they had been just 14–13 the year before. But they had a young center in Mike Gminski who really blossomed in his second year. Duke had three future pros in Gminski, Jim Spanarkel, and freshman Gene Banks. Banks had made

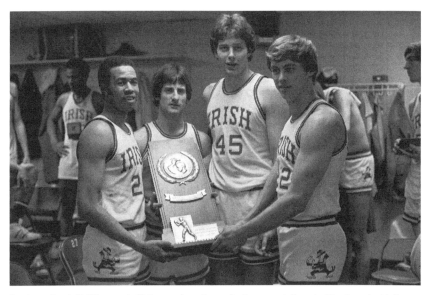

Seniors Duck Williams, Jeff Carpenter, Dave Batton, and Randy Haefner hold the trophy that signifies Notre Dame's first and still only trip to the Final Four. *Notre Dame Archives*

a big difference for Duke and some thought he compared favorably to Adrian Dantley.

Duke was dominant in the first half and had a 43–29 lead at halftime. They still held that 14-point lead (80–66) with four minutes left. But the Irish did not give up and it appeared Notre Dame's depth advantage was having an impact.

The Irish cut the lead to just two points, 88–86, with 27 seconds left. Phelps substituted freshman New York native Stan Wilcox to help with the press, just as he had brought in freshman New York native Ray Martin in 1974 versus UCLA.

Sure enough, Wilcox intercepted the in-bounds pass. He got the ball to Duck Williams who had an open shot to tie the game with 16 seconds left, but the left elbow jumper missed. Duke got the rebound, hit two free throws, and won, 90–86.

Notre Dame's depth almost pulled it off. Gminski (29), Banks (22), and Spanarkle (20) all had at least 20 points for Duke, while five Notre Dame players scored in double figures. Duke shot 32-for-37 from the foul line and 55 percent from the field. The Irish had a +7 turnover margin advantage, but still lost.

The season was not over, for in those days the NCAA Final Four had a consolation game. The Irish had another game against a three-headed scoring monster in Arkansas. It was another game that came down to the last shot. But this time Arkansas had the ball with the score tied. Ron Brewer, their outstanding point guard, who had made just 6 of 15 shots to this point in the game, nailed a 20-footer as the horn sounded to give Arkansas a 71–69 win.

Notre Dame had lost two games at the Final Four by six total points with both games coming down to the final 15 seconds.

It was disappointing but at 36 years old and with probably the best freshman class in Notre Dame history coming back for three more years, surely the Irish would return soon.

Unfortunately for Irish fans, the weekend of March 24–26, 1978 is still Notre Dame's only Final Four experience.

CHAPTER 14

The Legacy of the 88-Game Streak and the Notre Dame Streak Breakers

THE GREATEST STREAK?

UCLA's 88-game winning streak in college basketball is among the most celebrated in the history of sports, college or professional. It is not the longest in the history of sports, it isn't even the longest basketball winning streak. That distinction is held by the UConn women's basketball program that won 111 in a row between the 2013–14 and 2016–17 seasons.

The Indiana men's swimming program once won 140 consecutive dual meets and the Miami (Fl) men's tennis team captured 137 in a row between 1957 and 1964.

But those streaks still aren't as celebrated as the 88-game streak of John Wooden and the UCLA Bruins because those sports just aren't as prominent on the athletic landscape.

A look to some data about the 88-game streak puts it in perspective as one of the great team accomplishments in American sports history.

DATA ON UCLA'S 88-GAME WINNING STREAK

- There were 1,092 days in between losses and 1,084 days from the first win of the streak against UC Santa Barbara on January 30, 1971, until the 88th victory over Iowa in Chicago on January 17, 1974.

- UCLA's average margin of victory for the 88 games was 23.5 points per game.

- In the 50 years since the record was set, only one team has recorded a streak that is more than halfway to the record and that is by just one game. UNLV won 45 consecutive games from 1989 to 1991 before losing to Duke in the 1991 national championship game.

- The second longest streak in men's college basketball history is still the 60-game streak by San Francisco in the Bill Russell era, but it is still 28 games short of the UCLA streak.

- UCLA entered the last 86 games of the streak ranked as the top team in the nation. So, obviously every game they had a target on their backs, but still managed to win.

- UCLA had a streak of 46 consecutive polls as the No. 1 ranked team in the nation during the 88-game streak, still 19 polls longer than the second longest in history, 27 straight polls by Ohio State in the early 1960s.

- Over the course of the streak, UCLA was 18–0 versus AP top 20 teams, 12–0 versus top 10 and 7–0 versus top 5.

- UCLA won 29 games during the streak by 30 points and 17 by single digits. They had just eight wins by five points or less.

- During the 1971–72 season UCLA had a segment in which they won by at least 25 points in 18 of 19 games.

- UCLA defeated 45 different teams during the streak, including seven different Big 10 teams and five different ACC teams.

- The Bruins were 41–0 vs. the other Pac-8 schools during the streak.

- While Notre Dame had the victories at either end of the streak, UCLA did beat the Irish four times by a total of 128 points during the streak.

- Twenty-six times during the streak UCLA won a game with no days to prepare. (It should be noted the conference opponents also had no days to prepare, but this is still quite an accomplishment.)

- Twelve of the 88 wins were in the NCAA Tournament and 10 of those 12 wins were against teams ranked in the top 20 entering the game.

- A testament to not taking an opponent too lightly, UCLA won 70 in a row during the streak against unranked opponents.

- Only five of the 88 games were one-possession games and only one of the last 75 of the streak, a one-point win over Maryland, was a one-possession game.

- UCLA scored at least 100 points in 19 of the games and at least 90 points in 37 of the 88 games.

- UCLA won 40 of the 88 games away from home.

- 31 different UCLA players played in at least one of the 88 games, and 13 of the 31 went on to play in the NBA.

- Of the 13 who went on to play in the NBA, nine played at least 300 games and six played at least 10 years.

The above are all impressive notes on the streak, but is this really the greatest streak in men's college basketball history?

When ESPN did a feature on the greatest sports dynasties, UCLA's 10 national championships in a 12-year period was one the selections along with Notre Dame's football dynasty. In an interview for the piece, famed announcer Dick Enberg gave the impression that UCLA's 38-game winning streak in NCAA Tournament games might be even more impressive.

When you look at the magnitude of the games, especially considering seasons ended with a loss, it just might be a more impressive streak.

Here are some facts about UCLA's 38-game winning streak in the NCAA Tournament:

- UCLA's 38-game winning streak in the NCAA Tournament over a span of 10 years (1964–74) included 26 wins over teams ranked in the top 20 of the AP poll. That means Wooden and the Bruins beat a top 20 team 68.4 percent of the time during that streak. During the 88-game winning streak in all games between 1971 and 1974, UCLA only played 18 top 20 teams or 20.4 percent of the games.

- UCLA was 10–0 in national championship games during this 38-game NCAA Tournament streak.

- The 26 wins over top 20 teams included 15 wins over top 10 teams, 10 over top five, and two over the nation's number-one team, a No. 1–ranked Michigan team in the 1965 championship game and a No. 1–ranked Houston team in the 1968 semifinals.

- As you can see by the chart below, the second-longest NCAA Tournament winning streak is 13 by Duke between 1991 and 1993. That is basically only a third of the way to UCLA's record streak.

- UCLA was dominant in these NCAA games. They had to win by five points or less or in overtime just six times. The closest they came to a loss was a triple overtime game against Dayton in the 1974 tournament, a game UCLA won by 11. But it would be considered the closest of the 38 games because it was the only game that went to overtime.

- UCLA's 38-game streak was ended by NC State in the 1974 national semifinals, 80–77 in double overtime. UCLA then won the consolation game over Kansas, then won five straight the next year to win the national championship in Wooden's last game, meaning UCLA won 44 of 45 NCAA Tournament games to end Wooden's career. And the only loss was in double overtime to an NC State team that was playing what amounted to a home game in Greensboro, North Carolina.

Consecutive Wins in NCAA Tournament Play

Team	Years	Games	Ended by
UCLA	1964-74	38	NC State, 80–77 (2OT)
Duke	1991-93	13	California, 82–77
Cincinnati	1960-63	12	Loyola (Chicago), 60–58 (OT)
Florida	2006-07	12	Brigham Young, 99–92 (2OT) (2010)
Kentucky	1945-56	12	Iowa, 89–77
Arkansas	1994-95	11	UCLA, 89–78
Kentucky	1996-97	11	Arizona, 84–79 (OT)
Kentucky	2012-14	11	UConn, 60–54
San Francisco	1955-57	11	Kansas, 80–56
Georgetown	1984-85	10	Villanova, 66–64
Michigan State	2000-01	10	Arizona, 80–61
UNLV	1990-91	10	Duke, 79–77

With the explosion of sports media over the years, there have been many lists that attempt to document the greatest coaches, teams, and players. In 1999, ESPN celebrated the turn of the century with its *SportsCentury* series. One of the programs selected the top 10 coaches in any sport for the 20th century.

John Wooden was selected as the No. 2 coach in any sport for the century behind NFL coach Vince Lombardi. Wooden was lauded for his 10 national championships between 1964 and 1975, including a record seven in a row between 1967 and 1973. Most feel neither one of those records will ever be broken. This book of course documents they have already stood for 50 years.

Wooden was also recognized in 1986 in a *Sport* magazine list of the top 40 people who changed sports. It considered athletes, administrators, commissioners, broadcasters, agents; anyone who had to do with sports to that point in history. Wooden was selected No. 12 in that list, just ahead of Jack Nicklaus and just behind Wilt Chamberlain.

ESPN *SportsCentury* Top 10 Coaches of the 20th Century

1. Vince Lombardi, pro football

2. **John Wooden, college basketball**

3. Red Auerbach, pro basketball

4. Dean Smith, college basketball

5. Bear Bryant, college football

6. John McGraw, baseball

7. George Halas, pro football

8. Don Shula, pro football

9. Paul Brown, pro football

10. Knute Rockne, college Football

40 WHO CHANGED SPORTS
Sport **magazine, December 1986**
(Top 20 listed below)

1. Jackie Robinson, baseball

2. Muhammad Ali, boxing

3. Pete Rozelle, NFL commissioner

4. Arnold Palmer, golf

5. Vince Lombardi, football coach

6. Branch Rickey, Brooklyn Dodgers president

7. Red Auerbach, Boston Celtics coach and general manager

8. Marvin Miller, MLB players' union leader

9. Bill Russell, basketball player and coach

10. Billie Jean King, women's tennis

11. Wilt Chamberlain, basketball

12. **John Wooden, basketball coach**

13. Howard Cosell, sports television personality

14. Jack Nicklaus, golf

15. Roone Arledge, sports television producer

16. Ted Williams, baseball

17. Willie Mays, baseball

18. Chris Evert, women's tennis

19. Joe Namath, football

20. Bobby Orr, hockey

Wooden passed away at the age of 99 in Los Angeles in 2010. He was lauded throughout the world, not just by basketball players or sports personalities. The list of people quoted in an ESPN obituary included then President Barack Obama, who issued a public statement upon Wooden's passing, an indication of the national respect for the former UCLA coach:

> I'm saddened to hear of the passing of an incredible coach and an even better man, John Wooden. As a basketball fan, I remember fondly his 10 NCAA championships, his unrivaled winning streak at UCLA, and the caliber of players he mentored.
>
> But as an American, I salute the way he achieved all that success, with modesty and humility and by wholeheartedly dedicating his life to the betterment of others. Even after he became one of the game's early heroes, he worked as a high school teacher. And for the rest of his life, on and off the court, he never stopped teaching. He never stopped preparing his players and everyone he met to be their best. Despite all the records and the championships, he once said that it wasn't the tournaments or the games he missed the most, it was the practice and the preparation.
>
> He is reunited with his beloved wife Nell now, and my thoughts and prayers are with his children, James and Nancy, his grandchildren and great-grandchildren, and all whose lives were forever changed because John Wooden lived his so well.

Longest Win Streaks by Various College Sports

Men's Basketball: UCLA, 88 (1970–71 to 1973–74), ended by Notre Dame, 71–70

Women's Basketball: UConn, 111 (2013–14 to 2016–17), ended by Mississippi, 66–64 (OT)

Football: Oklahoma, 47 (1952–57), ended by Notre Dame, 7–0

Baseball: Florida Atlantic, 34 (1999), ended by Jacksonville, 2–1 / Texas, 34 (1977), ended by Rice, 4–3 (14 innings)

Softball: Oklahoma, 53 (2023, still active entering 2024)

Men's Tennis: Miami (FL) 137 (1957–64), ended by Princeton, 5–4

Men's Gymnastics: Oklahoma, 121 (2015–19), ended by Stanford, 415.222 to 414.556

Women's Soccer: North Carolina, 92 (1990–94), ended by Notre Dame in 0–0 tie

Women's Volleyball: Penn State, 109 (2007–10, ended by Stanford, 3–0

Men's Swimming: Indiana, 140 (1966 to 1979)

Women's Ice Hockey: Minnesota, 62 (2012–13), ended by North Dakota, 3–2

ESPN's Greatest College Basketball teams
ESPN The Magazine, 2016

UCLA, 1971–72 (30–0)

Indiana, 1975–76 (32–0)

UCLA, 1972–73 (30–0)

San Francisco, 1955–56 (29–0)

UCLA, 1967–68 (29–1)

UCLA, 1966–67 (30–0)

Texas Western, 1965–66 (28–1)

North Carolina, 1956–57 (32–0)

North Carolina, 1981–82 (32–2)

NC State, 1973–74 (30–1)

UCLA, 1968–69 (29–1)

San Francisco, 1954–55 (28–1)

Kentucky, 1995–96 (34–2)

Cincinnati, 1961–62 (29–2)

Duke, 1991–92 (34–2)

Kentucky, 2011–12 (38–2)

UCLA, 1970–71 (29–1)

UCLA, 1963–64 (30–0)

UCLA, 1969–70 (28–2)

Kentucky, 1977–78 (30–2)

UCONN, 1998–99 (34–2)

Ohio State, 1959–60 (25–3)

UCLA, 1964–65 (28–2)

Duke, 2000–01 (35–4)

Arkansas, 1993–94 (31–3)

*Boldface: John Wooden–coached team

NCAA Record for Most Consecutive College Basketball Team Victories

Team	Years	Wins	Ended by	Score
UCLA	1971-74	88	Notre Dame	71-70
San Francisco	1955-57	60	Illinois	62-33
UCLA	1966-68	47	Houston	71-69
UNLV	1990-91	45	Duke	79-77
Texas	1913-17	44	Rice	24-18
LIU Brooklyn	1935-37	43	Stanford	45-31
Seton Hall	1939-41	43	LIU Brooklyn	49-26
UCLA	1968-69	41	Southern California	46-44
Marquette	1970-71	39	Ohio State	60-59
Kentucky	2014-15	38	Wisconsin	71-64
North Carolina	1957-58	37	West Virginia	75-64
Cincinnati	1962-63	37	Wichita State	65-64

NOTRE DAME'S LEGACY AS A STREAK BREAKER

When Notre Dame ended UCLA's 88-game winning streak, it received considerable national attention, not only because it ended the longest streak in college basketball history, but also because it had the victories at both ends of the streak.

It received further attention because the Notre Dame football program had done the same thing in regards to the longest college football streak in history. Oklahoma had a 47-game winning streak in college football (still the longest in history) between 1952 and 1957.

Research shows Notre Dame has been ending streaks for years in all sports, making the program truly the all-time streak breaker of college athletics. And head coach Digger Phelps is associated with the Notre Dame basketball streaks, not just for ending the 88-game winning streak, but he also led the Irish to many other noteworthy streaks, as we see below.

NOTRE DAME STREAK BREAKERS BY SPORT
Men's Basketball

- **January 23, 1971—Notre Dame 89, UCLA 82 at Notre Dame, Indiana**

This win over the number-one ranked and four-time defending national champion UCLA ended the Bruins' 19-game overall winning streak and its 48-game non-conference winning streak.

- **January 13, 1973—Notre Dame 71, Marquette 69 at Milwaukee, Wisconsin**

  The Irish snapped Marquette's 81-game home winning streak at the Milwaukee Arena. Dwight Clay's left corner jumper with four seconds left gave the Irish the victory. It is still the fifth longest homecourt winning streak in Division I college history.

- **December 11, 1973—Notre Dame 73, Indiana 67 at Bloomington, Indiana**

  The Irish victory ended Indiana's 19-game home winning streak at Assembly Hall. Bobby Knight's team had gone to the Final Four the previous year. John Shumate led the way with 26 points.

- **January 19, 1974—Notre Dame 71, UCLA 70 at Notre Dame, Indiana**

  The Irish ended UCLA's 88-game overall winning streak, the longest in college basketball history. The Bruins had also won 40 consecutive games away from home. Dwight Clay's right corner jumper with 29 seconds left proved to be the game winner.

- **February 16, 1974—Notre Dame 72, South Carolina 68 at Columbia, South Carolina**

  Digger Phelps's third team broke another streak on this day, ending a 34-game home winning streak for the Gamecocks team coached by Frank McGuire.

- **December 11, 1976—Notre Dame 66, UCLA 63 at Pauley Pavilion, Los Angeles, California**

  Notre Dame ended UCLA's 115 game non-conference home winning streak. It was the first home non-conference loss in the history of Pauley Pavilion.

Football

- **November 9, 1946—Notre Dame 0, Army 0 at Yankee Stadium, Bronx, New York**

  Notre Dame tied the two-time defending national champion Army team 0–0 at Yankee Stadium to end the Cadets' 25-game winning streak. Notre Dame was voted number one the next week and would win the national championship.

- **October 24, 1953—Notre Dame 27, Georgia Tech 14 at Notre Dame, Indiana**

  Notre Dame's victory ended Georgia Tech's 31-game unbeaten streak. This was a battle between Hall of Fame coaches Frank Leahy and Bobby Dodd.

- **November 16, 1957—Notre Dame 7, Oklahoma 0 at Norman, Oklahoma**

  Dick Lynch scored a late touchdown to give the Irish the 7–0 win and end Oklahoma's 47-game winning streak, longest in college football history. The Irish had been the last team to beat Oklahoma when they were victorious by a 27–21 score on November 8, 1952.

- **January 1, 1971—Notre Dame 24, Texas 11 at Dallas, Texas (Cotton Bowl)**

  The Irish ended the Longhorns' 30-game winning streak. All the points were scored in the first half. It was the first loss for Texas and coach Darrell Royal since they installed the wishbone offense.

- **October 27, 1973—Notre Dame 23, Southern California 14 at Notre Dame, Indiana**

  Notre Dame ended Southern California's 23-game unbeaten streak. Southern California was the defending national champion. Eric Penick's 85-yard touchdown run in the third period was the key play. Notre Dame went on to win the national championship.

- **October 15, 1988—Notre Dame 31, Miami (FL) 30 at Notre Dame, Indiana**

Notre Dame ended Miami's 36-game regular season winning streak and 20-game road game winning streak with this one-point victory at Notre Dame Stadium. The Irish went on to win the national championship.

- **November 7, 2020—Notre Dame 47, Clemson 40 (2OT) at Notre Dame, Indiana**

  Notre Dame ended Clemson's 36 game regular season winning streak with a 47–40 double overtime victory during the COVID-19–impacted season of 2020.

Fencing

- **February 15, 1975—Notre Dame 15, Wayne State 12 at Wayne, New Jersey**

  Notre Dame ended Wayne State's 44-match winning streak in Wayne State's home facility.

Women's Soccer

- **October 1, 1994—Notre Dame 0, North Carolina 0 at Chapel Hill, North Carolina**

  Notre Dame ended North Carolina's 92-game winning streak with this tie. North Carolina shots hit the crossbar twice in overtime, but did not go in the goal.

UCLA's 88-Game Winning Streak

No	Date	Opponent	Site	Ranks	UCLA-Op	Mar
1.	1/30/71	UC-Santa Barbara	H	2/NR	74-61	+13
2.	2/6/71	Southern California	A	3/2	64-60	+4
3.	2/12/71	Oregon	A	1/NR	69-68	+1
4.	2/13/71	Oregon State	A	1/NR	67-65	+2
5.	2/19/21	Oregon State	H	1/NR	94-64	+30
6.	2/20/71	Oregon	H	1/NR	74-67	+7
7.	2/27/71	Washington State	A	1/NR	57-53	+4
8.	3/1/71	Washington	A	1/NR	71-69	+2
9.	3/5/71	California	H	1/NR	103-69	+34

No	Date	Opponent	Site	Ranks	UCLA-Op	Mar
10.	3/6/71	Stanford	H	1/NR	107-72	+35
11.	3/13/71	Southern California	H	1/3	73-62	+11
12.	3/18/71	Brigham Young	N1	1/20	91-73	+18
13.	2/20/71	Long Beach State	N1	1/16	57-55	+2
14.	2/26/71	Kansas	N2	1/4	68-60	+8
15.	3/27/71	Villanova	N2	1/19	68-62	+6
16.	12/3/71	The Citadel	H	1/NR	105-49	+56
17.	12/4/71	Iowa	H	1/NR	106-72	+34
18.	12/10/71	Iowa State	H	1/NR	110-81	+29
19.	12/11/71	Texas A&M	H	1/NR	117-53	+64
20.	12/22/71	Notre Dame	H	1/NR	114-56	+58
21.	12/23/71	TCU	H	1/NR	119-81	+38
22.	12/29/71	Texas	H	1/NR	115-85	+30
23.	12/30/71	Ohio State	H	1/6	79-53	+26
24.	1/7/72	Oregon State	A	1/NR	78-72	+6
25.	1/8/72	Oregon	A	1/NR	93-68	+25
26.	1/14/72	Stanford	H	1/NR	118-79	+39
27.	1/15/72	California	H	1/NR	82-43	+39
28.	1/21/72	Santa Clara	H	1/NR	92-57	+35
29.	1/22/72	Denver	H	1/NR	108-61	+47
30.	1/28/72	Loyola (Chicago)	A	1/NR	92-64	+28
31.	1/29/72	Notre Dame	A	1/NR	57-32	+25
32.	2/5/72	Southern California	H	1/NR	81-56	+25
33.	2/11/72	Washington State	H	1/NR	89-58	+31
34.	2/12/72	Washington	H	1/NR	109-70	+39
35.	2/19/72	Washington	A	1/NR	100-83	+17
36.	2/21/72	Washington State	A	1/NR	85-55	+30
37.	2/25/72	Oregon	H	1/NR	92-70	+22
38.	2/26/72	Oregon State	H	1/NR	91-72	+19
39.	3/3/72	California	A	1/NR	85-71	+14
40.	3/4/72	Stanford	A	1/NR	102-73	+29
41.	3/10/72	Southern California	A	1/NR	79-66	+13
42.	3/16/72	Weber State	N3	1/NR	90-58	+32
43.	3/18/72	Long Beach State	N3	1/5	73-57	+16
44.	3/23/72	Louisville	N4	1/4	96-77	+19
45.	3/25/72	Florida State	N4	1/10	81-76	+5
46	11/25/72	Wisconsin	H	1/NR	94-53	+39

No	Date	Opponent	Site	Ranks	UCLA-Op	Mar
47.	12/1/72	Bradley	H	1/NR	73-38	+35
48.	12/2/72	Pacific	H	1/NR	81-48	+33
49.	12/16/72	UC-Santa Barbara	H	1/NR	98-67	+31
50.	12/22/72	Pittsburgh	H	1/NR	89-73	+16
51	12/23/72	Notre Dame	H	1/NR	82-56	+26
52.	11/29/72	Drake	N5	1/NR	85-72	+13
53.	11/30/72	Illinois	N5	1/NR	71-64	+7
54.	1/5/73	Oregon	H	1/NR	64-38	+26
55.	1/6/73	Oregon State	H	1/NR	87-61	+26
56.	1/12/73	Stanford	A	1/NR	82-67	+15
57.	1/13/73	California	A	1/NR	69-50	+19
58.	1/19/73	San Francisco	H	1/10	92-64	+28
59.	1/20/73	Providence	H	1/9	101-77	+24
60.	1/25/73	Loyola (Chicago)	A	1/NR	87-73	+14
61.	1/27/73	Notre Dame	A	1/NR	82-63	+19
62.	2/3/73	Southern California	A	1/20	79-56	+23
63.	2/10/73	Washington State	A	1/NR	88-50	+38
64.	2/12/73	Washington	A	1/NR	76-67	+9
65.	2/16/73	Washington	H	1/NR	93-62	+31
66.	2/17/73	Washington State	H	1/NR	96-64	+32
67.	2/22/73	Oregon	A	1/NR	72-61	+11
68.	2/24/73	Oregon State	A	1/NR	73-67	+6
69.	3/2/73	California	H	1/NR	90-65	+25
70.	3/3/73	Stanford	H	1/NR	51-45	+6
71.	3/10/73	Southern California	H	1/NR	76-56	+20
72.	3/15/73	Arizona State	H1	1/16	98-81	+17
73.	3/17/73	San Francisco	H1	1/20	54-39	+15
74.	3/24/73	Indiana	N6	1/6	70-59	+11
75.	3/26/73	Memphis State	N6	1/NR	87-66	+21
76.	11/30/73	Arkansas	H	1/NR	101-79	+22
77.	12/1/73	Maryland	H	1/4	65-64	+1
78.	12/8/73	Southern Methodist	H	1/NR	77-60	+17
79.	12/15/73	NC State	N7	1/2	84-66	+18
80.	12/21/73	Ohio	H	1/NR	110-63	+47
81.	12/22/73	St. Bonaventure	H	1/NR	111-59	+52
82.	12/28/73	Wyoming	H	1/NR	86-58	+26
83.	12/29/73	Michigan	H	1/NR	90-70	+20

No	Date	Opponent	Site	Ranks	UCLA-Op	Mar
84.	1/5/74	Washington	A	1/NR	110-48	+52
85.	1/7/74	Washington State	A	1/NR	55-45	+10
86.	1/11/74	California	H	1/NR	92-56	+36
87.	1/12/74	Stanford	H	1/NR	66-52	+14
88.	1/17/74	Iowa	N8	1/NR	68-44	+24

N1—NCAA TOURNAMENT AT HUNTSMAN CENTER, SALT LAKE CITY, UTAH

N2—NCAA FINAL FOUR AT HOUSTON, TEXAS (ASTRODOME)

N3—NCAA TOURNAMENT AT MARRIOTT CENTER, PROVO, UTAH

N4—NCAA FINAL FOUR AT LOS ANGELES, CALIFORNIA (LOS ANGELES SPORTS ARENA)

N5—AT SUGAR BOWL CLASSIC, NEW ORLEANS, LOUISIANA

N6—AT FINAL FOUR AT ST. LOUIS ARENA, ST. LOUIS, MISSOURI

N7—AT ST. LOUIS ARENA, ST. LOUIS, MISSOURI

N8—AT CHICAGO STADIUM, CHICAGO, ILLINOIS

H1—NCAA TOURNAMENT AT PAULEY PAVILION, LOS ANGELES, CALIFORNIA

About the Author

Tim Bourret worked 40 years in the Clemson Sports Information Office before retiring in July 2018. He came to Clemson as an assistant sports information director in September 1978, then became director in 1989. In 2013, he became the assistant athletic director for football communications working for national championship head coach Dabo Swinney. He held that position until he retired.

In June 2017, Bourret was inducted into the College Sports Information Director's (CoSIDA) Hall of Fame. In June 2019, he received a Lifetime Achievement Award from the same organization.

In May 2018 he was presented the Bobby Richardson Award by the South Carolina Athletic Hall of Fame for his contributions to athletics in the state of South Carolina.

Five times under his direction the Clemson Sports Information Office was named to the Football Writers Association's "Super 11" Team (2009, 2011, 2015, 2016, 2017). The award recognizes the top eleven SID offices in the nation for their service in working with media covering college football.

Bourret also has extensive experience in broadcasting. He has served as color commentator for more than 1,200 Clemson basketball games with more than 44 years behind the microphone. He also serves as the primary color commentator for Clemson football broadcasts, a task he handled between 1982 and 1988, and from 2019 to the present.

The native of West Hartford, Connecticut, earned both his undergraduate degree (1977) and master's degree (1978) from the University of Notre Dame. He worked in the Sports Information office for Hall of Fame SID Roger Valdiserri from 1975 to 1978.

88 and 1 is his seventh book. He joined former Notre Dame basketball Coach Digger Phelps and *Sports Illustrated*'s John Walters as coauthors of *Basketball for Dummies*. He is also the author of *Digger Phelps's Tales from the Notre Dame Hardwood*, and *Father Ted Hesburgh: He Coached Me*, a book of reflections by Phelps on the former Notre Dame president.

Bourret has authored two versions of *The Clemson Football Vault* in 2008 and 2018 through Whitman Publishing. The same company also published his work, *Clemson University: 2016 National Champions*. He is also coauthor with Sam Blackman of *If These Walls Could Talk: Clemson Tigers*.